MEANIN

MEANING

PAUL HORWICH

CLARENDON PRESS · OXFORD

OXFORD
UNIVERSITY PRESS

Great Clarendon Street, Oxford OX2 6DP

Oxford University Press is a department of the University of Oxford.
It furthers the University's objective of excellence in research, scholarship,
and education by publishing worldwide in

Oxford New York

Athens Auckland Bangkok Bogotá Buenos Aires Calcutta
Cape Town Chennai Dar es Salaam Delhi Florence Hong Kong Istanbul
Karachi Kuala Lumpur Madrid Melbourne Mexico City Mumbai
Nairobi Paris São Paulo Singapore Taipei Tokyo Toronto Warsaw

with associated companies in Berlin Ibadan

Oxford is a registered trade mark of Oxford University Press
in the UK and in certain other countries

Published in the United States
by Oxford University Press Inc., New York

First published 1998
Reprinted in paperback 1999

British Library Cataloguing in Publication Data

Data available

Library of Congress Cataloging in Publication Data

Data available

ISBN 0–19–823728–6
ISBN 0–19–823824–X (Pbk.)

Printed in Great Britain
on acid-free paper by
Biddles Ltd
Guildford and King's Lynn

To my uncle Moshe

Preface

The ideas in this book are the product of four factors. In the first place, there is an attempt to extend the minimalist theory of truth into a more general deflationary picture of the relations between language, thought, and reality. Minimalism was elaborated in my book, *Truth*, of which a revised edition is being published in conjunction with the present work. But, as several critics have pointed out, that theory can be credible only in the light of a consonant account of meaning—and so my primary aim here is to provide such an account. In the second place, I have had a long-standing sympathy for Wittgenstein's view that the meaning of a word derives from its *use*. This idea is the core of what follows (although the particular form that it takes, and the precision with which I have tried to articulate and defend it, may not have met with his approval). In the third place, I have tried to develop a picture that can accommodate the many 'discoveries' about meaning that have emerged from the considerable attention this topic has received during the twentieth century—particularly in the work of Frege, Russell, Wittgenstein, Carnap, Quine, Chomsky, Davidson, Dummett, Grice, Kaplan, Kripke, Putnam, Katz, Fodor, Schiffer, and Burge. Although my account diverges greatly from the theories these philosophers have advanced, it attempts to incorporate the insights that motivated them. Finally, and again under Wittgenstein's influence, my goal has been non-revisionary—not to rectify our naive view of meaning, but to vindicate it. We imagine meanings as weird entities somehow attached to what would otherwise be 'dead' noises—entities that can somehow be combined with one another to produce the meanings of sentences; and we suppose that the meaning of a sentence somehow determines, given the nature of the world, whether that sentence expresses something true or false and hence whether we ought or ought not to endorse it. These sentiments are no more than common sense; but they can easily come to seem inexplicable and deeply paradoxical. The fourth aim of this work is to defuse these paradoxes; to take the mystery out of meaning.

The structure of the book is as follows. Chapter 1 runs quickly through the main issues to be addressed and the proposals to be advanced. Chapter 2 offers a compressed version of my overall argument: it sets out seven constraints on a good account of meaning, indicating how each tends to be misconstrued and made to seem virtually impossible to satisfy. The succeeding chapters concentrate, one at a time, on these constraints and show in detail how, once properly understood, they can easily be met. In particular, Chapter 3 focusses on the need to account for the explanatory relationship between the meaning of a word and its use, and to that end it elaborates my version of the use theory of meaning. Chapters 4 and 5 present deflationary views of truth, satisfaction, and reference, and thereby accommodate the representational power of meaning. Chapter 6 acknowledges the *epistemological* implications of understanding a language, but argues against the common idea that substantive a priori knowledge may derive from it. Chapter 7 explains the compositionality of meaning in a highly deflationary and non-Davidsonian way. Chapter 8 shows how meaning may have normative import without being intrinsically normative. Chapter 9 offers a reconstruction of Quine's 'indeterminacy' considerations, exposing some critical flaws in them. And Chapter 10 looks with a sceptical eye at Kripke's arguments against 'facts of meaning'. These chapters develop a continuous line of thought; but each one is self-sufficient and they can well be read out of order.

I am very grateful to the many colleagues and friends who have helped me with this project. Rather than bury them in a long list, I will be referring to them at appropriate points later on, where I can be more specific about the character of their contributions. But now is the right time for particular thanks to Samira Atallah for invaluable moral support, to Ned Block and Scott Sturgeon, who gave me good, detailed comments on the entire manuscript, and to the participants in my seminars at the Massachusetts Institute of Technology, the CNRS Institut d'Histoire et Philosophie des Sciences et Technique, and the University of Sydney. Despite all this help and my own best efforts, I am afraid that what follows is not as clear and simple and accessible to non-specialists as I would have liked it to be. To some extent this is because the topic is approached from an unfamiliar angle—one from which a number of gestalt shifts are required. I hope that those who persevere will find that this new perspective on the problems of meaning is worth the work needed to achieve it.

Contents

1

Introduction

What is meaning? Why are some sounds imbued with it and others
not? How, for example, does it come about that the word "dog"
means precisely what it does? How is it possible for those intrinsically inert ink-marks (or some associated state of the brain) to reach
out into the world and latch on to a definite portion of reality:
namely, the dogs? This issue, which might perhaps strike some as
small and arcane, is on the contrary one of the most urgent of philosophical questions. Witness the variety and depth of the problems on
which an answer to it depends. What is the nature, if any, of objective truth? Are some sentences guaranteed to be true, regardless of
what the world is like, simply by their having certain meanings? Can
this give rise to a kind of knowledge that is not based on experience?
Does it make sense to hypothesize that we are always dreaming, or
that we are artificially stimulated brains in a Martian vat? Do scientific theories describe the real, underlying structure of the world, or
are they nothing more than useful but meaningless instruments for
the organization of data? Will competing theories inevitably engender different languages? What is thought? Can it be inexpressible?
Are we able to discern the special qualities of our own sensations and
coherently wonder whether other people's are the same? Do moral
pronouncements articulate ethical facts or merely express the desires
of the speaker? Can there be such a thing as conceptual analysis?
Does ontology merely recapitulate philology? Is 'language on holi-
day' the peculiar source of philosophical puzzlement? Evidently
these problems comprise a good proportion of the most important
issues in philosophy. And evidently the approach we take to them will
depend on what we assume about the nature of meaning—on how
we answer the question with which I began.

Unfortunately the extensive discussion which this fundamental
question has justifiably received in the last hundred years or so has

done more to complicate the issue than to resolve it. The leading philosophers of the twentieth century have devoted much of their efforts to the study of meaning. However, their legacy has not been a definitive theory—far from it—but rather a series of observations about meaning, providing an accumulation of increasingly severe constraints on an adequate account of it. Thus we have (in cartoon form) Frege's problem, to deal with the difference in significance between "*a* is *f*" and "*b* is *f*" which exists even when "*a*" and "*b*" refer to the same thing; Brentano's problem, to explain how thoughts, which are mental events, can be about objects external to the mind; Wittgenstein's problem, to reconcile our feeling that our use of words is *guided* by what they mean, as if by a set of instructions, with the regress-threatening fact that any such instructions would already need to be understood; Carnap's problem, to show how there can be 'truth in virtue of meaning alone', and hence a priori knowledge; Quine's problem, to find an objective basis for deciding when given expressions have the same meaning; Davidson's problem, to show how the meanings of sentences are composed of or derived from the meanings of their component words; Dummett's problem, to ensure that we are able to acquire new terms without altering the meanings of the words we have already learned; Grice's problem, to specify the connection between language and thought; Kaplan's problem, to characterize the relationship between the meaning of a sentence, the context in which it is uttered, and the proposition it expresses; Putnam's problem, to do justice to the 'twin earth' thought experiments suggesting that what a given speaker means by a term is not 'in his head' but depends upon aspects of his physical and social environment; and Kripke's problem, to explain how, if there are non-normative, non-semantic properties underlying a word's meaning, they could determine when the word *ought* to be deployed. Quite a daunting array! One might be excused for despairing that any theory could possibly resolve such a morass of problems, and for concluding that the phenomenon of meaning will remain forever obscure.

But this sort of defeatism would be too hasty. After all, it must be acknowledged that questions in philosophy are sometimes based on confusion rather than ignorance. In such cases, straightforward answers are misconceived; the right approach is rather to expose and eliminate the muddles and mistaken presuppositions from which the questions emerge. This is the deflationary spirit in which I think we can profitably address our long list of adequacy conditions on a theory of meaning. It will lead us, I believe, towards ways of construing those constraints under which they are not at all hard to meet. Thus we will be able to arrive at a satisfactory account of meaning and thereby to demystify the philosophically problematic relations between language, thought, and reality.

More specifically, the picture of meaning to be developed here is inspired by Wittgenstein's idea that the meaning of a word is constituted from its use—from the regularities governing our deployment of the sentences in which it appears. This idea has not won the acceptance it deserves because it has been thought to be ruled out by the above constraints. It has been felt that the idea is too behaviouristic and holistic, incapable of accommodating the representational, compositional, epistemological, and normative aspects of meaning, and intolerably vague to boot. My view, however, is that these objections are founded on distorted, inflated versions of the adequacy conditions. My plan, therefore, is to suggest how the constraints really ought to be construed, and to offer a formulation of the use theory of meaning that is perfectly able to satisfy them.

One of the more easily avoidable sources of confusion in this area is that the word 'meaning' is deployed ambiguously, both in ordinary language and by theoreticians, to pick out various related but different phenomena. An expression's 'meaning' may be the concept it standardly manifests, or else the thing in the world to which it refers, or the propositional element that (given the context) it expresses, or what the speaker (perhaps mistakenly) takes it to be about, or what the speaker intends his audience to infer from its use. In order to avert premature objections, I want to be clear from the outset that I am primarily concerned with the first of these notions, which is the one I take to be fundamental: namely, the literal, semantic meaning of an expression type; that which is expressed independently of the speaker's intentions, beliefs, or context, and is known by anyone who understands the language. The other notions are quite legitimate, and it is not normally wrong to characterize them as 'meaning'. But for the sake of disambiguation I will use terms such as "reference", "propositional meaning", "speaker's meaning", "pragmatic meaning", and "implicature" for these other phenomena. As we shall see, they are best understood on the basis of an adequate account of semantic meaning, and I will reserve the word "meaning" for that notion.

Let me quickly run through the main elements of the theory to come. I apologize in advance to those who will find this summary too cryptic to follow, or who will jump to an oversimplified picture of the theory. But I am afraid that what I will be proposing has a large number of complicated, interlocking elements, many of them quite unfamiliar and initially implausible. So the theory—even when articulated at length—will inevitably be hard to understand, and my hope is that most readers will be helped by an initial overview of it.

(1) *Non-revisionism.* Attributions of meaning in the style of '"dog" means DOG', '"Il pleut" means IT'S RAINING', and so on, will be taken at face value as claiming, in each case, that the relation '*x* means *y*' links a certain noise or mark (such as the English word 'dog' or the French sentence 'Il pleut') with a further, more mysterious entity—a *meaning* (such as DOG or IT'S RAINING). Thus the account is not revisionary: it seeks to understand our common-sense commitments to meanings and to their association with words, not to correct them.

(2) *Meanings = concepts = properties.* I shall identify meanings with concepts (complex and simple), which I shall take to be abstract objects of belief, desire, etc., and components of such objects (i.e. propositions and their constituents). For example, the concept DOG is an ingredient of the proposition that dogs bark, and hence an ingredient of the state of 'believing that dogs bark'. Moreover, I will suggest (in Chapter 2) that properties should be identified with such concepts—e.g. that the property of doggyness (i.e. the property 'being a dog') is the same thing as the concept DOG.

(3) *Univocality of '*x* means *y*'.* The meaning relation, '*x* means *y*', will be treated (contra Grice) as univocal—the same in semantic contexts (e.g. "dog" means DOG) as in non-semantic contexts (e.g. Smoke means fire). As we shall see in Chapter 2, this relation may be construed in both contexts along the lines of '*x* indicates *y*'—or, more specifically, 'Occurrences of *x* provide reason to believe in the presence of *y*'. Thus '"dog" means DOG' amounts, roughly speaking, to 'Occurrences of the word "dog" provide reason to believe in the presence (within the thought of the speaker) of the concept DOG'. Note that what is indicated by the word is not the presence of a concrete dog—not an *exemplification* of doggyness—but rather the

presence of that property (an abstract universal) in some proposition that is thought by the speaker.

(4) *Non-nominalistic reductionism.* Meanings cannot be straightforwardly reduced to non-semantic entities. For example, the concept DOG (i.e. the abstract property of doggyness) cannot be identified with some physical or mental object. Instead, each concept may be characterized indirectly by reference to the situations in which it would be expressed or meant—that is, by reference to the circumstances in which a word or a complex expression would indicate its engagement by the speaker's mind. Thus, although there are no nominalistic reductive analyses of meaning *entities*, such as DOG, there are reductive analyses of meaning *properties*, such as 'x means DOG': there are theories along the lines of "x means DOG = $u(x)$", where '$u(x)$' involves no semantic notions. And concepts may then be characterized in light of those theories: e.g. DOG = the thought constituent whose presence is indicated by tokens of any expression type with property '$u(x)$'. Thus I will be proceeding somewhat counterintuitively. Instead of constructing the analyses of meaning properties from analyses of their constituents—which are concepts and the meaning relation—I will derive (by 'subtraction') an account of each concept from a theory of the corresponding meaning property and a theory of the meaning relation.

(5) *Impossibility of explaining why a given underlying property engenders a given meaning.* Contrary to what is widely presupposed in the literature, I hold that no analysis of the schema "x means f-ness" is either possible or necessary: no theory should be expected whose form is "x means f-ness = $T(x, f)$"—for example, "x means f-ness = tokens of x are caused by things that are f". To put the point another way, it is wrong to take for granted (as is done, for example, by Fodor, Dretske, Millikan, Papineau, and Jacob) that for a word to mean f-ness is for it to stand in some non-semantic relation to certain instances of f-ness. As a consequence, there is no reason to think that one should be able, on the basis of the underlying, non-semantic, meaning-constituting property of a word, to read off, or to explain, which particular meaning property it constitutes. For example, we should not expect to be able to explain why '$u(x)$' constitutes 'x means DOG', but merely to justify our judgement that it does. I will suggest in Chapter 10 that Kripke's principal argument in favour of

meaning scepticism is invalidated by his failure to recognize this point.

(6) *Meaning as use.* Instead of offering a reductive analysis of the form 'x means F (= x means f-ness) = $T(x, f)$', I argue that the non-semantic characteristic to which the meaning property of a word reduces is the property of *its use being governed by such-and-such regularity*—or, more specifically, the property that every use of the word is explained in terms of the fact that we accept certain specified sentences containing it. In the case of some words, these explanatorily basic use facts may indeed turn out to concern their deployment in circumstances characterized by using those very words: perhaps what constitutes the meaning of "red" is the explanatory role of our tendency to accept "That's red" in the presence of red things. Such examples may fan the temptation always to seek out analyses of the form, "x means f-ness = $T(x, f)$". But the facts that govern the use of other words may well have an entirely different shape—perhaps *non*-relational. For example, what explains the use of the word "true" is arguably our tendency to accept instances of "The proposition *that p* is true if and only if *p*". (Please bear in mind that this is an enormously simplified sketch of what will be argued in Chapter 3. Note in particular that the notion of 'acceptance' involved here is a psychological attitude, not to be identified with 'utterance'; and that the story will need to be further complicated in order to account for 'incomplete' understanding and the social determination of meanings.)

(7) *Adequacy.* The use theory is attractive in so far as it alone meets the principal substantive adequacy condition on an account of meaning: namely, that a good theory is one that is able to accommodate the explanatory relationship between meaning and use—that is, to account for the fact that we apply each of our words as we do in part because of what we mean by it. This implies that the meaning-constituting property of a word should be identified with whatever best explains the word's overall deployment. And that, quite plausibly, is the fact that its uses all stem from the acceptance, in certain conditions, of certain sentences containing it.

(8) *Objectivity of meaning.* In this way we can argue against Quine (in Chapters 3 and 9) that it is indeed possible to draw an objective

distinction between those features of a word that constitute its meaning and those that do not, but which are mere consequences of that meaning: for we may single out those patterns of usage that are *explanatorily fundamental*. Therefore, even granting Quine's pragmatic deconstruction of meaning—his insistence that meaning is merely what is preserved in translation, that translations are correct in so far as they are useful, and that useful translation manuals may be recognized as such merely through the observation of behaviour—it none the less emerges that translation is predominantly objective and meanings perfectly real.

(9) *Deflationary determination of reference*. The line between proper and improper applications of a predicate is determined by its basic use regularity, but only in the following deflationary way (elaborated in Chapter 4). First, the predicate's having that particular use constitutes its having a certain meaning. Second, the trivial meaning-to-*truth* schema, "*x* means *f*-ness → (*y*)(*x* is *true* of *y* iff *y* is *f*)", specifies the predicate's extension in light of that meaning. And third, assuming the desirability of truth, it is thereby determined when the predicate should and should not be applied. This approach to the so-called 'problem of error' rejects the need for a stronger (more explanatory) determination of a term's extension on the basis of its meaning-constituting property: we should not expect to be able to say, given a basic use regularity, what the extension would have to be of any word that is governed by that regularity. And this rejection hinges on taking a deflationary view of the truth-theoretic notions: that is, on taking the view that '*x* is true', '*x* is true of *y*' and '*x* refers to *y*' are irreducible. For in so far as we deny that '*x* is true of *y*' is analysable as '*x* bears relation *r* to *y*', we need not infer from the above meaning-to-*truth* schema that the meaning-constituting property of each predicate '*f*' must entail something of the form '(*y*)(*x* bears relation *r* to *y* iff *y* is *f*); so we will not be committed to the sort of meaning-constituting properties from which it would be possible to figure out the extensions of the words that possess them. Therefore deflationism enables us to resist inferring (from the meaning-to-*truth* schema) that one must be able to infer or explain—hence, in a strong sense, to 'determine'—a predicate's extension on the basis of its meaning-constituting property. Thus from a deflationary point of view, the problem of error is defanged: it cannot count against a candidate meaning-constituting property that we are unable to

specify and explain which applications are incorrect of the words
possessing that property.

(10) *No analyticity*. A couple of epistemologically significant
morals may be drawn from the deflationary/use-theoretic picture.
First, no sentence can be true in virtue of its meaning alone—not
even an implicit definition, i.e. a sentence whose acceptance determines the meaning of one of its constituent terms. For acceptance
does not imply truth; therefore, even though a word's meaning may
indeed derive from our *regarding as true* certain sentences containing
it, there is no need for those sentences *actually to be true*. A second
moral is that the constitution of meaning does not engender interesting a priori commitments. For although meaning-constituting
sentences (implicit definitions) are indeed a priori—i.e. they are not
adopted for empirical reasons—such sentences never express substantive claims of the sort whose justification has been of traditional
philosophical concern—e.g. claims of logic, arithmetic, or geometry.
Granted, a word's meaning may be fixed by the acceptance of substantive postulates containing the word. Nevertheless, in order to
give that meaning to the word, it is not *necessary* to accept those postulates: disagreement about whether they are true does not preclude
a common understanding of what they say. It is enough to commit
oneself to the conditional: *if* any word is to be deployed in that way,
this one will be. For example, in order to mean what we do by "phlogiston" we need not embrace the phlogiston theory; it suffices to
maintain that "If something satisfies that theory, it is phlogiston". In
general, in order to mean what we do by a term "f", which is
deployed within some theory "$\#f$", it isn't necessary to advocate that
theory; it will be enough to be committed to "$\exists x(\#x) \rightarrow \#f$"; that
conditional is the a priori implicit definition. Thus there is no route
from meaning constitution to substantive a priori knowledge as
imagined by the conventionalists and, more recently, by Peacocke
and Boghossian. These issues are the focus of Chapter 6.

(11) *Understanding as implicit knowledge*. To fully understand a
word is to attribute to it a meaning that coincides with its meaning in
the language. But such an attribution—such a belief about the meaning of a word—is *implicit* (as we shall see in Chapters 2 and 7). We
do not articulate these beliefs to ourselves. Rather, simply by virtue
of the fact that our use of a word is governed by a certain basic reg-

ularity, we are implicitly taking the word to have a certain meaning; and, to the extent that this basic regularity matches that of 'experts' within the community, we thereby qualify as implicitly knowing that it has that meaning. Thus, understanding is not a matter of explicit knowledge. (Consequently, we should not expect the explanatory relationship between our understanding of single words and our understanding of whole sentences to be mediated by inferential processes.)

(12) *Trivial compositionality.* In so far as truth is defined by the equivalence schema, "The proposition *that p* is true iff *p*", then the notion of proposition, and the intimately related notion of meaning, are conceptually prior to truth. Therefore, from our deflationary perspective on truth, it is necessary to reject the Davidsonian analysis of sentence meanings as truth conditions (whereby, for example, '*s* means that dogs bark' is explicated as '*s* is true if and only if dogs bark'). Consequently, we must find an alternative to Davidson's widely accepted explanation, based on that analysis, of the *compositionality* of meaning (i.e. of the fact that the meanings of sentences are engendered by the meanings of their component words). The alternative developed in Chapter 7 is that understanding a sentence consists, by definition, in nothing over and above understanding its constituents and appreciating how they are combined with one another. Thus the meaning of the sentence does not have to be *worked out* on the basis of what is known about how it is constructed; for that knowledge by itself constitutes the sentence's meaning. If this is so, then compositionality is a trivial consequence of what we mean by "understanding" in connection with complex expressions. It can put no constraint whatsoever upon how our *words* come to mean what they do—allowing, in particular, that the meaning of a word derives from its use.

(13) *Extrinsic normative import.* It is shown in Chapter 8 (contra Dummett, Wright, and Kripke) that the package consisting of deflationism about truth and the use theory of meaning is quite consistent with the *normative* import of truth and meaning: that is, with the fact that we *aim* for true beliefs, and that, depending on what a word means, it *ought* to be applied to some things but not others. The crucial idea here is that a property may have normative implications without being *intrinsically* normative; for it may be in virtue of the

non-normative character of a property that we would benefit from acting in a certain way on the things that possess it. For example, it is in virtue of the non-normative character of the property 'being an umbrella' that we benefit from carrying around something which possesses that property. Similarly, it may be in virtue of the non-normative basic use regularity of a word that we would profit from applying it in certain conditions. In this vein it can be shown that practical advantages do indeed accrue from ascribing predicates only to those things to which they truly apply. This is where the normative import of truth and meaning comes from; the notions themselves are non-normative.

I will begin to set out these ideas in the next chapter, sketching my argument to the effect that all but one of the traditionally presup-posed conditions on a good account of meaning have been miscon-strued and that the versions with which they should be replaced provide no constraint at all. The sole exception is that a satisfactory account must deal with the evident connection between the meaning of a word and the circumstances in which we are inclined to employ it; and this condition points us toward the use theory proposed in Chapter 3, which is the heart of the book. It articulates the theory, provides several arguments in its favour, and deals with a long series of actual and imagined objections. In subsequent chapters I return to give more thorough attention to how accounts of meaning may and may not be constrained by its relations to surrounding concepts. Thus there are discussions of truth and representation (Chapter 4), names and reference (Chapter 5), definition and a priori knowledge (Chapter 6), compositionality of meaning (Chapter 7), and linguis-tic norms (Chapter 8). And in the final two chapters I respond to the sceptical challenges posed by Quine and Kripke.

Finally, a note on the term "deflation". The deflationary view of truth is so called because it renounces the demand for any theory of the form 'x is true = x is such-and-such', and makes do instead with something obvious: 'The proposition *that p* is true if and only if *p*'. Similarly, the use theory of meaning involves the rejection of many widely assumed constraints on a good account. It minimizes theor-etical aspirations by renouncing the demand for (a) any nominalistic reduction of meaning entities, (b) any analysis of the schema 'x means f-ness', (c) any explanation of substantive a priori knowledge, (d) any non-trivial account of compositionality, and (e) any intrinsically normative meaning-constituting properties. In these respects the use theory of meaning is indeed deflationary. On the other hand, I am not supposing, as I do in the case of truth, that some trivial schema (such as ' "*e*" means *E*') can provide the whole story. Granted, it might come to seem obvious (after various confusions have been removed) that the meaning of a word derives from its having a certain basic use regularity. But, even so, we are left with the hard problem of spelling out what these use regularities are— whereas the question of what it is for a specified proposition to be true can be fully settled without any difficulty at all, simply by reference to the equivalence schema. Thus the use theory of meaning is, by that standard, not especially deflationary. None the less, in virtue of the respects in which it *is* deflationary, and given that the use theory of meaning and the deflationary view of truth together form a natural, mutually supporting pair of ideas, I propose to refer to the combination of them as "semantic deflationism".

2

Pseudo-Constraints on an Adequate
Account of Meaning

A vital fact about the English word "dog" is that it has a specific meaning—a meaning different from that of "cat" but the same as the Spanish "perro". More generally, there exists a range of *meaning properties* which words and their compounds can have, and a given language is determined in part by fixing which of them are exemplified by each of its phonological objects. Thus the English "dog" has one of these meaning properties (call it "meaning DOG"), which the Spanish "perro" also has, whereas the English "cat" has the property of meaning CAT.

The main philosophical problem of meaning is to characterize these properties—to specify how they are constituted. Are they physical, mental, or abstract? Do they have some irreducibly semantic nature? Are they normative, descriptive, or both? Are they individualistic or social, intrinsic or relational? Do they relate expressions to the aspects of reality that the expressions designate? To what extent is their application objective and determinate? Such questions, and more, are what philosophers have struggled, and are still struggling, to answer.

This problem has been thought both extremely important and extremely difficult. And it is certainly important; for it lies at the centre of the philosophy of language, which itself occupies the centre of philosophy. So there are few deep philosophical issues that do not hinge in one way or another on which account of meaning is adopted. But whether the problem is really as tough as has been thought is what I want to call into question here.

Why the problem of meaning has been *taken* to be so difficult is clear enough. It has been assumed that a satisfactory solution—an adequate philosophical account of meaning—would have to satisfy (or at least provide the basis for satisfying) a broad range of substantive constraints, notably the following:

(1) *The Understanding Constraint.* The theory must explain how facts about meaning can be known; for understanding a language involves knowing what its words mean.

(2) *The Relationality Constraint.* The theory must specify the general nature of the relation between terms and their meanings; that is, it must provide some analysis of the notion, '*x* means *y*'.

(3) *The Representation Constraint.* The theory must explain how language can represent reality—how, in virtue of their meanings, singular terms are used to refer to objects in the world, predicates pick out sets of things, and sentences express thoughts that are true or false.

(4) *The Aprioricity Constraint.* The theory must accommodate the arbitrary, conventional, a prioristic character of the meanings of words. For the choice of which language to use to express one's empirical beliefs is not itself an empirical matter.

(5) *The Compositionality Constraint.* It must explain how meanings are compositional—how it happens that the meanings of complex expressions are determined by the meanings of their parts.

(6) *The Normativity Constraint.* It must explain how meanings can have normative consequences—how it is, for example, that given what the word "dog" means, one *ought* to apply it to this thing but not to that.

(7) *The Use Constraint.* It must account for the relationship between the meaning of an expression and its use—the possibility of explaining the way words are used on the basis of how they are understood.

These constraints on an adequate theory of meaning have been regarded as hard to meet, even taken one at a time; so the prospect of finding an account that would meet all at once has seemed rather remote. I want to suggest, however, that the situation is actually not so bleak. For I believe that none of these constraints, when properly understood, poses serious problems. The trouble, I shall argue, is that they have been misconstrued and wrongly thought to imply certain further adequacy conditions which are indeed difficult (perhaps impossible) to satisfy. Understood as they should be, however, each of these seven observations about meaning is perfectly correct and easily accommodated.

In the present chapter I begin to substantiate this claim, thereby providing a sketch of the overall argument of the book. In later chapters the constraints are examined one at a time and in detail. So readers finding themselves impatient for a more thorough treatment of any of them can jump ahead to the appropriate point.

Terminological Preliminaries

The facts whose nature we are investigating are those regarding the meanings of words and their compounds—facts articulated by sentences such as

> The English word "dog" means DOG;
> Pierre's word "chien" means DOG;
> The sentence most often uttered in Seattle means IT'S
>   RAINING;
> The schema "*p* and *q*" means *P* AND *Q*;

and, in general,

> *S*'s expression *x* means *E*,

where what replaces "*S*" picks out a person or set of people, what replaces "*x*" picks out a type of phonological object, and what replaces "*E*" designates a meaning.

The types with whose meanings we are concerned are identified solely on the basis of their shape or sound (or some analogous feature). I shall describe them variously as *words*, *complexes*, *sentences*, *expressions*, etc., and I shall use double quotation marks (as in "bank") to name them. In addition we can recognize a related but importantly different linguistic type, which is individuated in terms of both sound and meaning. I shall use star quotation marks (as in *bank**) to designate these things. Thus in the sentence

"yank" rhymes with *bank*

the first quote-name unambiguously designates a single type, not all of whose tokens have the same meaning; whereas the second quote-name is ambiguous—in some contexts it refers to a type whose tokens, besides having a certain shape in common, all pick out a kind of financial institution, and in other contexts it refers to a type whose tokens have exactly the same shape, but which can pick out the side of a river.

I am adopting the convention of capitalizing an English expression in order to designate its meaning or meanings. Thus "DOG" names the meaning of the word "dog", and "BANK" ambiguously designates the two meanings of "bank". Putting it schematically, I introduce the capitalized term "*E*" in order to name whatever it is that the English expression "*e*" means—where "*e*" covers every type of meaningful expression, including predicates, names, sentences, connective schemata such as "*p* or *q*" and "All *f*s are *g*", and morphemes such as "un–" and "–able".

Although the facts with which we will be concerned have the form

S's expression *x* means *E*,

allowing that *x* may have different meanings in different linguistic communities, I will usually simplify this formulation by suppressing the explicit reference to *S*. I will take it that, for example,

"dog" means DOG

and

"Il pleut" means IT'S RAINING

articulate meaning facts. In such cases there is tacit reference to a particular person or community.

Let us now consider the various above-mentioned constraints on an adequate account of such facts.

1. Understanding

In some sense, no doubt, to *understand* something is to know what it means—which is presumably to know something about it of the above sort. However, a difficulty straight away emerges: it is not easy to identify the fact regarding, say, the word "dog", the knowledge of which constitutes our understanding that word. The obvious candidate is the fact that it means what it does, i.e. the fact that "dog" means DOG. But there appears to be a decisive objection to this suggestion—as clearly correct as it may initially seem. For in light of how the meaning designator, "DOG", has been introduced (as a name for whatever may be the meaning of "dog"), it is a trivial matter to work out that "dog" means DOG. Even those who do not understand the word (i.e. do not know what "dog" means) might nevertheless be fully aware of *that* fact. So it cannot be that understanding the word "dog" consists in knowing that "dog" means DOG.[1] But this is puzzling; for what other fact could possibly be relevant?

Suppose that the word means what it does in virtue of some more basic fact about it: namely, that it has property '$u(x)$'. One might be tempted to think that something of this sort is what is known by those who understand it. But that won't do either. For a sophisticated scientific inquiry might be required in order to reach the conclusion that "dog" has property '$u(x)$'; yet without having pursued any such inquiry, we nevertheless understand the word perfectly well. Nor can one reply that the inquiry is needed only to make us consciously aware of the fact that "dog" has '$u(x)$'—a fact which is already known unconsciously by anyone who understands the word. For the postulation of any such unconscious knowledge is a matter of scientific speculation; whereas we feel certain that there is something we

---

[1] One might be tempted to reply that if someone doesn't understand the word "dog" then he is not really in a position to work out (from the capitalizing convention) that "dog" means DOG, for he would not be able to understand the term "DOG" and so (assuming he has no other language) would not be capable of having the thoughts it may be used to articulate. This reply is not correct, for one can be aware that "DOG" is the name of whatever "dog" happens to mean—and hence understand "DOG"—without knowing what that meaning is. But even if it *were* correct it would merely open the door to another objection—equally effective. Namely, that our understanding the word "dog" cannot consist in our knowing that it means DOG, for that knowledge itself depends on understanding the word "dog". Similarly, understanding "dog" cannot consist in knowing that it means doggyness, or in knowing that it is true of dogs. Granted, such items of knowledge are not trivial; but that is because they are possible only for those who *already* understand the word "dog" (or some synonym of it).

know when we understand a word. So it remains to specify what are the properties of words the recognition of which constitutes understanding. On the one hand, it would seem that they must be meaning properties of the form 'x means E'; but on the other hand it would seem that they cannot be.

This paradox, I want to suggest, is the result of our having misconstrued the Understanding Constraint. No doubt we do 'know', in some sense, what our words mean. But there is no reason to presuppose, as we have been, that this knowledge is *explicit*—that the propositions we know to be true are propositions that we articulate to ourselves either consciously or unconsciously. On the contrary, it is that very presupposition which is leading us into trouble. For the explicit knowledge that "dog" means DOG is trivial and neither necessary nor sufficient for understanding. What we can and should suppose, rather, is that the knowledge in question is *implicit*. More specifically, the fact that the expert and hence communal deployment of "dog" is the result of the word's having use property '$u(x)$', constitutes the fact that it means what it does—i.e. that it means DOG— in the communal language. If a community member's deployment of the word results from the same property '$u(x)$', then the meaning of "dog" in his idiolect will be the same as its meaning in the communal language. He will then qualify as knowing *implicitly* what the word means, and thereby as understanding it. This explains why someone who works out explicitly (from the capitalizing convention) that "dog" means DOG does not thereby understand it.[2]

More accurately, understanding is a matter of degree: it is possible to have full knowledge, incomplete knowledge, or hardly any knowledge at all of what a word means in a communal language, and thereby to have full, incomplete, or minimal understanding of it. The degree to which an individual understands a word is constituted by the degree of similarity between what it means in his idiolect and

[2] It might be felt that the resort to implicit knowledge does not succeed in fully rooting out our initial difficulty. For in so far as the fact that "dog" means DOG is trivial—amounting to no more than the tautology that "dog" means what it means—then it is *necessary* and can have no substantive explanation; so it could not be the fact we are interested in. But this worry is unwarranted. It is indeed easy to reach the conclusion that "dog" means DOG. But this does not make it a necessary truth. Just as the President of the United States (i.e. Clinton) might not have been the President of the United States, so the meaning of "dog" (i.e. DOG) might not have been the meaning of "dog". Nor are we precluded from giving an account of what is required to possess that meaning; and in terms of that account we can give a substantive explanation of why "dog" means what it does.

what it means in the communal language. And this degree of similarity in meaning is in turn constituted by the degree of similarity
between the explanatorily basic use property, $u(x)$, that determines
the word's overall deployment in the community and the use property that determines its deployment by the individual. Just as long as
the individual has acquired the word from the community and has a
minimal understanding of it, the communal language meaning may
be correctly attributed to him—he means by it what everyone else
means. But he *knows* what it means only to the extent that whatever
constitutes its meaning in his idiolect resembles whatever constitutes
its meaning in the communal language.

The position I am urging here is sometimes expressed (but not, I
think, quite correctly) by saying that understanding is merely a form
of *knowing how* and not a form of *knowing that*: i.e. that it is a skill
or practical ability with no propositional content, something like
knowing how to juggle.[3] But a better way of putting the point (that
is, more faithful to the conceptual equivalence of 'understanding a
word' with 'knowing what it means') is that although understanding
is indeed a practical ability, it may none the less be characterized as
an instance of 'knowing that'—providing we recognize that the
knowledge is *implicit*. Moreover, it is perfectly consistent with this
position that the causal/explanatory basis for the implicit knowledge
should sometimes turn out, under scientific investigation, to involve
a body of unconscious *explicit* knowledge. For our question concerned what is presupposed in our ordinary conception of understanding, not the character of its hypothetical causal antecedents.[4]

2. Relationality

On the face of it, attributions of meaning, such as "The word "perro"
means DOG", "The schema "p and q" means P AND Q", and "The
sentence he uttered means SNOW IS WHITE", have a relational

---

[3] See, for example, Michael Devitt's *Coming to our Senses* (Cambridge: Cambridge
University Press, 1996), ch. 2.
[4] This issue is taken up again in Chapter 7, together with its import for how to
account for the compositionality of meaning. In so far as our understanding of primitive terms and the complexes they form requires merely *implicit* commitments, then it
should not be expected that the explanatory links between these commitments will
involve inferential processes.

structure: they say that the relation 'x means y' holds between a phonological type, x, and some other entity, y (for example, DOG, P AND Q, or SNOW IS WHITE), belonging to the category, meanings.[5] Consequently, two questions arise. What is the nature of these entities, the meanings? And what is the nature of the relation of 'meaning' in which terms stand to the meaning entities?

The second of these questions is not as hard as the first one. When we say

> Smoke means fire

we employ a concept of meaning whose character is explicable in terms of the notion of evidence: we are saying, roughly, that

> The observation of smoke *indicates* (i.e. should justify a belief in) the presence of fire.

Similarly (and contrary to Grice's influential view), when we specify the meaning of a word we are also making a claim about what is to be inferred from its occurrence: we are specifying what a person who uses the word should be expected to 'have in mind'. Thus the intuitive construal of

> "perro" means DOG

is something along the lines of

---

[5] The superficial impression that meaning facts are relational is confirmed when we consider their logical properties. We are inclined to infer

> x means something

from

> x means DOG

and to infer

> x and y mean the same thing

from

> x means DOG and y means DOG.

And such inferences are most readily accommodated by supposing that the logical form of a meaning fact is 'x means y': i.e. that meaning facts are indeed relational. (Remember that these formulations suppress reference to the person or persons whose words are at issue. Thus, strictly speaking, the inference is from "S's word x means DOG" to "S's word x means something", etc.)

The utterance of "perro" indicates (i.e. justifies belief in) the presence (within some mental state of the speaker) of the concept, DOG.[6]

The rough idea is that certain mental characteristics (for example, 'x believes that dogs bark') are composed of elements (for example, the concept, DOG), and that these elements may be associated with words in such a way that the employment of a word indicates the presence of its associated concept.

I should mention that in supposing that meanings are *concepts* I

---

[6] In his influential essay, "Meaning" (*Philosophical Review* 66 (1957), 377–88), Paul Grice maintains that the word "means" is ambiguous: that the notion we typically use in connection with language (what he calls *non-natural* meaning) is not the same as the notion (*natural* meaning) we deploy in speaking of the implications of natural phenomena (as in "Smoke means fire"). He bases this view largely on the following sort of argument. The sentence, "Her words mean she is angry", is clearly ambiguous. One might use it to say that her words have, in her language, the meaning SHE IS ANGRY. Or one might use it to say that one can reasonably infer from her choice of words that she is angry. Now, according to Grice, the way we should account for the ambiguity of this sentence is to suppose that the constituent word "means" is ambiguous. In the first sense (non-natural meaning), what is meant need not obtain: the statement might well be true even if no particular woman is angry. In the second sense (natural meaning), what is meant must obtain: the statement would be false if she were not in fact angry. Thus we can conclude that the word "means" is ambiguous, because this would best explain how the sentence containing it comes to be ambiguous. But this is a fallacious argument. Granted, the sentence in question is ambiguous. And granted, this is best explained in terms of an ambiguity in one of its constituents. But we can suppose that the guilty party is not the word "means", but rather the expression "she is angry"—which can refer either to the complex concept, SHE IS ANGRY, or to the fact of her being angry. In the former case we are saying that her words indicate the presence of the concept, SHE IS ANGRY, and in the latter case that her words indicate the presence of anger. In both cases the word "means" means "indicates", "reveals", or "gives reason to believe in the presence of". In both cases what is meant must obtain. Thus both cases employ what Grice calls *natural* meaning. There is no reason to think that in linguistic contexts we deploy a distinct notion of non-natural meaning. Needless to say, this is not to deny that there certainly do exist notions that are deployed in connection with language which are distinct from the notion of natural meaning. For example, the notion of reference—as when we say, "The word "Aristotle" refers to Aristotle". Nor is it to deny that the word "meaning" is ambiguous—in some contexts (for example, "I was meaning to phone") it has nothing to do with 'indication'. But these observations are irrelevant to the point at issue, which is whether the word "means" displays a certain ambiguity—more specifically, whether the concept of meaning that we employ in saying e.g. "The word "chien" means DOG" and "The expression "John is angry" means JOHN IS ANGRY", is distinct from natural meaning. I am suggesting that Grice's main argument in favour of that thesis is mistaken, and that we have no reason to depart from the naive view that meaning is, in both contexts, a species of *indication*.

do not intend to deny that they might also be *properties*: e.g. that the meaning of "dog" might be the property of 'being a dog' (i.e. dogginess). Of course, this can be so only if the term "property" is deployed in a sufficiently fine-grained sense (so that, for example, the property of 'being water' is taken to differ from the property of 'being made of H_2O'). In that sense, the identity conditions of properties are given by

The property f-ness = the property g-ness $\leftrightarrow$
   the predicate "f" means the same as the predicate "g",

and I see no good reason not to identify properties with concepts. If they are identical, then 'x means F' will amount to 'x indicates the presence, in some mental state of the speaker, of the property f-ness' (which will, of course, have to be sharply distinguished from 'x indicates an *exemplification* of the property f-ness').

Thus it is not hard to characterize the relation 'x means y' and thereby to satisfy the Relationality Constraint on an adequate account of meaning. It would be a serious mistake, however, to transform this thesis, which concerns the *superficial composition* of meaning properties, into a constraint on their *underlying nature*. We cannot infer, from the fact that 'x means DOG' contains the relation 'x means y', that whatever (at any level) constitutes that property must also contain that relation or else something which constitutes that relation. Consequently (as we shall now see), there is going to be no reason to think that 'x means DOG' reduces to some non-semantic relation between x and *dogs*.

What is wrong with these inferences? The basic error is that of supposing that reductive analysis must preserve logical structure. In other words, it is a fallacy to assume that whenever a fact has a certain component, then whatever constitutes this fact must contain either that same component or alternatively something that constitutes it. In particular, we cannot take for granted that in order for a property to constitute 'x means DOG' (i.e. 'x means doggyness') one of the components of that reducing property must be either the relation 'x means y' or something constituting it. Failure to appreciate this point leads, by the following route, to the conclusion that 'x means DOG' reduces to something of the form '$T(x, \text{dog})$'. It will be appreciated that in order to obtain a fully non-semantic reduction of the meaning property, i.e. of

x means doggyness,

and given the nominalistic irreducibility of the concept DOG (i.e. the property of dogginess), the relation

x means y

will have to be analysable into something of the form

x bears relation T^* to (certain specified) exemplifications of y

(where T involves only non-semantic terms). For such an analysis would enable a reduction of

x means doggyness

to

x bears relation T^* to (certain specified) exemplifications of doggyness,

which is equivalent to the patently non-semantic

x bears relation T^* to (certain specified) dogs

or

$T(x, \text{dog})$.

Thus, if it is assumed that reductive analysis preserves logical form, then fully non-semantic reductions of meaning properties can be obtained only on the basis of the above analysis of the meaning relation. This is the reason, I suspect, that it is so often presupposed that an adequate theory of meaning must take the form

x means $F = T(x, f)$,

where T may be dependent upon "f" and involves only relatively unproblematic (i.e. non-intensional) notions. And the problem becomes that of specifying T. It is this common view of the problem—this strong conception of the Relationality Constraint—that I am calling into question.

Before going further into what is wrong with it, I want to emphasize that the Strong Relationality Constraint is satisfied by just about every theory that has ever been seriously entertained. One prominent example is the Davidsonian 'truth-conditional' theory, whereby

> Predicate *x* means *F*

is analysed as

> (*y*)(*y* is *true* of *x* ↔ *y* exemplifies *f*-ness)

i.e.

> (*y*)(*y* is *true* of *x* ↔ *f*(*y*))

(where "*true*" is taken to express a primitive, naturalistic, explanatorily active property of utterances). Other examples are provided by the correlational (informational) theories of Stampe and Fodor, according to which

> Predicate *x* means *F*

is analysed, roughly speaking, as

> Instances of *f*-ness cause (under appropriate conditions)
>   utterances of *x*,

i.e.

> (*y*)(*y* is *f* → *y* would, in appropriate conditions, cause a
>   tokening of *x*).

Also governed by this constraint are the teleological theories of Millikan, Dretske, Papineau, and Jacob, whereby

> Predicate *x* means *F*

comes out roughly as

The evolutionary function of x is to be applied in the presence of fs.

And finally there is Kripke, whose argument *against* the naturalistic reduction of meaning-facts is based implicitly on the Strong Relationality Constraint. He assumes that in order for some property of a word to constitute its meaning, it would have to be possible to, as he puts it, *read off* from that property exactly which meaning it constitutes. And this 'reading off' requirement is tantamount to the view that a reductive theory of meaning properties would have to have the form: x means $F = T(x, f)$. Given the plethora of such examples, it is fair to regard it as a widespread assumption that an adequate account of meaning should satisfy the constraint of Strong Relationality.[7]

Notice, however, that this is a very substantive commitment, and that it stands in need of justification. For why should it not be, on the contrary, that although there is *perhaps* some relation to dogs that constitutes the property of meaning DOG, this is completely different from the relation to tables that constitutes the property of meaning TABLE? And why should there not be predicates "*f*"—maybe the majority of them—such that the property of meaning what they do is not constituted by *any* relation to *f*s? The answer offered above came from the idea that *surely* any non-semantic analysis of '*x* means

[7] See D. Davidson, *Inquiries into Truth and Interpretation* (Oxford: Clarendon Press, 1984); F. I. Dretske, *Knowledge and the Flow of Information* (Cambridge, Mass.: MIT Press, 1981); D. W. Stampe, "Toward a Causal Theory of Linguistic Representation", in P. French, T. Uehling, and H. Wettstein (eds.), *Midwest Studies in Philosophy* 2 (Minneapolis, Minn.: University of Minnesota Press, 1977); J. Fodor, *Psychosemantics* (Cambridge, Mass.: MIT Press, 1987); D. Papineau, *Reality and Representation* (Oxford: Blackwell, 1987); R. Millikan, *Language, Thought and Other Biological Categories* (Cambridge, Mass.: MIT Press, 1984); P. Jacob, *What Minds can Do* (Cambridge: Cambridge University Press, 1997); S. Kripke, *Wittgenstein on Rules and Private Language* (Oxford: Blackwell, 1982). For an elaboration of this critique of Kripke's argument see Chapter 10 below, and my "Meaning, Use and Truth", *Mind* 104 (1995), 355–68.

Here I am merely suggesting that such 'Strongly Relational' theories are ill-motivated. To appreciate how unsuccessful they are see, for example, Barry Loewer, "From Information to Intentionality", *Synthese* 70, (1987), 287–317; Fred Adams and Ken Aizawa, "Fodorian Semantics", and Peter Godfrey-Smith, "A Continuum of Semantic Optimism", both in Stephen Stich and Ted Warfield (eds.), *Mental Representation*, 223–42 and 259–77, respectively (Cambridge, Mass.: MIT Press, 1994); and Robert Cummins, "The Lot of the Causal Theory of Mental Content", *Journal of Philosophy* 94 (1997), 535–42.

F' must be the product of some non-semantic analysis of 'x means y'. But I have been suggesting that this intuition is based on the fallacious assumption that reductive analysis preserves logical form.

To see why this 'Constitution Fallacy' is indeed a fallacy, we should remind ourselves of what it takes, in general, for a relatively superficial property '$s(x)$' to be *constituted* by an underlying property '$u(x)$'. If we examine some paradigm examples of this relation—e.g. 'being water'/'being composed of H_2O' and 'being red'/'emitting light of such-and-such wavelength'—it becomes clear that the conditions necessary and sufficient for '$u(x)$' to constitute '$s(x)$' are that

(1)   '$u(x)$' and '$s(x)$' apply to the same things

and

(2)   facts about '$s(x)$' are explained by (1).

So, for example, (1') all water is made of H_2O molecules and vice versa; and (2') this is why water is transparent, why it boils at 100°C, etc. Note moreover that fact (1') (as opposed to the fact that we *believe* it) is not subject to explanation. Thus '$u(x)$' constitutes '$s(x)$' when their coextensiveness is the basic explanation of facts involving '$s(x)$'.[8]

Now the important point, in the present context, is that these conditions do not require any commonality of logical form between '$s(x)$' and '$u(x)$'; nothing precludes the possibility that the superficial property '$s(x)$' be a relation—articulated as '$s*(k,x)$'—and that the underlying property '$u(x)$' be monadic and not divisible into a part that constitutes k and a part that constitutes '$s*(y,x)$'. Consider, for example, the thesis that

x exemplifies f-ness

is constituted by

$f(x)$.

---

[8] Some philosophers speak of "property identity" rather than "property constitution" in such cases. As indicated above, I am reserving the former term for the stronger relation that obtains only when the predicates standing for '$u(x)$' and '$s(x)$' are synonyms.

This is intuitively plausible. Moreover, it satisfies our pair of conditions on 'property constitution'. Yet the underlying property may be essentially monadic whereas the superficial property is relational. By the same token, it is perfectly possible that 'x means DOG' be constituted, despite its relational form, by a monadic property '$u(x)$', which does not relate x to dogs or to dogginess. Consequently there is no need to base our account of the meaning property, 'x means DOG', on a prior analysis of the meaning relation—an analysis which, as we have seen, would have to take the form

$$x \text{ means } y = x \text{ bears relation } T^* \text{ to certain instances of y.}$$

It is worth noting that either way—whether or not '$u(x)$' is strongly relational—the meaning entity, DOG, is most directly identified as

That which is meant (i.e. indicated) by a word with '$u(x)$'.

And, generalizing, our concept of *concept* will be explained by the schematic principle

The concept F = that which is meant (i.e. indicated) by our word "f" and by any word with the same meaning-constituting property.

Thus we cannot arrive at the underlying analysis of, for example, 'x means DOG' in the way suggested by its superficial form—that is, by adding an analysis of the component, 'x means y', to an analysis of the concept, DOG. Rather, we must first uncover the nature of meaning properties and then arrive (by 'subtraction' as it were) at the character of meaning entities (i.e. concepts).[9]

In summary, then, we can indeed regard 'x means F' as express-

---

[9] The Strongly Relational theories I have mentioned (of the form 'x means F = $T(x, f)$') are not based on a prior nominalistic analysis of meaning entities. Consequently there is a certain inconsistency in their motivation. For although (in so far as it is presupposed that reductive analysis preserves logical form) it is insisted that the analysis of 'x means f-ness' involve a prior analysis of the constituent 'x means y', that presupposition is nevertheless flouted when it is not required that there also be a prior analysis of the *other* constituent—namely, the concept F. On the contrary (as we saw above), these theories rely on the idea that 'x exemplifies f-ness' reduces to '$f(x)$'— an idea which goes against the rationale for Strong Relationality.

ing a relation between x and F—between a phonological type and a meaning; but the relation is simply that of *indication*; the Relationality Constraint is trivially satisfied. It is a mistake, however, to conclude that what constitutes such facts must share this relational form; or, in other words, to infer from the logical structure of a meaning attribution that one of the constituents of its analysis is an analysis of the relation, 'x means y'; or, to put it another way, to assume that there are any worthwhile relational accounts of the form

x means $F = T(x, f)$.

Thus the Strong Relationality Constraint is not motivated by considerations of logical form. In the next section we shall see whether the need to explain *representation* can provide an alternative rationale for it.

3. Representation

Language is often used to represent components of reality. Names may refer to particular objects, predicates stand for properties exemplified by some things and not others, sentences sometimes describe facts—and it is because of the meanings of such marks and sounds that this occurs. Thus a satisfactory account of meaning properties must explain how it comes about that a certain noise, in virtue of possessing one or another of them, comes to designate this or that aspect of the world.

So much is reasonable and uncontroversial. However, I believe there has been a prevalent tendency to mistakenly transform this adequacy condition into a version of the Strong Relationality Constraint: specifically, that the meaning properties of terms must reduce to *relations* between those terms and the aspects of reality to which they apply.

Consider, for example, some word that means DOG. Its meaning determines its extension[10]—i.e.

---

[10] For the sake of simplicity, I confine attention to predicates whose extensions are context-insensitive.

x means DOG $\rightarrow$ x expresses a concept that is true of all and
only dogs

or, in other words,

x means DOG $\rightarrow$ x is *true* of all and only dogs,

where, by definition, a predicate is *true* (italicized) of a thing if and
only if the concept it expresses is true of that thing. Moreover, 'x is
true of y' is an extensional relation. So, given generally naturalistic
sympathies, we tend to expect there to be some underlying analysis
of it—some account of the form

x is *true* of y = x bears r to y

where '$r(xy)$' is a naturalistic (causal) relation of some sort.
Consequently, we are tempted to suppose that whatever property
may constitute 'x means DOG', it must entail

x bears r to all and only dogs.

Therefore the reductive analysis of 'meaning DOG' must take the
form

x means DOG = x bears r to all and only dogs, and . . .

which has the more general form

x means DOG = $T(x, \text{dog})$.

Some such analysis appears to be needed to explain how the meaning of the predicate determines its extension. Thus the Representation Constraint is taken to imply the Strong Relationality
Constraint. It seems that only if meanings are natural relations to
what is designated can we understand how the relation between a
predicate and its extension is guaranteed by its meaning. And, as we
have seen, there are indeed quite a few theories of meaning that
appear to have been designed accordingly.

However, this entire line of thought involves a highly dubious
'inflationary' assumption: namely, that the truth-theoretic prop-

erties—*truth*, reference, and satisfaction—are analysable in non-semantic terms. It is assumed, in other words, that there are reductions of the form

x is *true* = $t(x)$
x is *true* of (satisfied by) y = $r(x,y)$
x refers to y = $c(x,y)$

where t, r, and c are non-semantic (causal) properties of one sort or another. But this assumption is by no means obviously correct. On the contrary, it can be argued (and will be in Chapters 4 and 5) that our inclination to suppose that the truth-theoretic predicates express substantive properties (with underlying natures) is the product of linguistic illusion; and that the real function of these predicates in our language is to provide devices of semantic ascent and hence mechanisms by means of which certain generalizations may be formulated. It can then be shown that no more of a theory of truth than the trivial equivalence schema

The proposition *that p* is true iff *p*

is needed to account for this function.[11] And parallel things can be argued regarding reference and satisfaction: for example, that the notion of 'being true of' is entirely captured by our accepting the instances of

(y)(The concept F is true of $y \leftrightarrow f(y)$).

and the notion of reference is defined by

---

[11] For a more detailed and exact characterization and defence of the deflationary position, as I see it, see Chapter 4 below and also my *Truth* (2nd edn., Oxford: Oxford University Press, 1998). For other versions of the view see W. V. Quine, *Pursuit of Truth* (Cambridge, Mass.: Harvard University Press, 1990), ch. 5; Stephen Leeds, "Theories of Reference and Truth", *Erkenntnis* 13 (1978) 111–29; Scott Soames, "What is a Theory of Truth?" *Journal of Philosophy* 81 (1984) 411–29; also his "The Truth About Deflationism", in E. Villanueva (ed.), *Philosophical Issues* 8 (Atascadero, Calif: Ridgeview, 1997); Hartry Field, "The Deflationary Conception of Truth", in Graham MacDonald and Crispin Wright (eds.), *Fact, Science, and Morality* (Oxford, Blackwell, 1986); and Field, "Deflationist Views of Meaning and Content", *Mind* 103 (1994), 249–85.

(y)(The singular concept N refers to $y \leftrightarrow y = n$).

If this *deflationary* view of the truth-theoretic notions is correct, then the representational power of language does not imply that meaning properties are strongly relational. For in so far as we have no reason to think that

x is *true* of all and only dogs

consists in a naturalistic relation between x and dogs, then the conditional

x means DOG $\rightarrow$ x is *true* of all and only dogs

will not suggest that the meaning property has any sort of strongly relational structure.

None the less this conditional, which partially defines "is *true* of", can provide a trivial explanation of a word's representational character. It doesn't matter what kind of property 'means DOG' turns out to be. Suppose it is constituted by a monadic, intrinsic, non-semantic property, '$u(x)$'. If so, the explanation of why a word possessing that property is *true* of dogs would be simply (1) that any word with property '$u(x)$' is a word that means DOG, and (2) that any word that means DOG qualifies as being *true* of dogs.

We may conclude, therefore, that, in light of deflationism about truth, the representational character of language provides no reason to think that meaning properties should have a strongly relational form.[12]

4. Aprioricity

The fact that a word means what it does is a matter of arbitrary stipulation—a freely changeable linguistic decision, unconstrained by

---

[12] Let me emphasize that I have not tried (at this stage) to *refute* the thesis that meaning properties are strongly relational, but merely to undermine the only motives I can think of for insisting that they must be. In Chapter 3 when we come to consider, in a more constructive spirit, what properties *do* constitute meanings, it will become clear that many such properties do not relate predicates to the members of their extension, and those that do, do so in a far from uniform way.

empirical considerations, hence a priori. Consequently, if a predicate "*f*" derives its meaning from the fact that we articulate certain commitments by means of it—if, in other words, these commitments provide an *implicit definition* of "*f*"—then they must be a priori.

So far, so good. However, there is a common tendency for this observation to be extended in two questionable directions. First, it is thought, quite plausibly, that *substantive postulates* (such as laws of logic, arithmetic, and geometry) suffice to fix the meanings of some of their constituent terms—from which it is inferred that they must be held a priori. And, second, it is thought that knowledge of the truth of any such implicitly defining postulates may be derived from knowledge of their meanings. For it is assumed that the meaning bestowed on an implicitly defined term must be that meaning which would make the defining postulates correct. However, both of these extensions of the original observation (about the aprioricity of meaning-constituting assertions) run into difficulties, and make that constraint seem much more difficult to satisfy than it really is.

In the first place, as Quine showed, there is good reason to doubt that the postulates of logic, arithmetic, or geometry are a priori (at least, those that are deployed in science). For our set of scientific beliefs forms an interconnected system evolving through time subject only to the desiderata of empirical adequacy, overall simplicity, and conservatism; therefore any of our commitments—including even a principle of logic—might be abandoned in light of experience, for a substantial gain in global simplicity might be achieved by doing so. However, in accepting this conclusion, we are not compelled to give up the idea that implicit definitions are a priori; nor need we deny that we can fix the meanings of terms by accepting certain postulates containing them. What we must say (following Carnap, Russell, Ramsey, and Lewis)[13] is that the commitment to a substantive theory of *f*-ness, "#*f*", is the product of two independent decisions: one of them is to hold true the existential thesis "$\exists x(\#x)$" (i.e. to believe that

---

[13] See B. Russell, *The Analysis of Matter* (London: Allen & Unwin, 1927); R. Carnap, *Der Logische Aufbau der Welt* (Berlin: Schlachtensee Weltkreis-Verlag, 1928); F. Ramsey, "Theories" (1929), reprinted in his *Foundations*, ed. H. D. Mellor (London: Routledge & Kegan Paul, 1978); D. Lewis, "How to Define Theoretical Terms", *Journal of Philosophy* 62 (1970), 427–66. See also my "How to Choose amongst Empirically Indistinguishable Theories", *Journal of Philosophy* 79 (1982), 61–77; and my "A Defense of Conventionalism", in G. MacDonald and C. Wright (eds.), *Fact, Science and Morality* (Oxford: Blackwell, 1986).

there exists a property which has the characteristics '#—' specified by
the theory); the other is to hold true the conditional "$\exists x(\#x) \to \#f$"
(i.e. to decide to call that property "f", *if* there is such a thing). Thus
our acceptance of the substantive theory "$\#f$" is *sufficient* to fix the
meaning of "f" in virtue of the fact that it implies the acceptance of
the conditional "$\exists x(\#x) \to \#f$"; but only the latter commitment is
needed to constitute "f"'s meaning. Thus the real implicit definition
is indeed a priori—but it is not substantive.

In the second place, it is commonly but mistakenly supposed that
in order for certain postulates to implicitly define a term, they must
be true. For it is taken for granted that the meaning conferred on a
term when we implicitly define it is whatever meaning it would need
to have for the defining postulates to be rendered true. In fact, however, the meaning is given to "f" by our *regarding* the postulates as
true, quite independently of whether they really are true. Even if they
are not, our holding them true will succeed in giving "f" a meaning:
their actually being true plays no role in the meaning fixing. The
character of implicit definition and its bearing on a priori knowledge
are the focus of Chapter 6.

5. Compositionality

The meanings of complex terms are typically explained by the meanings of their parts. For, as Davidson has emphasized, how else are we
to explain in a reasonable way that speakers of a language attach
meanings to so many different expressions (including ones they
haven't encountered before), unless we regard this ability as a consequence of their attaching meanings to the (relatively few) basic terms
of the language?[14] So meaning is compositional. And it has been
thought that this fact severely constrains what sort of thing a meaning property might reduce to. Thus Davidson takes it to be a strong
point in favour of his explication of sentence meanings in terms of
truth conditions that it explains compositionality, since he can think
of no other way of doing so.

---

[14] See Davidson, *Inquiries into Truth and Interpretation*.

The Compositionality Constraint may be formulated as follows.

> An adequate theory of meaning must enable us to see how the meanings of complex terms may be determined, and thereby explained, by the meanings of their parts.

Fair enough. But we may wonder how difficult it really is to satisfy this constraint. Are there many (or any) otherwise plausible theories of meaning that are disqualified by their failure to satisfy it?

No doubt the compositionality constraint is not entirely vacuous. Theories of meaning have often been proposed that take the form

> For all expressions, e—whether primitive or complex—the meaning property of e is constituted by that characteristic of e which satisfies condition G,

where, depending on the theory, the property-selecting condition G may be 'being the *truth*/reference condition of e', 'being the assertibility condition of e', 'being the stereotype associated with e', 'being the use of e', etc. And for any such theory the possibility of a conflict with compositionality is clearly left open. We might well find a complex expression, c, which results from the combination of constituents i, j, and k, such that the alleged meaning-constituting properties of these four items are (respectively) g_4, g_3, g_2, and g_1, and such that the fact that

> c results from applying i to j and k

in combination with the fact that

> $g_1(k)$ and $g_2(j)$ and $g_3(i)$

does *not* explain why it is that

> $g_4(c)$.

To give a well-known example, consider a partial theory of meaning according to which the meaning of a sentence is fixed by the set of evidential conditions that each provides the sentence with a high probability of being true. This account is inconsistent with compositionality because the conditions which render a *conjunction* of sentences highly probable are not easily derived, hence not explained, by the conditions which render its conjuncts highly probable.[15]

Thus the compositionality constraint does have a certain bite. I want to suggest, however, that it is by no means as hard to satisfy as has often been assumed. To see this, notice that it will be met by any theory of meaning that takes the following three-stage form. The theory first describes the syntactic structure of the language: it specifies the primitive terms from which expressions are composed, and it shows how each expression of the language may be constructed out of these elements. Secondly, the theory analyses the meaning properties of the primitive elements. It may say, for example, that

> The name "Socrates" means SOCRATES in virtue of the fact that p_1("Socrates");
>
> The predicate "wise" means WISE in virtue of the fact that p_2("wise");
>
> The predication schema "x is f" means what it does in virtue of the fact that p_3("x is f");

where '$p_1(x)$', '$p_2(x)$' and '$p_3(x)$' are underlying meaning-constituting properties of words. And thirdly, for each complex term, the theory says that the fact that the term means what it does is constituted by the fact that it is constructed by combining certain primitive terms in a certain order, together with the facts regarding the meanings of the words involved. It says, for example, that

> "Socrates is wise" means SOCRATES IS WISE in virtue of the fact that "Socrates is wise" results from applying a schema meaning what "x is f" means to a sequence of words meaning what "Socrates" and "wise" mean.

And given what has already been said about the meanings of the primitives, this implies that

---

[15] See Chapter 7, n. 6, for substantiation of this point.

"Socrates is wise" means SOCRATES IS WISE in virtue of
the fact that it results from applying a schema with property p_3 to a sequence of words with properties p_1 and p_2.

Thus the property of meaning SOCRATES IS WISE, which an
expression, x, in some language may have, is constituted by the property

x results from applying a schema whose meaning-constituting
property is p_3 to a sequence of words whose meaning-
constituting properties are p_1 and p_2.

In that case, given premises about how the sentence "Socrates is wise"
is constructed, about what its constituents mean, about how those
meanings are constituted, and about how the property 'x means
SOCRATES IS WISE' is constituted—given all these premises—it
follows that "Socrates is wise" means SOCRATES IS WISE. Thus
compositionality holds. And it holds no matter what p_1, p_2, and p_3
may turn out to be.

Theories of this type do not propose a *uniform* condition for being
the meaning-constituting property of a term—a condition, G, that is
intended to pick out the meaning-constituting property of *any* term
no matter whether it is primitive or complex. More generally, they
don't provide a way of picking out, independently of compositionality considerations, which property of each complex engenders its
meaning, in such a way that there arises a substantive question as to
whether the compositionality requirement is satisfied. Instead these
theories *compose*, from the facts underlying the meanings of the
primitives, the facts underlying the meaning properties of complexes.
Thus the compositionality constraint is automatically satisfied.

Let me stress that nothing at all has been assumed about the
nature of the meaning properties of the *primitive* terms. Thus the
compositionality constraint leaves entirely open the metaphysical
character of meaning properties—whether they are physical, mental,
abstract, irreducibly semantic, monadic, relational, social, descriptive, normative or whatever. Nor, even once we have settled the metaphysical issue, does compositionality *per se* constrain to any degree
which *particular* properties to associate with the meanings of the
primitives.

Therefore Davidson and his followers would appear to be quite

mistaken in supposing that compositionality provides a compelling
rationale for embracing the truth-conditional account of meaning.
The arguments (spelled out in a series of papers by Jerry Fodor and
Ernie LePore)[16] to the effect that word meanings cannot be constituted by such things as prototype structures, inferential roles, or
recognitional capacities each make the uniformity assumption just
challenged. If that assumption is indeed false, then there is no need
for prototypes (or inferential roles, or recognitional capacities, etc.)
themselves to be compositional in order for them to be what provide
words with their meanings.

Consider—to mention the alternative I will be pursuing—the view
that the meaning of a word resides in some fact about its *use*.
Suppose that

> "Socrates" means what it does in virtue of its use being gov-
> erned by regularity U_1,

where U_1 is a specific use property of the word "Socrates"; and suppose similarly

> "wise" means what it does in virtue of its use being governed
> by regularity U_2;

> "x is f" means what it does in virtue of its use being governed
> by regularity U_3.

Compositionality will be satisfied as long as the fact that constitutes
the meaning of "Socrates is wise" is entailed by the fact that

> U_1("Socrates") & U_2("wise") & U_3("x is f") & "Socrates is
> wise" is formed by putting "Socrates" for "x" and "wise"
> for "f" in the structure "x is f".

And this entailment is secured by *identifying* these facts. On this view

---

[16] See J. Fodor and E. LePore, "Why Meaning (Probably) isn't Conceptual Role",
Mind and Language 6 (1991) 328–43; J. Fodor and E. Lepore, "The Pet Fish and the
Red Herring: Why Concepts Aren't Prototypes", *Cognition* 58 (1996), 243–76; and J.
Fodor, "There are no Recognitional Concepts; not even RED", in E. Villanueva (ed.),
Philosophical Issues 9 (Atascadero, Calif.: Ridgeview, 1998).

there is nothing more to meaning what we do by "Socrates is wise" than using the words "Socrates" and "wise", and the operation of predication, in the ways that are constitutive of their meanings, and in appreciating how the sentence is constructed from those three elements.

I don't mean to suggest that it is a trivial matter to articulate the compositional structure of our language. For in the first stage of the three-stage approach that I am recommending, it is necessary to discover how each sentence is constructed from some stock of primitive terms. And at the second stage it is necessary to attribute meaning-constituting properties to these elements, by finding which such attributions will best explain our use of the complexes they form. Evidently these tasks are far from simple. What *is* simple, however, is to find accounts of word meaning consistent with the fact that the meanings of words engender the meanings of sentences. For an extended examination of this approach to compositionality, see Chapter 7.

6. Normativity

Certain normative consequences flow from the fact that an expression has a particular meaning. For example, given what the word "dog" means, it would be correct to apply it to certain things, and a mistake to apply it to others. In some sense, one *ought* to apply it to some things but not to others. Therefore, whatever kind of property a meaning property reduces to, it must be capable of having some such normative import. And various philosophers (beginning with Kripke)[17] have suggested that this constraint may be extremely severe. They think it may be impossible to find *any* naturalistic (factual) property that could satisfy it.

This concern is misguided, it seems to me. For to concede, as we should, that meaning has normative consequences, is not to concede that meaning properties are *intrinsically* normative—i.e. that the right analysis of, for example,

x means DOG

---

[17] See Kripke, *Wittgenstein on Rules and Private Language*.

will take the form

   x ought to be applied only to dogs; and . . .

or will, in some other way, involve explicitly normative notions. It may be, rather, that, even though

   x means DOG

has a purely 'factual' analysis, it none the less has the normative implication

   x ought to be applied only to dogs.

And, generalizing, it may be consistent with the *non*-normative nature of meaning that predicates should be applied only to things of which they are true.

The existence of fact-to-value principles that attribute normative import to situations that are characterized in non-normative terms is quite familiar. Think of ethics and aesthetics. Of course, in any such case the question may be raised as to why the principles hold. Why should we think and act, in those naturalistically characterized circumstances, in the way that the principles dictate? In some cases we can explain the principles on the basis of more fundamental ones; in other cases we cannot. But we are never constrained to say that a principle's correctness hinges on the fact that its characterization of the antecedent circumstances is itself covertly normative.

In the present case, we can explain why, from a pragmatic point of view, it is beneficial to have true beliefs: one is more likely to get what one wants.[18] Therefore, in so far as having certain beliefs is correlated with assenting to certain sentences (in virtue of their meanings), it must be a good idea to assent to some sentences and not others. Thus it is not hard to see where the above norm of predicate application comes from—at least if it is construed pragmatically. If it is not—if someone holds that, regardless of the practical consequences, one should believe the truth—then her 'fact-to-value' assumption may be more difficult to explain. None the less we can easily see, given that

---

[18] See Chapter 8 below, and my *Truth*, for elaboration of this point.

assumption, why meanings will have normative implications, and nothing about the underlying nature of meaning properties need be presupposed. Thus the normative import of meaning does not preclude a reduction of meaning properties in non-semantic, non-normative (e.g. use-theoretic) terms. See Chapter 8 for elaboration of this line of thought.

7. Use

The thrust of my discussion so far has been that we have made the problem of meaning unnecessarily difficult by imposing various misconceived constraints on an adequate solution to it. I have discussed six such pseudo-constraints. In the first place, it is wrongly presupposed that the knowledge in which understanding a word consists is explicit. In fact, implicit knowledge of its meaning suffices, and this is constituted merely by the word's having the same meaning in a speaker's idiolect as it has in his language. In the second place, it is wrongly supposed that some analysis of "*x* means *y*" must be a component of the analysis of each specific meaning attribution. But this is a product of the Constitution Fallacy. In the third place, it is wrongly inferred from the representational power of language that meaning properties must be relations between words and the entities to which they refer. This line of thought overlooks the deflationary theory of truth. In the fourth place, it is wrongly thought that the postulates used for implicit definition are substantive theories that must be true—hence that implicit definition provides interesting a priori knowledge. But in fact, implicit definitions are insubstantive conditionals (of the form '$\exists x(\#x) \rightarrow \#f$') and they constitute the meanings of words by being *regarded* as true, not by *being* true. In the fifth place, it is wrongly assumed that the compositionality of meaning is to be accommodated by first proposing a uniform account of meaning—the same for complexes as for words—and then showing, by means of substantive arguments, that compositionality may be explained. But, on the contrary, a theory of meaning might satisfy compositionality automatically, by building it into its characterization of the meanings of sentences. And in the sixth place it is wrongly inferred from the normative import of meaning properties that they have an intrinsically normative character. Actually, it is in virtue of fact-to-value conditionals (e.g. that one ought not to believe what is false) that what one means has implications for what one should say.

Once these pseudo-constraints are removed, we are in a position to reassess accounts of meaning that have been unfairly dismissed for violating them. And I would like to end this chapter on a more positive note by introducing one such theory: the use theory of meaning. This approach is motivated by a further constraint: namely, that a decent theory be able to account for the relationship between the meaning of a word and its use. More specifically: the fact that someone means what he does by his terms is part of what explains the way he uses them; conversely, we infer what someone means by his terms from his linguistic behaviour; and a satisfactory account of meaning must accommodate these facts.

Of course the simplest explanation is to say that the meaning *is* the use—to say, more accurately, that there exists a range of use properties (i.e. ways of using words, regularities in the use of words) and to suppose that these are what constitute meaning properties. In the past this approach has been denounced for not squaring with the graspable, relational, representational, aprioristic, compositional, and normative character of meaning. But, as we have seen, these criticisms are well off target. It is true that those who understand a word need have no *explicit* knowledge of its use properties; that such properties do not generally relate words to their referents (and certainly not in a uniform way); that they don't provide substantive a priori knowledge; that the theory does not single out, independently of compositionality, which of a complex expression's properties constitutes its meaning; and that use properties are not intrinsically normative. But the constraints of understanding, relationality, representation, a priority, compositionality, and normativity are none the less satisfied. And since it also accommodates the Use Constraint just about as well as anything could, it seems to me that the use theory of meaning deserves another chance.

Not that there aren't many questions that will have to be addressed in articulating and defending such an account. Let me say very briefly what I take some of the main ones to be, and how I think they might be dealt with. In the first place, the terms in which use properties are to be characterized will have to be specified. Here it seems clear that, in so far as we are aiming for a general explanation of the nature of meaning and its causal relation to linguistic behaviour, then one requirement should be that *intensional* notions be prohibited: the relevant use properties must be characterized in physical, behavioural, and psychological terms. Secondly, there is the question of which of the many such properties of a given word is to be the one associated with its meaning. The right answer, I shall argue, is that we want the property that is *explanatorily basic*: the one that best explains all the other use properties of the term. If we think of this as a generalization regarding the use of the word, then the one we choose is the one that provides the simplest account of all the word's individual uses. The fact that there may well be no such thing—but only a range of equally good choices—is what constitutes the *indeterminacy* of meaning. But the fact that this range of equally good explanations does have its limits shows that the distinction between change of meaning and change of belief can nevertheless be preserved (although with some borderline cases), and so holism is not a consequence of the theory.[19] Thirdly, one might wonder if the environmental and social aspects of meaning can be accommodated. But this is a problem only for 'narrow conceptual/inferential role' versions of the use theory. We can and should allow that characterizations of use refer to the speaker's surroundings, and that members of a linguistic community can mean the same thing by a word even if they don't all conform to its meaning-constituting regularity of use.[20] Of course, each of these points needs fleshing out. This sketch is intended merely to give a rough indication of the sort of account that can meet our constraints and that should therefore be taken more seriously than it has been. The next chapter offers a more detailed articulation and systematic defence of the use theory of meaning.

[19] Thus I disagree with Fodor and Lepore, who argue that use theories lead inevitably to an intolerable holism. See their *Holism: A Shopper's Guide* (Oxford: Blackwell, 1991). For more on this point, see Chapter 3, the responses to Objections 2 and 3.

[20] This book is focused on our ordinary conception of the meanings of terms in common, public languages, such as English and Spanish. However, the line of thought carries over fairly straightforwardly to I-languages (in Chomsky's sense). In that context, also, it is reasonable to suppose that a good account of meaning should meet the constraints of understanding, aprioricity, relationality, representation, compositionality, normativity, and use; we are similarly tempted to misconstrue them; but when understood correctly they point us in the direction of a use theory. The main difference between I-language meanings and public language meanings, I would argue, is that I-language meanings are basic regularities of internal use in the conceptual system of the individual; whereas public language meanings are observable, communal patterns of linguistic behaviour. For further discussion, see Chapter 3 (response to Objection 14) and my "Meaning and its Place in the Language Faculty", in L. Anthony and N. Hornstein (eds.), *Chomsky and his Critics* (Oxford: Blackwell, 1999).

The deflationary conception of truth is so called mainly because it says that much less of a theory of truth is needed than has traditionally been expected. It says that certain traditionally assumed constraints on what a good theory of truth must be like are improper, and that once these are removed the search for a good theory becomes easy; for all we will need to accommodate is the equivalence schema, "The proposition *that p* is true if and only if *p*". Moreover, according to deflationism, the truth of the proposition that snow is white consists in snow being white, the truth of the proposition that lying is wrong consists in lying being wrong, and so on; but there is no uniform analysis of the property of 'being true'. Analogously, the use theory becomes plausible only when various misconceived adequacy conditions—applied, in this case, to theories of meaning— have been dropped. And this leaves us with the Use Constraint which, by itself, is easy to satisfy. Moreover, according to the use theory, although there exists a substantive property underlying the meaning of "dog" and another substantive property underlying the meaning of "electron", and so on, there is no uniform analysis of "*x* means *f*-ness". Thus the use theory of meaning is indeed deflationary. Moreover, it is partially motivated by deflationism about truth; for, as we have seen, it would only be from an inflationary perspective on truth that one would have reason to expect a substantive, relational analysis of meaning. We arrive, therefore, at a natural and plausible conjunction of ideas, which might well be called "semantic deflationism": that truth is captured by the equivalence schema and that the meaning of a word is engendered by its use.[21]

---

[21] Of course, the aptness of the term "deflationary" will depend on prior expectations: there do exist proposals about meaning that have even fewer theoretical aspirations that mine has—proposals that renounce the prospect of a reductive analysis of meanings to non-holistic, non-semantic features of use—and from that point of view, the account presented in this book may not seem especially deflationary. I will argue, however, that these more sceptical proposals are ill-motivated, and that they leave it mysterious how what we mean by a word can be responsible for the ways in which we use it. I have in mind W. V. Quine's *Word and Object* (Cambridge, Mass.: MIT Press, 1960); Kripke's *Wittgenstein on Rules and Private Language*; Stephen Schiffer's *Remnants of Meaning* (Cambridge, Mass.: MIT Press, 1987); Mark Johnston's "The End of the Theory of Meaning", *Mind and Language* 3 (1988), 28–42; and Hartry Field's "Deflationist Views of Meaning and Content", *Mind* 103 (1994), 249–85.

3

Meaning as Use

What I shall be calling "the use theory of meaning" is intended to answer the question: in virtue of which of its underlying properties does a word come to possess the particular meaning it has? The theory I am going to articulate bears certain affinities to ideas in the works of Wittgenstein, Sellars, Field, Harman, Block, Peacocke, Brandom, Cozzo, and other philosophers whose views could reasonably be labelled *use* theories of meaning.[1] But when I deploy this term I will be referring to my own specific version of the approach. My plan for this chapter is to sketch the main features of this account, to supply several arguments in its favour, to compare it with alternative theories, and to clarify and defend the proposal by responding to a large collection of old and new objections.

---

[1] See L. Wittgenstein, *Philosophical Investigations* (Oxford: Blackwell, 1953); W. Sellars, "Some Reflections on Language Games", *Philosophy of Science* 21 (1954), 204–8, his "Language as Thought and as Communication", *Philosophy and Phenomenological Research* 29 (1969), 506–27, and his "Empiricism and Abstract Entities", in P. A. Schilpp (ed.), *The Philosophy of Rudolf Carnap* (La Salle, Ind.: Open Court, 1963), 431–68; H. Field, "Logic, Meaning and Conceptual Role", *Journal of Philosophy* 69 (1977), 379–409; G. Harman, "Conceptual Role Semantics", *Notre Dame Journal of Formal Logic* 23 (1982), 242–56, and his "(Nonsolipsistic) Conceptual Role Semantics", in E. LePore (ed.), *New Directions in Semantics* (London: Academic Press, 1987); N. Block, "Advertisement for a Semantics for Psychology", in P. French, T. Uehling, and H. Wettstein (eds.), *Midwest Studies in Philosophy* 10 (Minneapolis, Minn.: University of Minnesota Press, 1986); C. Peacocke, *A Study of Concepts* (Cambridge, Mass.: MIT Press, 1992); R. Brandom, *Making it Explicit* (Cambridge, Mass.: Harvard University Press, 1994); and C. Cozzo, *Meaning and Argument*, Stockholm Studies in Philosophy no. 17 (Stockholm: Almqvist & Wiksell International, 1994).

A Sketch of the Theory

The picture I intend to develop involves three principal claims.

(I) *Meanings are concepts.* A word or phrase—whether it be spoken, written, signed, or merely thought (i.e. an item of 'mentalese')—expresses a 'concept', which is an abstract entity from which beliefs, desires, and other states of mind are composed. Thus, what a linguistic expression *means*—what it gives us reason to regard as present in the mental state of the speaker—is a concept. For example, the property of believing one has a dog consists in standing in the belief relation to the concept, I HAVE A DOG, i.e. to the meaning of "I have a dog".[2] And such concepts, expressed by sentences, are somehow engendered by the concepts expressed by words. Thus the concept, I HAVE A DOG, is made in part from the concept DOG, which is the meaning of "dog". I would argue, moreover, that one can identify *properties* with predicative concepts (that, for example, DOG = doggyness); but this further suggestion will play little role in what follows.

(II) *The overall use of each word stems from its possession of a basic acceptance property.* For each word there is a small set of simple properties which (in conjunction with other factors and with the basic properties of other words) explain total linguistic behaviour with respect to that word. These explanatorily basic properties fall into various kinds—the so-called phonological, syntactic, semantic, and pragmatic—where each such kind is defined by the distinctive

---

[2] Belief states are normally categorized in one of two alternative ways. One way is in terms of the proposition believed—e.g. the state of believing *that I have a dog*—a state which anyone who has that belief about me will share, though he might articulate it by thinking to himself, "He has a dog", or "Paul has a dog", etc. The other way is in terms of how the belief is articulated—e.g. the I-have-a-dog belief state which is shared by anyone who thinks to himself either "I have a dog", "Ho un cane", or something else with that meaning. Adapting Kaplan's terminology, the first is a relation to a thought content; the second a relation to a thought character. When I say that concepts are the constituents of belief states, I have in mind the latter kind. More specifically, they are the constituents of the second abstract relatum in such states—a thought character. Although we cannot generally identify the constituents of propositions with concepts, this may be possible for context-insensitive constituents of *de dicto* propositions. The relationship between meanings and propositions is discussed later in this chapter, in the response to Objection 12.

form of its members and by the range of phenomena they are needed to account for. The present theory is focused on the *semantic* feature of a word. The distinctive form of that feature is that it designates the circumstances in which certain specified sentences containing the word are accepted; and the primary explanatory role of a word's acceptance property is to account for the acceptance of other sentences containing the word. For example, it may be that

(a) the acceptance property that governs a speaker's overall use of "and" is (roughly) his tendency to accept "*p* and *q*" if and only if he accepts both "*p*" and "*q*";

(b) the explanatorily fundamental acceptance property underlying our use of "red" is (roughly) the disposition to apply "red" to an observed surface when and only when it is clearly red;

(c) the acceptance property governing our total use of the word "true" is the inclination to accept instances of the schema 'the proposition *that p* is true if and only if *p*'.

Thus for each word, *w*, there is a regularity of the form

All uses of *w* stem from its possession of acceptance property $A(x)$,

where $A(x)$ gives the circumstances in which certain specified sentences containing *w* are accepted. Think of all the facts regarding a person's linguistic behaviour—the sum of everything he will say, and in what circumstances. The thesis is that this constellation of data may be unified and explained in terms of a relatively small and simple body of factors and principles including, for each word, a basic use regularity. Statements (a), (b), and (c) indicate (to a first approximation) the sort of generalizations I have in mind. It is not implausible that something like these regularities are what explain our overall use of the words "and", "red", and "true".[3]

---

[3] For an important refinement of this position see Objection 17, and a fuller discussion in Chapter 6. In a nutshell: a fundamental acceptance property will not imply substantive commitments, but will merely specify how such commitments are to be

(III) *Two words express the same concept in virtue of having the same basic acceptance property.* Thus *w* expresses the same concept as "dog"—hence *w* means DOG—because a certain acceptance property is responsible for the overall use of *w*: namely, the one that is responsible for the overall use of "dog". Therefore the meaning property of a word is constituted by its having a certain basic acceptance property (or, in other words, by its conforming to the regularity, 'All uses of *w* stem from such-and-such acceptance property'). For example, the properties, '*x* means AND', '*x* means RED', and '*x* means TRUE' are constituted by something like the use properties described in (II). Note that the thesis is not that meanings are uses; nor is it even that meaning properties are identical to use properties. The proposal is rather that meaning properties are constituted by use properties of roughly the sort just illustrated. The relevant notion of 'constitution' is quite familiar. (I give a brief account of it in section 2 of Chapter 2, and later in the present Chapter, in the response to objection 4.) Just as 'being water' is constituted by 'being made of H_2O molecules' and 'being red' is constituted by 'emitting light of such-and-such a wavelength', so 'meaning AND' is constituted by the property characterized in (a) above.

These three theses form the core of the theory of meaning that I want to propose. I will elaborate them in the course of giving various reasons for believing the theory and in responding to a series of twenty-four objections.

Seven Arguments in Favour of the Use Theory of Meaning

(1) *The Univocality-of-"Meaning" Argument*

As we saw in Chapter 2, one thing to be said on behalf of the use theory—especially the first component of it—is that it accommodates our ordinary way of speaking of *meanings* as a species of entity

---

formulated if they are adopted. For example, what constitutes the meaning of "true" is the conditional commitment to accept instances of 'The proposition *that p* is true iff *p*' *given* a commitment, for some $, to accept instances of "The proposition *that p* is $ iff *p*".

to which words stand in the relation 'x means y'. Moreover it makes do with the familiar, non-semantic use of the word "means". When we say, for example, that black clouds mean it will rain, or that the expression on his face means that he is sad, we are deploying a notion of *means* which is, roughly speaking, the notion of *indication*. To say, in this sense, that x means y, is to say, roughly, that x provides a good reason to believe in the presence of y. Now, according to the above theory, when we specify the meaning of a word, we are claiming that someone's use of the word would provide a good reason to expect the occurrence in his mental state of a certain concept. Thus, according to this account, the notion of meaning we deploy in connection with language—in speaking of the meanings of words—is exactly the same as the notion we deploy in non-semantic contexts. It is a virtue of this account that it respects the relational appearance of meaning attributions and that it calls for no special, *ad hoc* assumption about the meaning of "means" in semantic contexts.

(2) *The Explanation Argument*

One of the properties of meaning that we recognize pretheoretically is that what people say is due, in part, to what they mean. For example, I assent to "That's red", when I do, partly because of what I mean by the word "red". And this explanatory feature of meaning is immediately accounted for by the use theory. For the central component of that theory is that the property which constitutes a word's having the meaning it does is that its use is governed by a certain explanatorily fundamental acceptance property. And it is indeed quite clear (as we have just seen) how the total use of a word might be derived, in light of circumstantial factors, from a basic 'law' of use—whereas it is relatively unclear how any other sort of property of a word (such as a reference, a normative characteristic, or some neurological correlate) would constrain its overall use.

Notice, by the way, that there is no conflict between my proposal to reduce meaning properties to use properties and the present observation that meaning explains use. For the aspect of use to which meaning properties reduce is quite different from the aspects of use that meaning properties explain. The former are generalizations to the effect that every use of a given word stems from a specified acceptance property; the latter are particular uses of that word. So it is

perfectly natural to explain one in terms of the other. The generalizations about use explain particular utterances; therefore the theory
that meaning properties are constituted by such generalizations
accommodates the intuition that the things we say may be explained,
in part, by reference to what we mean.

(3) *The Meaning-Attribution Argument*

Another strong argument in favour of the use theory is that it ratio-
nalizes our practice of meaning attribution: it squares with the procedures we actually follow to arrive at judgements about the
meanings of words. For clearly we do establish what is meant by a
word by observation of how it is used—more specifically, by recognizing an appropriate similarity between its use and the use of one of
our already understood terms. Thus we judge that the Italian "cane"
means DOG on the basis of discovering an appropriate similarity in
the use of "cane" and our use of "dog". Such 'appropriate' similarity does not preclude divergences in use—just as long as they can be
explained away as resulting from circumstantial differences. For
example, the fact that someone accepts "It is true that God exists"
while someone else denies it, is not taken to show that they mean different things by "true", because this difference in their use of the
word is explained by the fact that one of them accepts "God exists"
while the other does not. Similarly, a disagreement about whether to
apply "red" to the colour of some unexamined tomatoes in the fridge
would not suggest any variation in what is meant by that word. For
again the divergence in use is plausibly explained away as the product of differences that are unrelated to what the speakers mean. On
the other hand, if someone assents to the sentence "Even though it
is true that God exists, nevertheless God does not exist", we might
well conclude that he does not mean what we do by the word "true".
And if someone applies the word "red" to a surface that is obviously
green, we will be inclined to think that his understanding of the word
differs from ours.

These sentiments are exactly what one would expect in light of the
use theory. For the way we are deciding whether the use of one word
is 'appropriately' similar to the use of another is by determining
whether the divergence in their use can be explained away, i.e. recon-

ciled with there being an identity in the basic regularity that governs them. That is, their uses are regarded as 'appropriately' similar just in case they are governed by the same basic regularity. When this is thought to hold of some foreign term w and one of our words "f", then we conclude (as the use theory predicts) that the concepts expressed by w and "f" are identical—hence (since trivially "f" expresses the concept F) that w expresses the concept F—or, in other words, that w means F. (Davidson's account of meaning attribution, based on his Principle of Charity, does not significantly diverge from the present suggestion, as we shall see in the response to Objection 6.)

(4) *The Synonymy Argument*

A further piece of evidence derives from the fact that synonyms are pretty freely substituted for one another. Suppose that terms w and v belong to the same language and have the same meaning. In that case speakers of the language, when they are prepared to accept something containing w, will usually be just as prepared to accept the sentence derived from it by replacing w with v. And this fact about synonyms calls for explanation. What account of the nature of meaning properties will explain that if two terms have the same one then they are 'co-accepted' in this way? Notice that if understanding a predicate were simply a matter of knowing what it is true of, this phenomenon would remain unexplained. For one might perfectly well know of some object both that w is true of it and that v is true of it, yet not be aware that those words are true of the same thing. The use theory, on the other hand, provides a natural answer; for the co-acceptance of synonyms is exactly what one should expect if the meaning property of a word is constituted by whatever explains the assertive utterances in which it figures—that is, by the fact that a certain basic regularity governs its use. For if w and v are governed by the same *basic* regularity, then, provided that all the other factors influencing the deployment of those words are the same—as they will be for a single person at a single time—the overall dispositions for their use by a given person at a given time will be the same, and so they will indeed be co-accepted. Thus the use theory derives a good measure of confirmation from the co-acceptance of synonyms.

(5) *The Implicit Definition Argument*

A fifth source of support for the theory lies in the phenomenon of implicit definition. One may introduce a new term, "f", and give it a meaning, simply by accepting a body of postulates, "#f", containing the term. This is how the non-observation vocabulary of a scientific theory is typically defined. But there is a question as to how such 'definitions' could work. What does meaning have to be like in order for there to be a possibility of conferring it in such a way? And it is hard to think of a plausible alternative to the answer that

"f" means what it does

is constituted by the fact that

The basic acceptance property of "f" is that "#f" is regarded as *true*.

Thus "f" means what it does in virtue of possessing the property that accounts for its overall use. (This point is developed in Chapter 6.)

(6) *The Translation Argument*

The way in which we operate with manuals of translation (i.e. mappings that preserve meaning) is explained—and can only be explained—by means of the use theory of meaning. To see this, notice that a translation manual T (which maps our words, w_1, w_2, . . ., into foreign words $T(w_1)$, $T(w_2)$, . . . , and vice versa) is an instrument intended to enable us to manage successfully in a foreign community. To that end it is used as a device of 'expectation replacement': when we are abroad, instead of asserting *our* sentences, we assert the translations of them, supposing that this will generate the same relevant expectations in the audience as our sentences would at home. Conversely, when a foreigner says something, we are to have the expectations normally associated with the translation of what he said. What this suggests is that our expectations at home are engendered by an implicit psychological–behavioural theory, $\$[w_1, w_2, . . .]$, specifying the uses of our words, w_1, w_2, . . ., in relation to one another and to environmental and other circumstances; and that our deployment of translation manual T in a foreign community consists in our operating there with the same implicit theory, but transformed by T. That is, we operate abroad with $T(\$)$, i.e. with $\$[T(w_1), T(w_2), \ldots]$. And this is useful if $T(\$)$ is as good at enabling accurate predictions there as $\$$ is here—which will be the case if and only if $T(\$)$ is as true as $\$$. But the difference between $\$$ and $T(\$)$ is merely that the theory structure, $\$(x_1, x_2, \ldots)$, is occupied on the one hand by our words and on the other hand by the associated foreign words. That is to say, the property of w_1 that any adequate translation of w_1 must also have, is $(\exists x_2)(\exists x_3) \ldots \$(x_1, x_2, x_3, \ldots)$—which specifies a basic regularity of use. Thus the function of translation manuals (as devices of expectation replacement) is explained by the theory that a good translation manual preserves the basic explanatory roles of words—i.e. by the theory that meanings consist in basic regularities of use. (See Chapter 9 for further discussion.)

(7) *The Pragmatic Argument*

A related point in favour of the theory is that, in so far as it explains why we should seek manuals of translation, it explains, *a fortiori*, why it is valuable to possess the concept of translation and therefore the concept of meaning; hence it accounts for our having those concepts. In other words, there is a pragmatic rationale for our deploying the notions of meaning and translation that are characterized by my initial theses (I), (II), and (III). Since these use-theoretic notions are valuable for us to deploy, they are notions we can be expected to have. Thus the use theory explains the fact that we possess the concept of meaning.

Alternative Theories

At a different level, some support for the use theory derives from the inadequacy of its rivals. To see this, let us review a range of alternative proposals, indicating where they fall short. In this connection it should be borne in mind that so-called 'theories of meaning' divide into two groups. There are those, like the use theory, whose primary purpose is to specify the underlying non-semantic properties of expressions in virtue of which they possess their particular meanings; and there are those that remain at the semantic level, aiming at a systematization of familiar meaning facts in terms of theoretical semantic notions. Included in this second category are Frege's theory of sense, Katz's structural 'markerese', the Kripke/Lewis/Stalnaker possible-world approach, Barwise and Perry's situation semantics, and Davidson's truth-conditional theory of meaning. Such theories are not addressing the same question as the use theory, and so I will not consider them in the present survey of alternatives. Nor, for similar reasons, will I consider the Gricean approach, since, in not engaging the problem of how beliefs and their component concepts are constituted, it also offers no answer to the main question at issue here. Finally I will not at this point examine alternative use-theoretic accounts such as verificationism or the above-mentioned views of Wittgenstein, Sellars, Field, Harman, Block, Peacocke, Brandom, and Cozzo; the merits of the present version will emerge later. What I do want to consider briefly are some very different approaches to the issue of where a word's meaning comes from: specifically

1. *The Definition Theory*: that the meaning property of a word consists in there being a certain definition of it—i.e. in there being certain conceptually necessary and sufficient conditions for its applicability.

2. *The Mental Image Theory*: that the meaning property of a word consists in its being associated with a certain mental picture.

3. *The Prototype Theory*: that the meaning property of a word consists in there being certain paradigm cases of its applicability and there being a 'similarity metric' which determines how close other things are to these exemplars.

4. *The Informational Theory*: x means F = In 'suitable' circumstances instances of f-ness cause tokenings of x.

5. *The Teleological Theory*: x means F = The (evolutionary) function of x is to indicate fs.

Two principal considerations favour the use theory over these alternatives. In the first place, there is its generality. It is evident that none
of these rival accounts can purport to deal with the meanings of *all*
words. Definitions are notoriously few and far between; and even if
they were common, there would have to be a certain residue of
indefinable primitives. Not everything has an imaginable visual
appearance. Exemplars and similarity metrics seem out of place in
connection with the theoretical vocabulary of science. And the informational and teleological theories cannot aspire to deal with the
terms of logic and mathematics. Thus a virtue of the use theory is its
universal scope. It alone can hope to offer an account of every single
meaning property.

The second peculiar virtue of the use theory is its explanatory
power. Most of the arguments sketched above were inferences to the
best explanation. A range of phenomena were cited—such as the co-
acceptance of synonyms, the dependence of use upon meaning, the
possibility of implicit definition, and our methods of meaning attribution—and it was shown in each case how the use theory provides
an explanation. The present point—obviously crucial—is to suggest
that this explanatory prowess is not matched by the alternative theories of meaning. In fact it is not clear how any of them would reliably
explain any of the cited phenomena.

Consider, for example, the informational theory

> x means F = in conditions I, an F would cause a tokening
> of x.

How, on this account, might we account for the influence on linguistic behaviour of what we mean by our words? In particular, how
might we explain why virtually no one who understands the words in
the sentence "Some bachelors are married" will accept it? From a
use-theoretic perspective this is a relatively easy question; for it can
be supposed that the meaning of "bachelor" is constituted by the fact
that the basic regularity in its use is our maintaining "A bachelor is
an unmarried man". But from the informational perspective our
understanding of "bachelor" and "married" consists in the tendency
of their tokens to be produced by the presence of bachelors and married people. This, together with the fact that bachelors are unmarried, might perhaps explain a propensity to assert, after many
observations, "Bachelors are married" and hence a propensity to

deny "Some bachelors are married". But it does not explain the strength of that belief, nor the speed with which it is acquired.

I don't want to deny that some of the rival theories might roughly work some of the time—specifying more or less the correct meaning-constituting properties of certain terms. For example, perhaps the meaning of "bachelor" does consist in the above definition; perhaps the meaning of "red" derives from its tendency to be caused by red things. But this is no retreat from the use theory. For such successes will occur only if and when what is specified by the rival theory happens to correspond to the word's basic regularity of use. The general objection to the rivals is that the forms of meaning-constituting property to which they are committed will not *reliably* satisfy the explanatory demands on such properties (primarily, to account for the overall use of the words that possess them), unlike the use-theoretic answers, which are tailor-made to do so. And this is why the use theory alone will be able to accommodate the various phenomena (such as the co-acceptance of synonyms, the possibility of implicit definition, the methods by which meanings are inferred, and the utility of translation manuals) which were cited on its behalf above.[4]

Objections to the Use Theory of Meaning

Let me continue to flesh out the theory, and the above reasons for maintaining it, by saying something in response to each of the numerous difficulties that have been thought to preclude use-theoretic accounts of meaning. Some of these issues have already been mentioned, and some will need more detailed attention, which they will receive in subsequent chapters. But, at the cost of a certain repetitiveness, I think it worth while to assemble a fairly complete list of the objections that have been made against use theories of meaning, together with preliminary indications of how they can be deflected.

The complaints, in brief, are as follows:

(1) The notion of 'use' is too obscure for there to be such a thing as the so-called 'use theory' of meaning. (Quine)

---

[4] See Chapter 2, n. 7, for some references to literature critical of various non-use-theoretic theories of meaning.

(2) If meaning were use, then any change in what we say, no matter how minor (for example, our coming to accept a single sentence that we once denied), would entail at least *some* change of meaning—which is absurd. (Fodor and LePore)

(3) The radical indeterminacy of meaning precludes its constitution either by use or by any other non-semantic substratum. (Quine)

(4) Given any meaning-constituting property, one should be able to see *why* it constitutes the particular meaning that it does; but use properties would not satisfy this explanatory requirement. (Kripke)

(5) The use of a predicate cannot fix its extension, but its meaning can and does. (Kripke)

(6) The meanings of sentences are truth conditions and the meanings of predicates are satisfaction conditions. (Davidson)

(7) The meaning of a complex expression depends on the meanings of its parts and on how they are put together; but this fact cannot be squared with the use theory. In other words, use is not compositional, but meaning is. (Davidson)

(8) Even if compositionality *per se* does not preclude the use theory, still not all possible patterns of use for a word are consistent with the requirement of compositionality; therefore they cannot all constitute meanings. (Dummett)

(9) There are (very complex) expressions with meanings but no uses. (Katz)

(10) A characterization of the use of a word fails to provide it with a definition and hence fails to specify *what* it means. (Frege)

(11) A word type derives its meaning (or meanings, if it is ambiguous) from the meanings of its tokens; but a theory which constructs meanings from regularities of use must take type meaning to be fundamental.

(12) Even after ambiguities have been resolved, a given sentence (e.g. "I am at the bank") can express different propositions on different occasions; but the use theory gives no account of this fact.

(13) A word's usage may vary radically from one person to another, whereas its meaning is fixed by the linguistic community. (Putnam, Burge)

(14) A scientifically valuable account of meaning would have to be internalistic—the alleged meaning-constituting properties would have to be neural (or something like that); but use properties sometimes make reference to the environment—to the fact that certain sentences are asserted in certain external conditions. (Chomsky)

(15) The use theory cannot be applied to names, because they have referents but no meanings. (Kripke)

(16) We typically know the meaning of a word without knowing the regularities governing its use.

(17) Any alleged meaning-constituting use for a word (any postulates containing it) can be coherently doubted, and even rejected, without affecting the word's meaning. (Carnap)

(18) The use theory implies that certain terms are implicitly defined by the acceptance of postulates containing them—and those postulates must therefore be knowable a priori. But in light of epistemological holism (i.e. Quine's web-of-belief model) we can see that nothing is a priori.

(19) Use is not a normative notion, but meaning is; for the meaning of a word determines how it *ought* to be applied. (Kripke, Brandom, Putnam, Gibbard)

(20) A sound may be produced in accordance with some definite regularity, and yet none the less have no conceptual content.

(21) In so far as the uses of words are characterized by reference

to sentences containing them that are *accepted* (asserted, held true), then use is not fully explicable in non-semantic terms; for *acceptance* is a semantic notion.

(22) There are expressions (e.g. "and" and "but") with the same meaning (or semantic content, at least), but different uses. (Katz)

(23) The meaning of an utterance is the mental state it expresses, which is obviously not a use.

(24) The use theory implies that two predicates, "*f*" and "*g*", can have exactly the same meaning as one another. And given that the meaning of a word is the concept it expresses, such synonymy would imply their intersubstitutivity *salve veritate* in belief (and other propositional-attitude) contexts. But, as Benson Mates has shown, someone (somewhat confused) may come to believe that not all *f*s are *g*s, yet not be *so* benighted as to think that not all *f*s are *f*s.

1. *Obscurity*

It is often said that the trouble with the use theory is not so much *falsity* as *unintelligibility*, on the grounds that it is completely unclear what is meant by the "use" of a word. But this complaint is surely an exaggeration. After all, expressions of the form "the use of *X*" and "how *x* is used" are common bits of ordinary language (applied, for example, to tools or to pieces in a game); and there is no particular difficulty in understanding someone who says he is going to tell us how some unfamiliar word is used. Moreover, I can be quite specific about what sort of thing is intended, in the present theoretical context, by the "use" of a word.

To begin, I have in mind some property of a word *type*. This property is specified by a generalization about tokens of that type—by the claim that they are all explained in terms of a certain acceptance property, a property specifying the circumstances in which designated sentences containing the word are held true. A couple of examples of such explanatorily basic acceptance properties, already mentioned, are (a) that we have the disposition to assert "That is red" in the presence of evidently red things; and (b) that we have the tendency to accept instances of the schema, "The proposition *that p* is true if and only if *p*". Notice that what I am taking to be the meaning-constituting use of a word is not merely that the word *possesses* a certain acceptance property, but that this fact about it is *explanatorily basic*—that it accounts for all uses of the word.[5] Thus *w*'s meaning what it does is constituted by a regularity of the form, 'All uses of *w* stem from the fact that $A(w)$'—where $A(x)$ is an acceptance property.

Second, one should refrain from referring to such regularities as *rules*, so as not to encourage the idea that they are explicitly represented and deliberately followed. Such self-conscious following of rules for the use of words may sometimes occur, and may be associated with particular meanings; but it cannot constitute the meanings of *all* words because (as Wittgenstein emphasized) the rules themselves would have to be understood, and we would be faced with an infinite regress.

Third, a use property must be *non-semantic*. In order to specify one it will not do, for example, to say 'Instances of "bachelor" mean UNMARRIED MAN' or '"Napoleon" is used to refer to Napoleon'. For the whole point is to demystify meaning and affiliated notions by characterising them in such terms that their explanatory relations to verbal behaviour become understandable.

Fourth, a use property should be *readily detectable*. For we can tell whether someone understands a word by the way he uses it. Therefore a property such as 'associated with such-and-such brain activity' could not be a use property; whereas a property such as 'applied in the presence of red things' would be fine.

A fifth point is that uses need not be restricted to inference patterns, or other purely *internal* phenomena. That sort of restriction—which sometimes goes under the name, "narrow conceptual-role (or inferential-role) semantics"—provides a notion of use that is too weak to capture meaning in the ordinary sense of the word.[6] The

---

[5] The reason for supposing that *w*'s meaning is constituted by a regularity of the form '*w*'s possesssion of acceptance property $A(x)$ is explanatorily basic', rather than merely '*w* possesses $A(x)$', is that there could be another word, *v*, whose basic acceptance property is '$A(x)$ and $B(x)$', and in that case the second strategy would compel us to conclude, wrongly, that since *w* and *v* both possess $A(x)$, then *v* means the same as *w*. See Chapter 6, sect. I, for further discussion.

[6] See the response to Objection 14 for discussion of an attempt—known as the 'two-factor theory'—to rectify this weakness.

meanings of certain terms (e.g. "true") may be given by purely internal regularities of use; but others (e.g. "red") will call for reference to the environment. It should be noticed that given the above-mentioned point—namely, that the use regularities are not to be regarded as explicitly formulated, deliberately followed rules—there can be no objection (on grounds of circularity) to the idea that the use regularity of a given term may be characterized using that very term.

Finally, a use regularity for one word relates its occurrence to occurrences of other words. That is to say, the regularities governing the deployment of different words are not entirely separable from one another. In example (b) above, the regularity concerns not merely the word "true" but also the expressions "proposition" and "if and only if".

2. *Holism*

The fact that the regularities governing our use of any word will inevitably specify the occurrence of other terms (and hence the fact that the meanings of different words are inextricably interconnected with one another) provides one sense in which language is to some extent 'holistic'. But we can imagine a different, and more clearly implausible, form of holism; and it is sometimes alleged against the use theory of meaning that it must be wrong because it entails holism in this bad sense. Here is the argument.

If the meaning of a word were its use, then any discovery, in so far as it leads to the affirmation of previously unaffirmed sentences that contain the word, would give it a slightly new use—and therefore a slightly new meaning. But we do not regard such small changes of use as changes of meaning. So the use theory is false.

In response, it should be pointed out that one would not say, for example, that a hammer is being given a new use when it is used to hammer in a particular nail it has never hammered in before; one would not say that the queen in chess is being given a new use when it happens to be moved into a position that has never before been reached. And similarly, if a planet beyond Pluto were discovered, and we started to say "There are ten planets", we would not thereby have given the word "planet" a new use. So the objection fails.

But, it will be asked in reply, what is the basis of the distinction that is being assumed here between the use facts (like, perhaps, our disposition to accept "Planets orbit stars") which could plausibly be held to constitute *the use* of "planet", and other use facts (like our disposition to accept "There are nine planets") which surely could not? Are we not committing ourselves (as Fodor and LePore have argued),[7] to some form of the analytic–synthetic distinction which Quine has persuaded us does not exist?

Perhaps. However, the fact that we sometimes do, and sometimes do not, recognize that the use of a word has changed, suggests that we do draw some sort of distinction here. What we have in mind, I would suggest, in differentiating between those use properties which comprise what we call "*the* use" and those which do not is simply the difference between the *explanatorily basic* use property and the rest. In other words, the way to pick out the particular use property of a word that comprises what we call "the use" is to find the use property that provides the best explanation of all the others.

The outcome of this sort of procedure may no doubt be indeterminate. There will sometimes be alternative, equally good ways of finding a simple regularity in the use of a word that (in conjunction with the use regularities of other terms and with general psychological laws) will account for all other aspects of its use. Therefore there will sometimes be no objective fact of the matter as to where the boundary lies between the pattern of use that constitutes the meaning of the expression, and other facts about its deployment. But a distinction with unclear boundaries is a distinction none the less— one that puts us in a position to say of certain novel deployments of a word that they definitely do not amount to changes in its use. Thus the use theory of meaning does not in fact lead to the counter-intuitive form of holism.

3. *Indeterminacy*

I have conceded that there may be a degree of holism and indeterminacy in the constitution of meaning. But it might be thought, given Quine's profoundly sceptical analysis of meaning and translation, that the situation is much worse than this—that the indeterminacy-cum-holism with which we are faced is so radical as to preclude

---

[7] Fodor and Lepore, *Holism.*

altogether the naive assumption, endorsed by the use theory, that each word possesses its very own meaning.

In order to clarify and settle this matter it is vital to distinguish some very different forms of scepticism, holism, and indeterminacy regarding meaning.

First, there is what I will call MEANING HOLISM. This is the above-mentioned view that the meaning of a term depends on every single aspect of its overall use. It implies that no two people mean exactly the same thing by any of their words, and therefore that they never fully disagree with one another; similarly for a single person at two different times. Thus (*pace* Davidson and Block)[8] MEANING HOLISM is highly implausible. But as we have just seen, our version of the use theory does not entail it.

Second, there is the somewhat more palatable idea, MEANING INDETERMINACY, that there may be no objective fact of the matter as to whether a given property of a word is, or is not, part of what constitutes the meaning property of that word: for example, no objective fact as to whether a given acceptance property is explanatorily basic. Evidently, this view comes in degrees. In its extreme form it covers just about every word and just about every acceptance property of every word. Notice that MEANING HOLISM and MEANING INDETERMINACY (to whatever degree) are incompatible with one another. It would be a blunder to infer, from the impossibility of drawing a sharp line around the meaning-constituting uses of a word, that *all* uses are meaning constituting.[9]

Third, there is another position that is sometimes called "meaning holism" but which, for the sake of disambiguation, I will call MEANING INTERDEPENDENCE. This is the thesis that in order for a given meaning to be expressed, there must exist terms with certain other specific meanings. Suppose that what constitutes the meanings of a particular pair of words, w and v, is the (non-conjunctive) relational fact, Rwv. In that case, w's meaning-constituting property is $(\exists y)Rxy$, and v's is $(\exists x)Rxy$; therefore w can have the meaning it has only if there is a word with the meaning that v has, and vice versa. As we have seen, the use theory requires a

---

[8] Davidson, *Inquiries into Truth and Interpretation*; N. Block, "An Argument for Holism", *Proceedings of the Aristotelian Society* 95 (1994–5), 151–69.

[9] This fallacy is noted by Paul Boghossian in his "Analyticity Reconsidered", *Nous* 30 (1996), 360–91, at 384.

degree of MEANING INTERDEPENDENCE, because the meaning-constituting use regularity of a word will involve the acceptance
of sentences which inevitably contain certain other words as well. But
the use theory does not require the extreme version of the view—
namely, the thesis that every word's meaning is dependent on every
other word's meaning (which would be the case if the fact that constituted the meaning of all of the words $w_1, w_2, \ldots, w_N$ were the N-
place relational fact, $R^*(w_1, w_2, \ldots, w_N)$). Notice that, even in this
extreme form, MEANING INTERDEPENDENCE does not imply
MEANING HOLISM (though it is implied *by* MEANING
HOLISM). Two people may well both satisfy R^* (hence give the same
interdependent meanings to their words), yet not be disposed to
make all the same utterances; for there may well be a difference
between them with respect to the non-linguistic factors that determine (together with R^*) what they will be inclined to say.

Fourth, there is a view I will call MEANING DISTRIBUTION,
according to which a given word might not have any underlying
meaning-constituting property of its own; rather, the meaning-constituting fact might concern a pair, or cluster, of words, and be
'spread' over its members. To see what I have in mind here, imagine
that the above meaning-constituting relation, Rxy, is strongly *sym-
metric*: i.e. $Rxy = Ryx$. In that case, even though the words w and v
are not synonyms, the only available *individual* meaning-constituting
properties—which are $(\exists y)Rxy$ and $(\exists x)Rxy$—would be *identical*.
Consequently we cannot suppose that w and v have distinct meaning-
constituting properties; rather the meanings of the pair of terms $\langle w,$
$v \rangle$ are jointly constituted by their having the relational use property,
Rxy. It seems to me that MEANING DISTRIBUTION is the view
for which Quine argues in Chapter 2 of *Word and Object*.[10] He
assumes, moreover, that in such circumstances w and v would not
have distinct meanings; and since he argues that MEANING DIS-
TRIBUTION is a common phenomenon, he takes himself to have
undermined the naive idea (which he calls "the museum myth") that
each expression is associated with a distinct meaning. However, as we
shall see in Chapter 9, there is an alternative moral one might prefer
to draw from MEANING DISTRIBUTION. For, even in the face of
that phenomenon, one might nevertheless decide to retain the trivial

---

[10] See also his "Ontological Relativity", *Ontological Relativity and Other Essays*
(New York: Columbia University Press, 1969).

schema, "*f*" means *F*'. If so, one will maintain that *w* and *v* do have distinct meanings, while acknowledging that their individual meaning properties are not separately constituted.

It should be noted that this position is very different from what I called MEANING INDETERMINACY. For the latter does not deny the existence of individual meaning-constituting properties, but says rather that it can be objectively unclear what they are. Both positions, however, have implications for the indeterminacy of translation. MEANING INDETERMINACY with respect to a pair of terms, *e* and *f*, in different languages allows for the possibility that there may be no determinate fact of the matter as to which basic regularity governs the use of *e*—and similarly for *f*. Consequently there may be no determinate fact as to whether *e* and *f* are governed by the same basic use regularity, and hence whether they have the same meaning. MEANING DISTRIBUTION with respect to terms *w* and *v*, belonging to our language, implies that if there were a behaviourally identical linguistic community—but one that used *w** and *v** instead of our *w* and *v*—then there could be no determinate fact of the matter as to whether to translate *w** as *w* or as *v*.

However, it remains to be seen how often, if ever, instances of MEANING INDETERMINACY and MEANING DISTRIBUTION actually arise. According to Quine, MEANING DISTRIBUTION is pervasive: proxy functions provide an unlimited supply of examples (such as "rabbit" and "cosmic complement of a rabbit"). And if he is right, then words do not typically have individually constituted meaning properties. It seems to me, however, that Quine's argument takes too narrow a view of the linguistic data that are available for the identification of meanings (focusing exclusively on which sentences we would be disposed to accept under interrogation, and neglecting both what we spontaneously accept and the inferential relations amongst what we accept. When this situation is rectified, it becomes difficult (though not impossible) to find cases of MEANING DISTRIBUTION. (See Chapter 9 for extensive discussion of these issues.)

A fifth form of indeterminacy, quite different from the varieties just distinguished, concerns everyday properties (such as '*x* is red', '*x* is a table', etc.) rather than meaning properties (such as '*x* means RED', '*x* means TABLE', etc.). We have seen that it may be indeterminate what constitute the latter; for it may be indeterminate which regularities in the use of the words "red", "table", etc. are explanatorily basic. And this implies that there may be words such that it is indeterminate whether or not a given meaning property is exemplified by them. In addition, however—and this is a quite separate phenomenon—it may be indeterminate whether an ordinary predicate ("*x* is red", "*x* is a table", etc.) applies to a given thing. This will be so when the (determinate) basic regularities of use for the predicate (a) do not determine that it is applied to that thing, (b) do not determine that its negation is applied, and (c) will not determine either of these outcomes no matter what further discoveries are made.

Two forms of this fifth type of indeterminacy are notable. One of them occurs when the regularities for the use of a predicate say nothing and imply nothing about its application to a given object; they can yield *no* inclination either to apply or to withhold the predicate. Vagueness comes from this type of indeterminacy.[11] The other especially interesting case is when the regularities give rise to *conflicting* inclinations—both to apply the predicate and not to apply it. This can come about when the predicate is normally used within a certain restricted domain and when the simplest regularity that would accommodate that practice, if it were extended beyond that domain, would conflict with other use regularities. Philosophical paradoxes often originate in this way.[12]

In summary, I have distinguished five forms of indeterminacy/ holism phenomena and argued that none of them poses any difficulty for the use theory of meaning. The theory rules out MEANING

---

[11] The rough idea is that the explanatorily basic regularities of use, in the case of vague predicates, have a 'gappy' character, specifying that the predicate is applied to objects possessing some underlying property to a least a certain specified degree, *x*, and that its negation is applied to objects possessing that property to less than a certain specified degree, *y*, where *y* is less than *x*, and that neither the predicate nor its negation is applied to objects possessing the property to some degree between *x* and *y*. Therefore, in so far as the regularity is explanatorily fundamental, it can be seen that no further discoveries could alter that situation: there could never be a stable inclination to apply either the predicate, or its negation, to such objects. See my "The Nature of Vagueness", *Philosophy and Phenomenological Research* 57 (1997), 929–36.

[12] This is similar to Stephen Schiffer's diagnosis of philosophical paradoxes. See his "Contextualist Solutions to Scepticism", *Proceedings of the Aristotelian Society* 96 (1995–6), 317–33. Consider, for example, the 'liar' paradoxes. The fact that explains our deployment of the truth predicate in 'normal' contexts (i.e. to propositions that do not themselves involve the concept of truth) is that we accept all instances of the schema, 'The proposition *that p* is true if and only if *p*'. But if this regularity is extended beyond the normal domain (e.g. if we substitute "This proposition is not true" into the schema), then contradictions can be derived whose acceptance would be incompatible with the regularity underlying our use of the word "not".

HOLISM (whereby the meaning of a word depends on its *overall* use); it engenders only mild cases of MEANING INDETERMIN-ACY (whereby it is unclear whether a given property of a word does or does not help to constitute its meaning); it happily embraces a degree of MEANING INTERDEPENDENCE (whereby a word's meaning what it does depends upon there being words with certain other meanings); it allows for the very occasional case of MEAN-ING DISTRIBUTION (whereby the meanings of different words are not separately constituted); and it illuminates the special kinds of indeterminacy associated with vagueness and with philosophical paradoxes.

4. *Explanation*

It is commonly felt that if a meaning property, say

> x means DOG,

is to be constituted by some specific underlying property, '$u(x)$', then one should be able to *explain* why this is so: one should be able to explain why '$u(x)$' constitutes *that* meaning property rather than some slightly different one. As Kripke puts it: one should be able to scrutinize any given meaning-constituting property and "read off" which meaning it engenders.[13] This sentiment requires that there be a theory of meaning of the form

> x means $F = T(x, f)$,

where T is fairly independent of "f". For how else could we have a rule that puts us in a position to read off, for any given meaning-constituting property, which meaning it determines, and thereby puts us in a position to explain why that particular meaning should be the

---

[13] See his *Wittgenstein on Rules and Private Language*. As far as I know, Kripke's 'reading off' requirement has not been challenged by any of his other commentators. See Paul Boghossian's "The Rule Following Considerations", *Mind* 98 (1989), 507–50 (who explicitly endorses it) and also Simon Blackburn, "The Individual Strikes Back", *Synthese* 10 (1984), 281–301; Warren Goldfarb, "Kripke on Wittgenstein on Rules", *Journal of Philosophy* 82 (1985), 471–88; and Crispin Wright, "Kripke's Account of the Argument against Private Language", *Journal of Philosophy* 81 (1984), 759–78.

one that is determined? But the use theory does not have this form. It *may* happen that the use regularity constituting 'x means DOG' will advert to dogs in some way. But this need not be so. It all depends on what the explanatory basis for our overall use of the word "dog" turns out to be. And even if dogs do turn out to be an aspect of this regularity, we should not expect other meaning properties to be constituted in a similar way. We should not expect that the use regularity underlying 'x means ELECTRON' will advert to electrons in a way that parallels the reference to dogs in the regularity underlying 'x means DOG'. And we might expect there to be many meaning properties (e.g. 'x means TRUE') whose constituting use regularities make no reference at all to the kind of thing in the extension of words with those properties. Thus there will be no way to read off which meaning is constituted by a given use property. The best we can do, in order to get from one to the other, is to appreciate that some word (say, "glub") has the use property—i.e. actually to use it in that way; in which case we can deploy that very word to characterize the constituted meaning (as "x means GLUB").

Thus the use theory does indeed violate the commonly assumed requirement that there be explanations of the links between given meaning-constituting properties and given meanings. But this requirement is misconceived; so our violation of it is not objectionable. To see why this is so, notice, in the first place, that no such requirement is generally imposed in other contexts. We do not expect to be able to explain why 'being water' is constituted by 'being made of H_2O molecules', or why 'being red' is constituted by 'emitting light of such-and-such wavelength'. Nor, in such cases, is there any way of reading off which superficial property is constituted. All that can be explained is *why we suppose* that the relation of property constitution obtains—but not why it in fact obtains.

What no doubt seems relevantly different in the case of meaning is that the properties we are trying to reduce—e.g. 'x means DOG'— are *relational*. Consider, for example,

> x is the capital of England
> x is the capital of France
> . . . and so on.

Here we can expect a level of reduction to properties of the form

> x bears R to England

> *x* bears *R* to France
> ... and so on,

from any of which we can read off which 'capital property' is constituted. Moreover we can explain why

> '*x* bears *R* to England' constitutes '*x* is the capital of England'

in terms of the more basic fact that

> '*x* bears *R* to *y*' constitutes '*x* is the capital of *y*'.

Similarly, it might well be thought that the relational properties

> *x* means DOG
> *x* means ELECTRON
> ... and so on

must be constituted by relational properties of the form

> *x* bears *S* to DOG
> *x* bears *S* to ELECTRON
> ... and so on,

which, in order to eliminate all the semantic notions (and given the
identity of properties and concepts) must be reduced to

> *x* bears *T* to instances of doggyness
> *x* bears *T* to instances of electronhood
> ... and so on,

or in other words

> *x* bears *T* to dogs
> *x* bears *T* to electrons
> ... and so on.

And so we will be able to explain why

> '*x* bears *T* to dogs' constitutes '*x* means DOG'

in terms of the more basic fact that

'x bears T to fs' constitutes 'x means F',

i.e.

x means $F = T(x, f)$.

However, although this line of thought is natural, it is far from compulsory—and the use theory rejects it. As we saw in Chapter 2 (section 2), it is a fallacy to assume that what constitutes a given fact must have the same logical structure as that fact: "Fido exemplifies stinkiness" is constituted by "Fido stinks"; "The proposition that John loves Mary is true" is constituted by "John loves Mary". Similarly, 'x means DOG' may be constituted by some use regularity that does not amount to x standing in some non-semantic relation to dogs. That this is indeed the case can be established by showing that this use regularity accounts for the characteristics of the meaning property which it allegedly constitutes. If that is so, then we must abandon any expectation of there being a theory with the form

x means $F = T(x, f)$,

and therefore abandon any hope of being able to explain why certain non-semantic properties engender the meanings they do. The situation, rather, is that we will obtain a series of reductive analyses,

x means DOG $= u(x)$
x means ELECTRON $= v(x)$
. . . and so on,

where the underlying use regularities '$u(x)$', '$v(x)$', . . ., and so on, enable us neither to 'read off' nor to explain which particular meaning properties they constitute.

5. *Reference*

Here is a closely related objection. It is often said that the meaning of a word cannot be constituted by its use because its meaning determines its reference whereas its use could not do that. It is argued that, fallible finite creatures that we are, the set of things to which we are disposed to apply a predicate will inevitably diverge from its true extension. Thus the use of a predicate does not fix its extension, whereas its meaning obviously does.[14]

However, this reasoning is fallacious, for it equivocates on the sense of "determine". The meaning of a predicate does indeed determine its extension, in the sense that any two expressions with the same meaning must have the same extension (ignoring context sensitivity). But we have been given no reason to think that the use of a predicate fails *in that sense* to determine its extension. On the contrary, in so far as our predicates "f" and "g" have the same use, we must surely hold true "$(x)(fx \leftrightarrow gx)$", and so cannot suppose that their extensions diverge. What we have been given instead (but irrelevantly) is an argument to show that, in some much stronger sense of "determine" (call it "DETERMINE") the use of a predicate does not DETERMINE its extension.

Let me elaborate the notion of 'DETERMINATION' that appears to be presupposed in this argument. What seems to be understood by saying that the use of a predicate, x, must DETERMINE its extension is that there must be some use relation, '$a(xy)$', linking x with each member of its extension. It must be, in other words, that

x is *true* of y iff $a(xy)$,

where $a(xy)$ is some such relation as

We are disposed to apply predicate x to object y in (ideal) circumstances I.

And this requirement implies that

The extension of x is the set of fs iff $(y)[a(xy) \leftrightarrow y$ is $f]$.

But the meaning of x fixes its extension. The conclusion is therefore drawn that the meaning property

---

[14] This reasoning can arguably be extracted from Kripke's *Wittgenstein on Rules and Private Language*. A closer reading of his text is offered in Chapter 10. Kripke's difficulty, which is widely thought to plague all accounts of meaning constitution, is known as 'the problem of error'.

x means F

could be constituted by a certain use property only if that use property were to entail

$$(y)[a(xy) \rightarrow y \text{ is } f],$$

for only then would x's extension be DETERMINED by what constitutes its meaning. But it turns out that no such use properties can be found; and that is because we cannot think of any use relation, $a(xy)$, that connects each predicate with the members of its extension. So the use theory of meaning must be wrong.

The obvious response, however, is that in the absence of any initial reason to think that the extension of a predicate should be DETERMINED by the property constituting its meaning, the fact that it is not so DETERMINED by any use regularity provides no basis for doubting the constitution of meaning by use.

But perhaps there *is* some motivation for the DETERMIN-ATION requirement? Might one not argue as follows? Since 'x is *true* of y' surely has some sort of analysis—i.e. there is surely some underlying relation, $r(xy)$, such that

$$x \text{ is } true \text{ of } y = r(xy)$$

—then whatever constitutes

x means F

must indeed entail something of the form

$$(y)[r(xy) \leftrightarrow y \text{ is } f].$$

I suspect that this is indeed the implicit rationale for the DETER-MINATION requirement. I can think of no other motivation for it. However, it can and should be resisted. For the assumption that the relation

x is *true* of y

has a non-semantic analysis is highly controversial. Indeed, the next

chapter elaborates a *deflationist* view of the truth-theoretic properties, according to which there is no such analysis.

Such a view is an instance of what we saw in the previous section:
namely, that what constitutes a relational fact need not involve an
analysis of that relation. From the deflationary perspective, the fact
that constitutes "dog" being *true* of Fido does not incorporate any
analysis of "*x* is *true* of *y*"; what constitutes that fact, rather, is simply that Fido is a dog (and that "dog" means DOG). In general, "*x*
is *true* of *y*" is implicitly defined by a combination of the equivalence
schema

$$(y)(\text{Concept } F \text{ is } true \text{ of } y \leftrightarrow fy)$$

and the definition of "*true* of" for predicates in terms of "true of" for
concepts

$$(x)(y)[x \text{ is } true \text{ of } y \leftrightarrow (\exists z)(x \text{ expresses } z \ \& \ z \text{ is true of } y)].$$

Thus there is no non-semantic reductive analysis of "*x* is *true* of *y*";
so there is no reason to force the properties that constitute meanings
into the above mould. Consequently, the fact that the basic regularity of use of a predicate does not DETERMINE an extension provides no ground for denying that it constitutes the meaning property
of the predicate. For elaboration of this discussion, see Chapter 4.[15]

6. *Truth Conditions*

A very widespread opinion, promoted especially in the work of
Donald Davidson,[16] is that the meaning of a sentence is its truth condition: for example, that the meaning of "snow is white" consists in
the property of 'being *true* if and only if snow is white'. And it is generally taken to follow from this theory that the meaning of a sentence
does not derive from its use.

---

[15] Christopher Peacocke, in his *A Study of Concepts*, combines a form of the use
theory of meaning with the view that meaning-constituting properties must DETER-
MINE reference. From our point of view this position falls foul both of Kripke's arguments that no such DETERMINATION is possible, and of the present argument that
no such DETERMINATION is necessary.

[16] Davidson, *Inquiries into Truth and Interpretation*.

But, in the first place, this inference is far from obvious. As we saw earlier in this chapter, accounts of meaning that remain at the semantic level do not conflict with the use theory. On the contrary, they stand in need of some further theory that will characterize the underlying nature of whatever semantic properties they postulate. Thus, even if one accepts the Davidsonian picture, it remains to be said what it is for a sentence to have a certain truth condition: how does this come about? And the use theory offers an answer to this question: namely, that the property of 'being *true* if and only if snow is white' consists in the property of 'being constructed in a certain way from words with certain uses'. Indeed I believe that this account is what Davidson is committed to by his own way of answering the reductive question, which is based on the 'Principle of Charity'. For his view, put crudely, is that we should assign truth conditions to foreign utterances in such a way that as many of them as is reasonably possible turn out to be in accord with what we also hold *true*. But deciding what is '*reasonably* possible' involves (a) looking for a manual of translation that is simple (ideally, one that is induced by a word-to-word mapping) and (b) accommodating predictable disagreement (i.e. not expecting a foreigner to agree with us if we can see that his evidence is misleading, but translating his utterance into something we would accept in those circumstances). Implicit in this elaboration of the Principle of Charity, it seems to me, are the following ideas: (1) that what a person holds *true* is determined by various factors, including the observable circumstances, background beliefs, inferential propensities, and basic regularities of use of words—regularities that specify, as a function of the other factors, which sentences are held *true*; and (2) that a good assignment of truth conditions should 'optimize agreement' in the sense of preserving these basic regularities. Thus, once its precise content is elaborated, Davidson's Principle of Charity arguably boils down to the use theory of meaning. Consequently the truth-conditional and use-theoretic characterizations of meaning by no means preclude one another.

None the less, it must be conceded that there is some tension between the two approaches. For even if Davidson were to accept a use theory of *truth conditions*, this approach would conflict on the question of explanatory order with the use theory of *meaning*. For on the latter view a sentence's truth condition is a *consequence* of its meaning, not *constitutive* of it. More specifically, according to the use theory of meaning, our grasp of the truth condition of (say) "snow is white" is the product of the following three-stage process. First, we know the meaning of "snow is white" by knowing its mode of construction and the uses of its component words. Second, we know the meaning of *"true"* by accepting instances of 'The proposition *that p* is true iff *p*' and accepting '$(u)[u$ is *true* iff $(\exists x)(u$ expresses x & x is true)]', and then inferring instances of the disquotation schema, '"*p*" is *true* iff *p*'—including '"snow is white" is *true* if and only if snow is white'. And third, in so far as we understand all the constituents of that biconditional, we can be said to know *that "snow is white" is true if and only if snow is white*. Thus our knowledge of the truth conditions of "snow is white" *derives from* our knowledge of its meaning.[17]

A virtue of this way of thinking, as opposed to Davidson's, is that it gives a more plausible account of the relationship between meaning and truth conditions. It is agreed on all sides that

> *u* means that snow is white →
>   *u* is *true* if and only if snow is white.

But Davidson's approach requires that the truth condition of a sentence *constitutes* its meaning; and this is problematic since it is not the case that

> *u* is *true* if and only if snow is white →
>   *u* means that snow is white

For example, "grass is green" has the same truth value as "snow is white"; therefore, given the *material* construal of "if and only if" (which Davidson employs), "grass is green" is *true* if and only if snow is white: but obviously it is not the case that "grass is green" means that snow is white. In order to overcome this difficulty we would have to find a conception of '*x*'s truth condition is that *p*' that is stronger than '*x* is *true* iff *p*'. To this end Davidson has suggested 'It is a law of nature that *x* is *true* iff *p*'. But neither this suggestion, nor various other proposed manœuvres, look as though they will work. (Could it

---

[17] This anti-Davidsonian position is urged by Gilbert Harman in his "Meaning and Semantics", in M. K. Munitz and P. Unger (eds.), *Semantics and Philosophy* (New York: New York University Press, 1974); and in his "Conceptual Role Semantics".

ever be a *law of nature* that an expression has the truth condition that
it has? If it were, could it not be a law of nature that two distinct truth
conditions invariably coincide?) Faced with such difficulties, and the
series of revisions, objections and further modifications that they
provoke, the whole approach quickly loses its initial appealing simplicity and begins to look rather contrived and implausible. It seems
better first to explain meaning in terms of the use theory (or the
Principle of Charity), and then to derive truth conditions by means
of the disquotation schema. There is simply no need for a route from
truth conditions to meanings.[18]

7. *Compositionality*

But not so fast! A decisive advantage of the truth conditional
approach, according to Davidson, is that it alone can account for the
fact that each of us is able to understand a virtually limitless number
of expressions of our language, including sentences we have never
heard before.[19] The explanation proceeds in two stages. First, we postulate that the meanings of complex expressions are explained by the
meanings of their parts. If this is so, then anyone who has the (relatively simple) ability to use the *primitive* terms in accordance with
their meanings is in a position to understand all the complex expressions too. Second, this postulate of *compositionality* is in turn
explained by the truth-conditional approach. For Tarski showed how

---

[18] Davidson's position on the relationship between meanings and truth conditions
is not as unequivocal as this summary suggests. In some of his earlier writings he does
appear to maintain that the truth condition of a sentence is what constitutes its meaning. But in later writings (and presumably in reaction to the difficulties discussed in the
text) he appears to fall back on a more hedged and elusive position in which, although
it is still maintained that we somehow interpret a person's language (attributing meanings to his sentences) by invoking a Tarski-style truth theory, it is no longer so clear
how this happens—i.e. which truth-theoretic property of a sentence constitutes its
meaning. For useful discussion, see John Foster's "Meaning and Truth Theory", and
John McDowell's "Truth Conditions, Bivalence, and Verificationism", both in G.
Evans and J. McDowell (eds), *Truth and Meaning* (Oxford: Clarendon Press, 1975);
and Mark Sainsbury's "Understanding and Theories of Meaning", *Proceedings of the
Aristotelian Society* 80 (1979–80), 127–44.
[19] D. Davidson, "Truth and Meaning", in his *Inquiries into Truth and
Interpretation*. See also J. Higginbotham, "Knowledge of Reference", in A. George
(ed.), *Reflections on Chomsky* (Oxford: Blackwell, 1989); and R. Larson and G. Segal,
Knowledge of Meaning (Cambridge, Mass: MIT Press, 1995).

the truth (or reference) condition of each complex expression is entailed by the truth (or reference) conditions of its parts. Therefore, in so far as meanings are constituted by truth (or reference) conditions, we can see how the meanings of complexes are engendered by the meanings of their component words.

Unfortunately this explanation of our linguistic abilities suffers from the just-mentioned difficulty of needing, but not having, a satisfactory conception of *truth condition*. Moreover, contrary to what is typically assumed, it is far from clear that the truth-conditional approach is really the only way to account for compositionality. In particular, it is a fairly simple matter to see how compositionality would arise within a use conception of meaning. For a reasonable assumption about the state of understanding a complex expression of our own language is that it consists in nothing more than understanding the parts of that expression and appreciating how they have been combined with one another. This idea is developed and defended in Chapter 7. If it is correct then we can see very easily how our knowledge of the uses of words (in so far as it engenders our understanding of them) gives rise to our understanding of sentences. Moreover, it is also a fairly simple matter to see how our vast linguistic repertoire—i.e. our ability to deploy such a huge number of complex expressions—can be explained on the basis of the use theory. For our knowledge of how to use our complex expressions is very plausibly a consequence of our knowledge of the uses of the relatively small number of primitives.

Consider, for example, the sentence "All emeralds are green". Suppose (enormously oversimplifying) that the meaning of "emerald" is given by the fact that

> There is a disposition to accept "Something is an emerald if and only if it has characteristics, f_1, f_2, and f_3".

Suppose that the meaning of "green" is given by the fact that

> There is a disposition to accept "That is green" in the presence of something clearly green, and otherwise to deny it.

And suppose that the meaning of "All As are Bs" is given by a tendency to conform to certain classical rules of inference, including, for example,

From "All As are Bs" infer "All CAs are Bs".

These facts constrain the use of "All emeralds are green". They tell us something about what will be inferred from it, and about the circumstances in which it will be accepted. They tell us, for example, that we will infer "All big emeralds are green" from it; and that, given the presence of a red object known to be $f_1, f_2,$ and f_3, we will deny the sentence. Thus, from the use-theoretic perspective, our grasp of the meanings of the constituents of the sentence will indeed determine the ways in which it is deployed.

Let us also suppose, in accord with the just-mentioned general view of what it is to understand a complex, that the meaning of "All emeralds are green" consists in nothing more or less than the fact that

> "All emeralds are green" results from substituting words meaning EMERALD and GREEN into a generalization schema whose meaning is ALL AS ARE B.

In that case it is a triviality that anyone who understands the constituents of the sentence and knows how it is put together from them will understand the whole sentence.

Thus, both the deployment of complex expressions and the compositionality of their meanings square perfectly well with a conception of meaning as use.

8. *Dummett's Objection*

Michael Dummett has argued that not every possible regularity of use for a word can establish a meaning, because not every such pattern of use is consistent with the compositional character of language. For he takes compositionality to imply not merely that the meanings of complex expressions are determined by the meanings of their words and by the way the words are combined with one another, but also that there cannot be a substantial degree of MEANING INTERDEPENDENCE amongst the words: there cannot be a 'large' class of words whose meanings can be expressed only because the meanings of the other words in the class are also expressed. What this amounts to is that in order for our language to be properly 'compositional', in Dummett's strong sense, there cannot be a 'large' class of words whose meaning-constituting regularities of use concern their deployment in relation to one another; it cannot be that their meanings are simultaneously determined by conditions for the acceptance of sentences containing them all. In particular, it cannot be that the meanings of all the logical constants (including "not" and "or") are constituted by the practice of conformity with the basic rules of classical logic (including the disposition to accept instances of "p or not p"). To the extent that this condition is violated then, according to Dummett, "the functioning of language [is] unintelligible".[20]

However, it is left quite unclear what it would be for "the functioning of language [to be] unintelligible" and why we should mind if this is so. Granted, any class of MEANING INTERDEPENDENT words has to be learned all at once; for if merely some of them are deployed initially, then acquisition of the others would dictate some revision in what is meant by the initially learned ones. But why should this need for simultaneous acquisition be thought either undesirable or mysterious? Why should it become problematic only when the class of such terms becomes 'large'? And how large is too large? In the absence of answers to these questions, we have no reason to think that language either *does* satisfy or *should* satisfy Dummett's strong compositionality requirement.

What *is* eminently plausible, as we have seen, is that the facts constituting our grasp of words and basic syntactic operations explain our capacity to understand and use the sentences that can be constructed from them. This is how compositionality is normally and properly understood. But compositionality, in this sense, does not preclude the possibility that, amongst the explanatorily basic, meaning-constituting facts there will be specifications of the *joint* use of several (indeed many) primitives in relation to one another. Therefore compositionality, as it uncontroversially holds, does not motivate 'atomistic' constitution of meaning. In particular, it could

---

[20] M. Dummett, *Elements of Intuitionism* (Oxford: Clarendon Press: 1977): "What would render the functioning of language unintelligible would be to suppose that the relations of (immediate or remote) dependence of the meaning of one word on that of another might not be asymmetrical, that, in tracing out what is required for an understanding of a given sentence, and, therefore, of the words in it, we should be led in a circle" (p. 368). See also his *The Logical Basis of Metaphysics*, ch. 10 (Cambridge, Mass.: Harvard University Press, 1991).

well be that the disposition to accept instances of "*p* or not *p*" is what, in part, fixes the meanings of "or" and "not". If so, then the meanings of "or" and "not" will be interdependent. But (as we saw in the response to Objection 3) this form of 'holism'—whereby the meanings of some words depend for their existence on there being words with other particular meanings—is neither bad nor implausible.

9. *Useless Expressions*

Consider: "The boy the cat the dog bit scratched cried." An objection made by Jerry Katz is that there are many such sentences which are too long and/or complicated to be used in ordinary language, but none the less have meanings. So their meanings cannot reside in their uses.[21]

The moral to be drawn from this point, I think, is that we have a notion of

> What complex expression *e* means in the *language* of speaker *S*

which differs from our conception of

> What *e* means to *S*

or

> How *S* understands *e*.

For what we are inclined to say about the incomprehensibly complex sentences to which Katz is alluding is that they might well have a definite meaning in a speaker's language despite meaning nothing to that speaker.

But this observation poses no threat to the use theory of meaning since *both* conceptions of 'the meaning of *e*' can be captured in use-theoretic terms. On the one hand

> *e*'s meaning what it does to *S*

---

[21] J. J. Katz, *Language and Other Abstract Objects* (Totowa, NJ: Rowman & Littlefield, 1981), and *The Metaphysics of Meaning* (Cambridge, Mass.: MIT Press, 1991).

is constituted by

> *S*'s taking it that *e* is constructed in a certain way from
> primitives with certain uses.

And on the other hand

> *e*'s meaning what it does in *S*'s language

is constituted by

> *e*'s being constructed in a certain way (given the syntactic
> rules that best explain the verbal behaviour of the speakers
> of the language) from primitives with certain uses.

(This view of how the meaning properties of complex expressions are constituted was mentioned in the response to Objection 7 and is defended at length in Chapter 7.) Thus it must be conceded that the meaning of a complex expression in a speaker's language is *not* necessarily manifested in his use of it. However, a use-theoretic property is none the less associated with it: namely, that it is constructed in a certain way from words with certain uses. And this, we can suppose, is the property in which its meaning in the language consists. We can suppose, in other words, that the syntactic principles that best explain linguistic behaviour will permit the composition of sentences so complex that an individual is not able to identify their mode of construction. In such a case, the sentence will not be understood and will not be used, but it none the less has a meaning in the speaker's language—a meaning that is constituted by the uses of its parts and the way those parts are combined.

10. *Definition*

It might be supposed that in order to specify the meaning of a word it is necessary to explicitly define it (in the style of "bachelor" means UNMARRIED MAN, and therefore that the use regularity of a word is inadequate in that it fails to provide any such formula. However, we must keep in mind that the two questions

What does "*f*" mean?

and

What provides "*f*" with its meaning?

are different from one another. The first is supposed to be answered in the form

"*f*" means *G*

—that is, via a synonym "*g*", a different expression with the same meaning. And of course there is often no such thing—in which case the question has no good answer. The second is answered by identifying the underlying characteristic that constitutes the meaning property, '*x* means *F*'. It is only this question that the use theory is intended to address, and so its inability to specify *what* a word means can be no basis for criticism.

Notice, moreover, that the explicit definition of a term should not be regarded as an alternative (let alone a *preferable* alternative) to the specification of its meaning-constituting use. For even when explicit definition is feasible—for instance, when we wish to introduce a new word with the same meaning as an existing expression—it can only be in virtue of some practice with the word—the instigation of some use regularity—that we succeed in giving it the desired meaning. See Chapter 6 for further discussion.

11. *Tokens, Types, and Ambiguity*

Which is more fundamental, the meaning of a word *token* or the meaning of the *type* to which it belongs? Should we first give an account of how a specific utterance, made at a definite place and time, means what it does, and then proceed to explain, in terms of that account, how it comes about that the general type that the utterance exemplifies has a certain meaning in the language? Or is it better to proceed in the opposite direction, beginning with a theory of what it is for a type of expression to have a certain meaning, and then deriving from that theory an account of how tokens of that type acquire their meaning?

Evidently the use theory, in so far as it supposes that meanings derive from *regularities* of use, is committed to the second of these strategies. And this may seem to be a mark against it, since the first approach might appear to be more logical and more promising. For it is tempting to suppose that a person can mean whatever he wants by a given utterance token, unconstrained by how physically similar utterances are typically meant. This intuition is bolstered by the phenomenon of ambiguity: some word types have more than one meaning; therefore it is mysterious how a token could inherit a definite meaning from its type; and so one is tempted to explain the various meanings of the type by reference to the different meanings that are given to its tokens.

However, on reflection it seems clear that these considerations are misleading, and that the correct explanatory order is from type meanings to token meanings—just as the use theory requires. For although ambiguity indeed exists, it is strikingly *limited*: there are billions more word tokens than there are word types. And this suggests that the physical character of a token—the type to which it belongs—plays a central role in determining its meaning. That indeed leaves us with the problem of ambiguity; but it can be handled as follows.

We must look for the simplest way of explaining the overall use of a given phonological type. Such a type has a single meaning when there is a single, simple acceptance property, such that all instances of the type may be explained in terms of it. However, if the type has more than one meaning this will be manifested by the need (for the sake of simplicity) to invoke more than one regularity of use in the explanation of its instances. In that case the phonological type divides into various subtypes, whose instances have in common that they stem from the same basic regularity of use. Thus the meaning of a token derives from the meaning of its subtype; and the meaning of that subtype is constituted by the regularity needed to account for the occurrence of its members.

12. *Propositions*

What about indexicals (such as "I", "now", and "here"), demonstratives (such as "this" and "that"), and other context-sensitive terms? On the face of it, each such term has a constant use which is mastered by those who understand it; yet what it 'means', in some sense, can vary from one occasion to another. For example, speakers of English know how to use "I am hungry"—they know its unique meaning. However, on different occasions it expresses different propositions: I used it yesterday to say *that I was hungry*; whereas John will use it tomorrow to say *that he is (then) hungry*. So it would seem that there is an important conception of 'meaning' on which the use theory sheds no light.

Certainly it is vital to distinguish between (1) the meaning (or meanings) of a sentence type, (2) the meaning of one of its tokens, and (3) the proposition expressed by that token. And similarly for the constituent words of a sentence. Moreover, we must acknowledge that the use theory applies primarily to the first of these notions, and derivatively to the second (in so far as the meaning of a sentence token is simply one of the meanings of the ambiguous sentence type). As for the third notion of meaning—the proposition expressed—the use theory does not purport to give a complete account of it. However, since the meaning of an utterance token is a major deter- minant of which proposition is expressed, it would be unjust to say that we can shed no light at all on the character of propositions and their constitutents.

Let me indicate how the use theory of meaning may be extended into an account of propositions. This is a big and complicated topic; and what follows is *very* sketchy indeed—but hopefully better than nothing.

The simplest way of accommodating the inferential character of belief attributions (e.g. that "John believes that dogs bark" entails "John believes something") is to suppose that such attributions have a relational form, i.e. to suppose that that-clauses are singular, refer- ring terms; and it is a matter of stipulation to call the entities to which they refer, "propositions". Thus propositions certainly exist; it merely remains to specify, for each such thing, the circumstances in which it is expressed and to indicate what kind of entity it is. When is it correct to deploy a given that-clause, "that p", to designate what is expressed by a given utterance, u? In other words, under which con- ditions is it correct to give an *interpretation* of u by saying

u expresses the proposition that p.

And what is the nature of the proposition (or propositions) desig- nated by such that-clauses?

As in the case of meanings, the proposition expressed by an utterance is determined by how that utterance is constructed from its parts and by which propositional constituents those parts express (see Chapter 7, Objection 12). For example, the proposition *that I am hungry* (which I express by now saying "I am hungry") is a function of the propositional constituents expressed by my words "I", "am", and "hungry"—call these constituents ⟨I⟩, ⟨am⟩, and ⟨hungry⟩. Thus our initial questions reduce to a pair of more fundamental ones—questions regarding words rather than sentences: namely, (1) what is the relation between a term, x, and one of our terms, "e", such that "e" may be deployed to give an interpretation of x; i.e. what relation between x and "e" must exist in order that

x expresses the propositional constituent ⟨e⟩;

and (2) what kinds of entity are designated by "⟨e⟩"—what sorts of things are propositional constituents?

If x is a predicate, the answers to these questions are relatively straightforward. In that case, we articulate what is expressed by x by using a term with the same meaning as x, i.e. the same use as x: for example

"rouge" expresses ⟨red⟩.

And as for the nature of that propositional constituent, it is a *meaning*: the predicate, x, expresses the meaning of x, for example

⟨red⟩ = RED.

If, on the other hand, x is a singular term, then the situation is complicated in a couple of respects. The first complication derives from the fact that x may or may not be *context-sensitive*. It may be a term, such as "I", "now", and "that", whose referent depends on the circumstances of utterance; or it may be a term, such as "Saturn" or "the smallest prime number", whose referent is constant. The second complication derives from the difference between three kinds of attitude attribution, known as *de dicto*, *de re*, and *de se*. For example, "Mary said that she saw the last dodo" is ambiguous. It may or may not be intended that Mary conceives of the last dodo using the concept, THE LAST DODO; perhaps she merely said *of* the last dodo (conceived of in some other way), that she saw it. Similarly, the word "she" may be intended merely to designate a certain person, and not to indicate how Mary thinks of that person. Alternatively, it may be intended to convey that Mary is thinking of herself from the first-person perspective, as "I".

In order to accommodate these phenomena we must acknowledge that when term "*e*" occurs within a that-clause it may articulate three distinct propositional constituents: namely, $\langle e \rangle (dd)$, $\langle e \rangle (dr)$ and $\langle e \rangle (ds)$. And we must distinguish, for each of these entities, the conditions in which a given singular term expresses it.

Consider, to begin, the *de dicto* case. In order that the singular term, x, expresses $\langle e \rangle (dd)$, it is necessary that "*e*" have the same meaning as x. But in addition it is necessary *either* that x and "*e*" be context-insensitive terms or, if they are not, that they be deployed in the same (relevant) context as one another. Thus, "You said that that man is Marlon Brando" will be a correct *de dicto* attribution by me, if the person I am addressing uttered something with the same meaning as "That man is Marlon Brando" and if this person was in the same context as I am when he made the utterance. As for the *nature* of the propositional constituents expressed, when "*e*" is context-insensitive (e.g. "Marlon Brando") then $\langle e \rangle (dd)$ is the concept e (e.g. MARLON BRANDO); and when "*e*" is context-sensitive (e.g. "That man") then $\langle e \rangle (dd)$ is an ordered pair consisting of the concept, E, and the context of x's deployment.

Second there is the *de re* case. In order that x expresses $\langle e \rangle (dr)$, it is necessary that "*e*" and x be coreferential. If x is context-insensitive, then what is required for such coreferentiality is (as we shall see in Chapter 5) that there be some singular term of ours, "*g*", such that (1) x and "*g*" have the same meaning, and (2) e is the same thing as g. Thus when Mary utters "I saw the animal pictured on page 341 of the *Encyclopaedia Britannica*", she is saying, *de re*, that she saw the last dodo. If x is context-sensitive—if it is an indexical or a demonstrative—then "*e*" is constrained by a batch of rules, including

x means I $\rightarrow [x$ expresses $\langle e \rangle (dr) \leftrightarrow e =$ the speaker of the utterance]

x means NOW $\rightarrow [x$ expresses $\langle e \rangle (dr) \leftrightarrow e =$ the time of the utterance]

x means THAT $F \rightarrow [x$ expresses $\langle e \rangle (dr) \leftrightarrow e =$ the F to which the speaker is attending].

As for the *identity* of a *de re* propositional constituent, it is simply the referent of the term used to articulate it. For example, what is expressed, *de re*, by "the animal pictured on page 341 of the *Encyclopaedia Britannica*" is simply the last dodo. And, in general, $\langle e \rangle (dr)$ is the same thing as *e*.

Finally there is the *de se* case: the case in which an element, "*e*", of a that-clause neither articulates the meaning of the term, *x*, which it is used to interpret, nor gives its referent, but is intended rather to indicate that *x* means the same as a certain indexical or demonstrative. For example, "Mary said that she was happy" can be understood *de se* to convey that Mary uttered something meaning "I am happy"; "John said that Fred is a doctor" might be intended to communicate that John uttered something meaning the same as "He is a doctor". Here, the condition for *x* to express $\langle e \rangle (ds)$ is that *x* and "*e*" be related by one of the above batch of principles for indexicals and demonstratives. However, in the present case, the propositional constituent is not an object, but (as in the case of *de dicto*, context-sensitive constituents) it is an ordered pair consisting of the meaning of *x* and the context of its utterance.

Let me repeat emphatically that these few cryptic remarks are not intended to comprise a theory of propositions, but merely to give some hint as to how such an account, based on a use theory of meaning, might be given.[22]

13. *Communal Meanings*

As Saul Kripke, Hilary Putnam, and Tyler Burge have made clear,[23] members of a linguistic community typically mean exactly the same

[22] Besides (i) the meaning of a sentence type in a language, (ii) the meaning of a given utterance of it, and (iii) the proposition expressed by that utterance, a further notion of meaning relates, somewhat vaguely, to what the speaker 'has in mind' in making the utterance—to what, putting it literally, he intends to communicate. For example, someone might say, "The Porsche is in a hurry," meaning (in this fourth sense), "The driver of the Porsche is in a hurry." The use theory does not purport to give an account of this phenomenon. It is plausible, however, that an analysis of the literal meaning of an expression type (which the use theory *does* provide) will be an important part of such an account. I owe this example to Jean-Yves Pollock, who cites Ray Jackendoff's *The Architecture of the Language Faculty* (Cambridge, Mass.: MIT Press, 1997).

[23] See S. Kripke, *Naming and Necessity* (Cambridge, Mass.: Harvard University Press, 1980); H. Putnam, "The Meaning of 'Meaning'", in his *Mind, Language and*

as one another by a given word, even when their uses of it diverge, not merely in superficial respects (which might be explained away on the basis of differences in evidential circumstances), but also in fundamental respects (stemming from different basic regularities). Thus someone may always be at a loss as to whether to apply "beech" rather than "elm", or may not appreciate that "arthritis" names a disease of the joints; yet he may none the less qualify as an English speaker who means what we do by these words.

This fact about meaning can be dealt with in use-theoretic terms by bringing to bear Putnam's idea of 'the division of linguistic labour'. In order for an individual member of the community to mean a certain thing by a given word, it is not necessary that he himself uses it precisely in accordance with the regularity that fixes the meaning of the word type. What is needed is, first, that there are acknowledged experts in the deployment of the term—experts whose usage is determined by some such regularity; second, that the individual is disposed to defer to the experts—i.e. to accept correction by them; and consequently, third, that his use of the term conforms to that regularity at least to some extent. In these circumstances, even when the speaker's use of a word is fundamentally abnormal, we none the less attribute the normal meaning to him; and that normal meaning is constituted by the regularity that explains the overall use of the word by those 'specialists' to whom the rest of us are prepared to defer.

14. *I-Language Meanings*

An objection from the opposite direction can well be imagined: namely, that the use theory is not internalistic enough; for the meaning-constituting regularities of use that it postulates sometimes relate the deployment of words to aspects of the environment. But, as Chomsky has argued,[24] the properties that are going to be explanatorily valuable in scientific linguistics are likely to be properties that supervene on internal states of the brain.

Reality: Philosophical Papers 2 (Cambridge: Cambridge University Press, 1975); T. Burge, "Individualism and the Mental", in P. French, T. Uehling, and H. Wettstein (eds.), *Midwest Studies in Philosophy* 4: 73–121 (Minneapolis, Minn.: University of Minnesota Press, 1979).

[24] See, for example, Chomsky's *Knowledge of Language* (New York: Praeger, 1986).

Chomsky's view strikes me as quite plausible, but not really to count against the theory under consideration. For the aim of the present use theory is to give an account of 'meaning' in the ordinary, non-scientific sense of the word—to say what we have in mind in our everyday attribution of meanings to expressions in public languages such as English and Spanish. The purpose of the account is not scientific explanation, but rather a demystification of the ordinary concept of meaning, followed by the philosophically beneficial consequences of that demystification: namely, solutions to the numerous problems (mentioned at the beginning of Chapter 1) that are produced, or at least exacerbated, by confusion about that concept. Thus the use theory is not intended to be a part of science, and so cannot be impugned for failing to meet Chomsky's constraints on an adequate linguistic theory, reasonable as they may be. Moreover, the present account, though perhaps unsuited, as it stands, to the needs of science, might none the less provide a helpful clue to the sort of meaning property that *will* be explanatorily valuable in linguistics. For some of the considerations that favour the use theory of public-language meaning will suggest an analogous account of the meanings of I-language expressions: namely, that they are basic regularities of *internal* use in the conceptual system of the individual.[25]

Some philosophers (for example, Ned Block, Brian Loar, and Colin McGinn)[26] have expressed sympathy for a so-called 'two-factor' theory of meaning according to which the meaning of each term is made up of two distinct components: (1) an internal conceptual role (intended to account for the causal/explanatory power of meaning); and (2) some relation between the term and the external world (intended to account for the reference-determining character of meaning). But this idea seems to me to involve various misconceptions. First, in so far as the aim of the theory is to account for meaning *in the ordinary sense*, then many of the uses of a word that its meaning should help to explain will *not* be internal—they will be uses of the word in relation to the environment. Consequently, the conceptual roles (= basic use regularities) needed to explain them will

---

[25] For further discussion see my "Meaning and its Place in the Language Faculty".

[26] See Block, "Advertisement for a Semantics for Psychology"; B. Loar, "Conceptual Role and Truth Conditions", *Notre Dame Journal of Formal Logic* 23 (1982), 272–83; C. McGinn, "The Structure of Content", in A. Woodfield (ed.), *Thought and Object* (Oxford: Oxford University Press, 1982).

also have to be not wholly internal. Second, we cannot expect to be able to *split up* the explanatorily basic use regularity of a word into an internal component (which will explain the internal use facts) and an external component (which will explain the relational ones). (How, for example, could such a division be made of the regularity: "Uses of the word "red" stem from the tendency to apply it to observed surfaces that are determinately red"?) Third, the problem with purely internal conceptual roles is *not* that they are incapable of fixing referential or truth-conditional properties. The problem is rather that purely internal conceptual roles do not constitute the ordinary meanings of our words. Consequently, it will be impossible for us to apply the schema

$$x \text{ has the same conceptual role as our } "f" \to x \text{ is } true \text{ of } f\text{s}$$

to the terms, x, with purely internal conceptual roles in order to articulate, in ordinary language, the referents and truth conditions of those terms. And fourth, not only is there no *need* to supplement the causal/explanatory aspect of a meaning with something to determine a referent, but there is little likelihood of being able to do so success- fully. In light of the plausibility of deflationism about the truth- theoretic notions, we should not expect to find any particular non-semantic relation that is responsible for reference.

15. *Names*

Names provide the occasion for two contrary objections to the use theory of meaning. On the one hand it might be thought that although any given name has a use, it does not (as Kripke has shown) have a meaning, but merely a referent.[27] On the other hand—and from the opposite direction—it might be alleged that although a name *does* have a meaning, no single use regularity could possibly constitute it; for the use of a name varies dramatically from one per- son to another—depending, for example, on whether the speaker is, or is not, acquainted with its referent.

But neither of these criticisms stands up to scrutiny (as we shall see in detail in Chapter 5). In the first place, Kripke showed merely

---

[27] Kripke, *Naming and Necessity*.

that names do not have the same meanings as definite descriptions; he gives no reason to think that they do not have meanings at all. And we do, after all, speak quite properly of translating names and of understanding them—i.e. of knowing their meanings. In the second place, the striking differences between various peoples' use of a given name can be explained away as various divergences from the common use of 'experts'—of those who are familiar with the referent—and it is the basic regularities in 'expert' use which constitutes the meanings of names.

16. *Knowledge of Meaning*

Surely, understanding a word consists in knowing what it means. But we generally do not know what are the fundamental regularities in the use of our words. Indeed, most of us would be hard-pressed to state any of them. So the use theory fails to specify correctly the knowledge we have about a word that constitutes our understanding of it. Or so it might seem.

However, although we are not normally in a position to articulate the regularities underlying the use of our words—and consequently cannot be said to have *explicit* knowledge of them—we can none the less be said, simply in virtue of implementing those regularities, to *implicitly* know what they are. Moreover, there is no compelling reason to think that the sort of knowledge of meanings that constitutes understanding must be explicit. And so it is not implausible that, when we speak of knowing the meaning of a word, what we have in mind is simply that we know implicitly how the word is used and hence what it means. This issue was discussed in more detail in section 1 of Chapter 2.

A related concern about our knowledge of what we mean derives from the 'externalist' character of certain regularities of use. For it might seem that, from the plausible premises

We know a priori that our word "water" means WATER

and

We know a priori that (x means WATER $\rightarrow$ water exists in the environment of x)

one could argue to the counterintuitive conclusion that

We know a priori that water exists in our environment.[28]

The trouble with this reasoning is that it again involves neglecting the distinction between explicit and implicit knowledge. Perhaps we do have explicit a priori knowledge that "water" means WATER; for that type of knowledge is arguably trivial—deriving from nothing more than the capitalizing convention for designating meanings. But explicit knowledge of the second premise—of how the property underlying 'x means WATER' is constituted (and, in particular, that it consists in some relation to environmental water)—is surely not a priori. In order to acquire it, one must first observe how the word "water" is deployed and then infer that the basic regularity for its use makes reference to water.

Perhaps ordinary, unreflective users of the word might be said to know such things *implicitly*. And any such knowledge would plausibly be a priori, since a person's implicit knowledge is not contained in his 'web of belief' and so is not hostage to considerations of empirical adequacy and overall simplicity. So let us concede that we do have implicit a priori knowledge that water exists in the environment of any word meaning WATER, and also that our word "water" means WATER. Moreover it is natural to regard implicit knowledge as closed under entailment. It would then indeed follow that we know a priori that water exists in our environment. But in so far as that knowledge is merely implicit (and in so far as all implicit knowledge is trivially a priori), such a conclusion is not at all counterintuitive.

17. *Scepticism*

Someone could surely mean what is generally meant by a word, even though he does not endorse the statements that would seem to provide its basic pattern of use. So, for example, we can mean PHLO-

---

[28] This argument comes (slightly modified) from Paul Boghossian's "What the Externalist can Know A Priori", *Proceedings of the Aristotelian Society* 97 (1996–7), 161–75, where it is deployed to show a tension between externalism regarding meaning and the doctrine that we know what we mean. See also M. McKinsey "Anti-individualism and Privileged Access", *Analysis* 51 (1991), 9–16.

GISTON by the word "phlogiston" even though we do not maintain the phlogiston theory which supposedly fixes the word's meaning. Similarly, it would seem that a fan of intuitionistic logic might be aware of the meanings of our words "not", "and", etc., despite rejecting the classical principles whose general acceptance implicitly defines these terms.

In order to accommodate this point, which is surely correct, it is necessary to distinguish two closely affiliated acceptance commitments of a word. First, there is the unconditional practice of using that word to formulate one's acceptance of certain substantive principles. Second there is the conditional commitment to use *that* word to articulate those principles *if* they are to be accepted. And it is the second of these commitments that is fundamentally meaning constituting. The first fixes meaning only in so far as it implies the second. Thus the word "phlogiston" may be used as the phlogiston theory specifies; and this unconditional regularity of use will indeed be sufficient to fix its meaning—but not necessary. What really constitutes the meaning of "phlogiston" is the conditional acceptance property: of using that word on condition the theory is accepted. In the first of these cases the word is given a meaning and that meaning (i.e. that concept) is canonically deployed; whereas in the second case the assigned meaning is not canonically deployed. It is like the difference between playing a game and merely being aware of the rules, or between employing a tool and merely knowing how to use it. Either way, the word is assigned a function—a conditional acceptance property specifying the circumstances in which certain sentences containing the word are accepted. But the resulting linguistic instrument may or may not be found attractive and put to normal work—the unconditional regularity may or may not be actualized. See Chapter 6 for further discussion.

18. *A Priori Knowledge*

Is the use theory of meaning able to account for a priori knowledge? And should it be able to? One might well suppose that it both can and must. For it might be thought that we would have a priori knowledge of any sentence whose acceptance constitutes the basic use of one of its constituent terms. After all, if the meaning of "f" stems from the decision to accept the sentence "$\#f$", then "f" will surely receive the meaning necessary and sufficient for "$\#f$" to be *true*; so given what it means, "$\#f$" must be *true*. How else are we to explain our a priori knowledge of logic, geometry, and arithmetic, amongst other things, if not as resulting in this way from the implicit definition of terms?

But this reasoning is defective. In the first place, even though our meaning-constituting commitments are maintained a priori, they may none the less be false—and this would not in the slightest diminish their capacity to confer meaning. For a term acquires its meaning from our *regarding* certain sentences containing it as *true*—from our using it in that way—independently of whether they are in fact *true*. So it is not the case that we can infer the truth of these sentences from the fact that they are implicit definitions.

In the second place, as we have just seen, the acceptance properties that are constitutive of a meaning are *conditional*. A meaning may indeed be associated with the role of a term "f" in a body of substantive postulates, "$\#f$". But in order to assign "f" to that role, hence to that meaning, it is not necessary to maintain those postulates; it suffices to be committed to the conditional "$\exists x(\#x) \rightarrow \#f$", which says that were anything to be given that role then "f" would be. Consequently, even though meaning-constituting commitments are indeed a priori, we cannot thereby demonstrate the aprioricity of logic, arithmetic, or geometry.

Moreover, we should not suppose that the use theory's failure to explain substantive a priori knowledge is in any way objectionable. For in light of Quine's web-of-belief model of theoretical development it is far from obvious that there is a priori scientific knowledge of substantive domains such as logic, arithmetic, and geometry; so it certainly can't be taken for granted that a decent theory of meaning must be able to account for such a thing. For elaboration of these points see Chapter 6.

19. *Normativity*

From the meaning of a word various conclusions about how it *ought* to be applied may be drawn; but no such conclusions flow from its actual use—or so it would seem. For example, if a word means DOG, then it is proper to apply it to dogs and it would be wrong to apply it to cats. But from the fact that the word is typically applied to dog-like objects and occasionally (in foggy conditions) to cat-like objects, nothing follows at all about how one *ought* to apply it: we cannot conclude that the cat applications are wrong. Thus it may seem that use and meaning have different normative implications and must therefore be distinct properties.

But there is a fallacy lurking in this line of thought. Let us allow that

> *x* means DOG → *x* ought to be applied only to dogs.

However, it is by no means evident that the explanation of this conditional is that the property '*x* means DOG' is constituted (in part) by the property '*x* ought to be applied only to dogs': the normative implications of the meaning property do not necessarily make it intrinsically normative. Therefore the fact that use properties are *not* intrinsically normative—the fact that nothing can be immediately deduced (i.e. without further premises) about how the words that possess them *ought* to be applied—does not disqualify them from being the basis of meaning. To nail down this conclusion, notice that no one would dream of arguing from the conviction that

> *x* is a human being → *x* ought to be treated with respect

to the conclusion that 'being a human being' could not be constituted by an intrinsically non-normative, biological property—perhaps something of the form 'possessing such-and-such genotype'. Similarly the normative import of a meaning property does not preclude its reduction to an intrinsically non-normative, use property.

But what, more specifically, could account for the normative import of a meaning property? A promising strategy is to begin with the *pragmatic* value of true belief and then to show, given the correlation between accepting a sentence and believing the proposition it expresses, that each predicate ought, in virtue of its meaning, to be applied to certain things and not others. This idea is developed in Chapter 8.

20. *Regularities without Meaning*

It seems clear that there are many possible regularities of use that do not coincide with meanings. For example, one might fall into the habit of making a certain noise while sleeping in the afternoon; and this practice would surely not provide that noise with any conceptual content.

We must grant, of course, that not every regularity of use constitutes a meaning of the relevant kind: namely a concept, a constituent of beliefs, desires, and so on. But we have been supposing all along that in order for a type of sound or mark to have the kind of meaning in which we are interested—that is, *conceptual* meaning—the regularity for its use must concern the circumstances in which certain sentences containing it are *accepted* (see the next section for an account of this notion). Moreover the use of a new term must cohere with the regularities that constitute the meanings of the other words. So, for example, in so far as we are disposed (in light of the meaning of "or") to accept instances of "*p* or not *p*", then, if "glub" is a new predicate, we must accept "That is glub or it isn't glub". Thus the particular use theory recommended here is not committed to the absurd claim that any old pattern of noise-making is associated with the expression of a concept.

There may be a residual doubt as to whether, even within our *restricted* class of use regularities, every member will constitute a meaning; for it may be thought that not all such regularities could determine a referent or extension. However, this doubt—as we saw in responding to Objection 5—derives from a misguided, 'inflationary' view of reference. From the deflationary point of view, the conceptually fundamental principle governing the relation 'being *true* of' is the schema

$$(y)(\text{Predicates meaning } F \text{ are } true \text{ of } y \leftrightarrow fy).$$

And this will trivially fix the extension of any predicate, regardless of how its meaning is constituted.

21. *Acceptance*

The regularities of use that (I am suggesting) constitute the meanings of words concern the circumstances in which specified sentences are privately *accepted* (i.e. uttered assertively to oneself). Therefore, in so far as the aim of the theory is to give a general account of meaning properties through a non-semantic reductive analysis of them, it is essential to make it plausible that the psychological relation 'Person *S* accepts the sentence "*p*"' can be explicated in non-semantic terms.[29]

To that end I would like to do two things: first, rebut a popular argument that is supposed to show that the relevant notion of acceptance *is* semantic; and second, sketch a positive account suggesting that it *isn't*.

The argument for the conclusion that 'acceptance' is a semantic concept goes like this. The difference between accepting a sentence and merely uttering it (e.g. as a joke, a linguistic example, etc.) consists in the presence or absence of a commitment to the sentence's being *true*; but *truth* is a semantic notion; therefore so is acceptance.

However, there is a decisive response to this line of thought. Granted, *accepting* a sentence goes hand in hand with accepting its *truth*. But, equally well, *supposing* something goes hand in hand with supposing its *truth*, *doubting* something goes hand in hand with doubting its *truth*, and so on. All of these correlations are fully explained by the obviousness of the schema

$$\text{``}p\text{''} \text{ is } true \leftrightarrow p.$$

Consequently, its relationship to truth is not what distinguishes acceptance from other attitudes (such as doubting, conjecturing, etc.) and does not help to constitute its nature. Thus the relevant concept of acceptance does not presuppose the notion of truth.

A reason for thinking, on the contrary, that acceptance is a *non*-semantic notion would be provided by an account of it in purely physical, behavioural, and psychological terms. Let me therefore offer an extremely crude first approximation of such an account: a functional theory that simultaneously characterizes 'acceptance', 'desire', 'observation', and 'action' by means of five principles that relate these notions to one another, to behaviour, and to environmental conditions:

---

[29] In ordinary language the word "acceptance" designates an attitude to *propositions*—one might accept, for example, *that dogs bark*. Here, however, I am using the word in a non-standard sense, to refer to the corresponding attitude to sentences—what Davidson calls "holding true". Thus in the sense deployed here one may 'accept' (i.e. hold true) "dogs bark" and thereby accept (in the ordinary sense) the proposition it expresses.

(1) For each observable fact O there is a sentence type "o" such that:

O is instantiated in view of $S \leftrightarrow S$ accepts "o".

(2) For each basic action type A there is a sentence type "a" such that:

S does $A \leftrightarrow S$ wants "a".

(3) The set of things S accepts conforms to principles of consistency, simplicity, and conservatism.

(4) S accepts "$p \rightarrow q$" iff S is disposed to accept "q" should he come to accept "p".

(5) (S wants "q" and S accepts "$p \rightarrow q$") $\rightarrow S$ wants "p".

Thus what S accepts may be inferred, given principles of inference and decision theory, on the basis of what he utters and what he does. No doubt this account is grotesquely over-simple. For one thing, the practical syllogism, expressed in (5), should be replaced with a more sophisticated decision theory, such as the principle of expected utility maximization. However, the theory does appear to capture some of the central characteristics of acceptance—and it does not presuppose any semantic ideas. Therefore one may not unreasonably hope that an adequate account, along roughly these preliminary lines, might be forthcoming. In which case acceptance is indeed a non-semantic notion and hence legitimate for deployment in a reductive account of meaning.

22. *The Semantic/Pragmatic Distinction*

If there are terms with the same meaning but different uses, then obviously meaning is not constituted by use; and it is often maintained—for example, by Jerry Katz[30]—that there exist many such pairs of words. Some alleged examples are:

and —— but

dog —— cur

American —— Yank

---

[30] Katz, *Language and other Abstract Objects* and *The Metaphysics of Meaning*.

For each such case, the claim is made that we must distinguish between the descriptive (semantic, truth-conditional) content (which is the same whichever of the words is used) and the further implications of selecting one way, rather than another, of expressing that content. Thus if one wants to warn the listener that the second conjunct is somewhat surprising given the first, one might use "but" instead of "and"; if one wants to be insulting, one uses "Yank" instead of "American", and so on. Consequently, the members of each pair have the same meaning but different uses.

An initial response to this objection would be to deny that the words in question are synonyms. It could be argued that there is a broad, non-technical notion of meaning in which the members of the above pairs of expressions do not have exactly the same meaning— and precisely because of the differences in how they are used; so meaning, in this broad sense, might well be identified with use. However this response would not be adequate as it stands. For it would leave unexplained the contrast between semantic and non-semantic (i.e. descriptive and non-descriptive) aspects of meaning. In so far as this distinction is intuitively clear, then the use theoretician owes some account of how, in his terms, it might be drawn.

However, the rough shape of such an account is not hard to discern. It is plausible to suppose that there are some facts regarding the use of a term that constitute its semantic content, and further facts that underlie other aspects of its meaning. The difference between these two different types of fact is that those constituting the semantic content of a word make reference merely to the beliefs of the speaker—to the circumstances in which certain sentences involving the word are accepted; whereas the other facts—those constituting non-descriptive content—specify the use of a word as a function of desires or intentions of the speaker that go beyond articulating his belief. For example, the use of both "and" and "but" may be governed by the acceptance property:

We tend to infer "p" and "q" from "p C q" and to infer
"q C p" from "p" and "q".

However, the overall use of "but" may be governed by the further principle:

"but" is used to warn the hearer that the second conjunct will be found surprising in light of the first.

Thus two words may have the same basic acceptance property; but given a speaker's desire not merely to describe a situation, but to effect some further speech act as well, he will pick one of these words rather than the other.[31]

23. *Thought*

Language is an expression of thought, a means by which statements are made, questions asked, instructions given, and so on. Therefore, to *understand* a language—to know the significance of its expressions—is to be able to tell which thoughts underlie their use: to know what is being asserted, asked, demanded, and so on. Thus the meaning of a sentence is the propositional character it typically expresses, and the meaning of a word is the element of such a character (i.e. the concept) that it expresses.

This eminently natural conception of meaning may appear to be quite distinct from, and incompatible with, the conception of meaning as use. But in fact these views are easy to reconcile with one another (as we saw in Chapter 2). For the concept DOG is most directly identified as the concept that is normally expressed in English by using the word "dog" and expressed in other languages by words with the same use as "dog". And on that basis, after the appropriate investigation into the nature of that shared use, we will be led to a characterization of DOG as that entity whose engagement by the speaker's mind is manifested by his deployment of a word with use regularity '$u(x)$'. In other words, we will arrive at a theory of the form

$$x \text{ expresses the concept DOG} = u(x)$$

which reduces the meaning property to a basic use regularity. Thus the natural view that the meaning of an expression is the concept it expresses is quite consistent with the further claim that such concepts are identified by means of the use regularities of the words that express them.

---

[31] David Ryan reminded me that some words (e.g. "hello" and "ouch") appear to have no descriptive content, though they are clearly meaningful. On the present account, what is special about the regularities of use that constitute the meanings of such terms is that they will not allude to the acceptance of sentences containing them.

Notice that, in so far as '*x* means *F*' implies a correlation between a speaker's use of the term, *x*, and his engagement with the concept, *F*, then there must also be a correlation between *acceptance* properties of the term and *belief* properties of the concept. Moreover, if it is explanatorily fundamental, vis-à-vis the overall use of *x*, that certain specified sentences containing it are accepted in certain specified circumstances, then it will be explanatorily fundamental, vis-à-vis the overall use of the concept *F*, that the correlated propositions are believed in those circumstances. Thus the use theory of meaning could equally well have been formulated by beginning at the level of thought and maintaining that each concept is individuated by certain explanatorily basic patterns of deployment, and then adding that the meaning of a term is the concept, so individuated, with which it is correlated. This (roughly speaking) is the way things are done by Christopher Peacocke.[32] Similarly, I see no fundamental difference between the use theory and the views of those (such as David Lewis and Frank Jackson)[33] who favour 'functionalist' accounts whereby each mental element is identified as that which plays a certain causal role, and the meaning of a term is then identified with the element it expresses.

---

[32] See Peacocke, *A Study of Concepts*. The principal difference between Peacocke's account and what is argued here concerns truth and reference. Peacocke supposes that there must be something he calls a "Determination Theory" whose job it is to explain, given the individuating ("possession") conditions for a concept, why it has the particular extension it does. More specifically, he assumes that if a concept is individuated by the acceptance of certain propositions containing it, then the extension it must have is the one that will render those propositions true. This assumption leads him to suppose that not every pattern of use can constitute a coherent concept (for not every such pattern will, given the Determination Theory, be able to have an extension). And on this basis he concludes that we know certain propositions a priori, in virtue of our possession of their constituent concepts; for when the acceptance of a proposition is an individuating condition for one of its constituents, then that proposition must be true. However, according to the account I am developing here, this line of thought goes wrong at the outset. For (as we saw in the response to Objection 4) the demand for a Determination Theory presupposes an *inflationary* view of truth and reference—a view that should be rejected. And in that case there will no reason to think certain patterns of acceptance cannot constitute concepts, and no basis for inferring that concept-possession engenders a priori knowledge. For further discussion of Peacocke's epistemological proposal, see Chapter 6.

[33] See F. Jackson, *From Metaphysics to Ethics* (Oxford: Clarendon Press, 1998), and D. Lewis, "Reduction of Mind", in S. Guttenplan (ed.), *A Companion to the Philosophy of Mind* (Oxford: Blackwell, 1994).

24. *Mates's Problem*

As Benson Mates first observed, no two expressions in the same language—even those regarded as synonyms—are reliably interchangeable *salve veritate*.[24] However close in meaning the predicates "*f*" and "*g*" may be, a given speaker might understand one of them imperfectly, leading him to say "Not all *f*s are *g*s", and leading us to suppose that

> He said that not all *f*s are *g*s, but he didn't say that not all *f*s are *f*s,

and to suppose moreover that

> He believes that not all *f*s are *g*s, but he doesn't believe that not all *f*s are *f*s.

This phenomenon evidently causes trouble for the thesis that the meanings of words are concepts—that is, the components of belief states. For if they are, then it follows from the assumption that "*f*" and "*g*" are synonyms that the state of believing *that . . . f . . .* is the same as the state of believing *that . . . g . . . .* Thus it would seem that we have either to deny that expressions can ever be synonyms or else to reject the Mates intuitions; and neither step is appealing.

The best way out of this dilemma, it seems to me, is to retain the idea that the meaning of a word is a concept (a constituent of propositional-attitude states), to accept that two terms "*f*" and "*g*" can have the same meaning, and to acknowledge with Mates that someone, perhaps somewhat confused, might none the less say and believe that not all *f*s are *g*s. However, it seems to me that we must then be prepared to allow that, *ipso facto*, the subject is saying and believing that not all *f*s are *f*s.

It can be no objection to this characterization of the situation that he did not utter the words "Not all *f*s are *f*s", because he did, after

---

[34] B. Mates, "Synonymy", in L. Linsky (ed.), *Semantics and the Philosophy of Language* (Champaign, Ill.: University of Illinois Press, 1952), 111–36.

all, utter something synonymous with that sentence. And such grounds are precisely the basis for maintaining, for example, that Pierre, who came out with "Il pleut", said that it is raining.

A deeper source of resistance to the suggestion, I would guess, is our reluctance to attribute self-contradictory beliefs to the subject. For although he is indeed making a mistake, it seems unfair to attribute such gross irrationality to him. In response, however, it is crucial to appreciate that not all self-contradictory belief is irrational. What certainly is irrational is *knowingly* believing a contradiction—a state which more or less coincides with thinking to one's self something of the form "p & $-p$", "Not all fs are fs", etc. But, as our example shows, it is quite possible to believe a contradiction without recognizing that one is doing so. And such a belief may well not be irrational. Thus no accusation of barefaced irrationality is implicit in supposing that our subject believes that not all fs are fs, and so we should not shrink, out of a reluctance to be unfair, from attributing that belief to him.

Thus the situation here resembles Kripke's case of Pierre, who asserts "Londres est joli" on the basis of hearsay but who comes to maintain "London is *not* pretty" after he has spent a little time there—not realizing that "Londres" and "London" name the same place.[35] There is overwhelming reason to suppose that Pierre believes that London is pretty (for he continues to accept "Londres est joli"), although he clearly also believes what he now says in English: namely, that London is not pretty. Again, our resistance to this natural characterization of Pierre's state of mind is the feeling that, misguided though he may be, he does not deserve to be convicted of contradicting himself. But this resistance should be dispelled once we appreciate that the 'crime' is deliberate self-contradiction, not contradictory belief *per se*.

I have attempted in this chapter to respond briefly to all the objections that I can imagine being made against the use theory of meaning. Amongst these difficulties, some are critical—namely those relating to truth, reference, a priori knowledge, compositionality,

[35] S. Kripke, "A Puzzle About Belief", in A. Margalit (ed.), *Meaning and Use* (Dordrecht: Kluwer, 1979), 239–83.

linguistic norms, the indeterminacy of translation, and the prospects for any non-semantic reductive analysis of meaning properties. These issues will be addressed thoroughly, one at a time, in the chapters that remain.[36]

[36] I would like to thank Malcom Budd, Jakob Hohwy, Pierre Jacob, Jerry Katz, Huw Price, and Barry C. Smith for suggestions that helped me improve this chapter.

4

Truth

This chapter will concern the relationship between three concepts: namely, TRUTH, ABOUTNESS, and MEANING. The aim will be to show how a certain philosophical view of truth—known as deflationism—helps to dissolve a certain problem regarding aboutness—the notorious problem of intentionality—and thereby puts us in a good position to discern the nature of meaning. So there will be three questions on the table. First: what is truth? What is the characteristic shared by 'Snow is white', 'Electrons are negatively charged', and other true propositions? Second: how can a word—a mere sound or mark—be *about*, or *represent*, a certain aspect of external reality? How is it possible for the word "Plato", that I might use here and now, to reach out through space and time and latch on to a particular person living a long time ago and a long way away? And third, the central problem of this book: which underlying, non-semantic property of a word provides it with the particular meaning it has? What is it about different words—"dog", "and", "good", and so on—that is responsible for their meaning what they do and that justifies the particular way in which we translate them into foreign languages? Addressing these questions in turn, I will proceed in three stages. First, I will say what I think is the essence of the deflationary perspective on truth, outlining the evidence in favour of adopting it. Second, I will show, from that perspective, how the problem of aboutness should be approached and dissolved. And third, I will indicate how this view of the problem encourages a use theory of meaning.

The basic thesis of deflationism, as I see it, is that the equivalence schema

The proposition *that p* is true iff *p*

is *conceptually fundamental.*[1] By this I mean that we accept its instances in the absence of supporting argument:[2] more specifically, without deriving them from any reductive premise of the form

For every x: x is true = x is such-and-such

which characterizes traditional ('inflationary') accounts of truth, such as the correspondence theory (x is true = x corresponds to a fact), the coherence theory (x is true = x belongs to a coherent system of beliefs), the verificationist theory (x is true = x would be verified in ideal circumstances), and the pragmatist theory (x is true = x is useful to believe). The evidence for this basic deflationist thesis is that our overall deployment of the truth predicate—the sum of everything we do with the word "true"—is best explained by taking the *fundamental* fact about its use to be our inclination to accept the instances of the equivalence schema.[3] And the evidence for this explanatory claim is that that regularity is necessary and sufficient to account for the *value* of our concept of truth: its utility as a device of generalization.

Let me elaborate. Deflationism about truth is partially inspired by Wittgenstein's caution against the temptation to overdraw linguistic analogies. For most familiar predicates—"dog", "car", "snow", etc.—are deployed in the service of categorization and explanation. And in any such case one might reasonably inquire into the shared

[1] The deflationary view of truth is articulated and defended in my *Truth* (Oxford: Blackwell, 1990) and further elaborated in the second edition (Oxford University Press, 1998). See also Quine, *Pursuit of Truth*, ch. 5; Leeds, "Theories of Reference and Truth"; Soames, "What is a Theory of Truth?" and "The Truth about Deflationism"; Field, "The Deflationary Conception of Truth" and "Deflationist Views of Meaning and Content".

Arguably the truth predicate is ambiguous: standing most often for a property of propositions, but sometimes for a corresponding property of utterances. Here I am using it in the first of these senses, and I use the italicized word "*true*" in the second sense: that is, to mean "expresses a true proposition".

[2] The instances of the equivalence schema that must be accepted by an English speaker, *S*, are obtained by replacing "*p*" (on the LHS of the material biconditional) with a sentence in *S*'s language, and replacing "*p*" (on the RHS) with another instance of that sentence—one which *S* takes to express the same proposition.

[3] As discussed in Chapter 3, I am assuming that linguistic behaviour is the product of a combination of facts and general principles, including an interlocking set of fundamental regularities governing the use of words (i.e. governing the acceptance of sentences containing them).

characteristics of the things to which it applies. But we should not assume that *all* predicates function in this way; in particular we should not assume that the truth predicate does—that it, like the others, is a device of categorization and explanation. But what in that case could its function possibly be?

An ingenious answer was first proposed by Quine, who observed that the truth predicate plays a vital role in enabling us to capture certain generalizations.[4] For we can generalize

The moon is subject to gravity

by saying

Every physical object is subject to gravity.

And similarly we can always obtain a generalization from a statement about a particular object by replacing the term referring to the object with a (restricted) universal quantifier: thus, '*a* is *H*' becomes 'Every *G* is *H*'. However, there is an important class of generalization that cannot be constructed in anything like this way: for example, the one whose instances include

(a) If dogs bark, then we should believe that dogs bark;
(b) If God exists, then we should believe that God exists;
(c) If killing is wrong, then we should believe that killing is wrong.

In this case, and in various others, the usual strategy does not work. How then can the generalization be formed? What is the single proposition—with which one might agree or disagree—that captures all these particular conditionals?

Quine's suggestion was that it is in order to solve this problem that we have the concept of truth. More specifically, what is needed is that there be a term "*K*"—in English, the word "true"—governed by the schema

The proposition *that p* is *K* iff *p*.

[4] See W. V. Quine, *Philosophy of Logic* (Englewood Cliffs, NJ: Prentice-Hall, 1970).

For in the light of its instances we can convert our original list, (a), (b), (c), etc., into an equivalent one

> If the proposition *that dogs bark* is true, then we should
>   believe *that dogs bark*;
> If the proposition *that God exists* is true, then we should
>   believe *that God exists*;
> If the proposition *that killing is wrong* is true, then we should
>   believe *that killing is wrong*,

in which the same property (namely, 'If x is true, then we should believe x') is attributed to objects of a certain type (namely, propositions). So this second list can be generalized in the standard way, as

> Every proposition is such that, if it is true, then we should
>   believe it,

or, more colloquially,

> We should believe the truth.[5]

The deflationist's contention (which is founded on a survey of linguistic usage) is that whenever we deploy the concept of truth nontrivially—whether in logic, ordinary language, science, or philosophy—it is playing this role: a device of generalization. Moreover, its doing so requires, as we have just seen, no more and no less than the equivalence schema. Thus the basis for our use of the truth predicate is indeed our acceptance of the instances of that schema, and *not* any principle of the form

> For every x: x is true = x is such-and-such.

---

[5] It was perhaps an exaggeration to have suggested that the concept of truth is *needed* for this purpose. An alternative strategy would be to introduce substitutional quantification, by means of which one could articulate the desired generalization by saying '(p)(If p, then we should believe that p)'. But in that case there would be required a battery of extra syntactic and semantic rules to govern the new type of quantifier. Therefore, we might consider the value of our concept of truth to be that it provides, not the only way, but a relatively 'cheap' way of obtaining the problematic generalizations—the way actually chosen in natural language. For further discussion see my *Truth*.

This core deflationary position has, I would argue, certain additional, distinctive implications about truth: first, regarding the *meaning* of the truth predicate (namely, that "true" is *implicitly defined* by the equivalence schema);[6] and second, regarding the *underlying nature* of the property of truth (namely, that it almost certainly does not have one).[7] But my concern here is neither with these more-or-less debatable consequences nor with how they might be derived. What I want to do, rather, is to examine the bearing of the core deflationary position on questions about the possibility of aboutness and the nature of meaning. How is it possible for a word to represent (refer to, be about) some specific aspect of the world? And in virtue of which of its underlying, non-semantic properties does a word come to have the particular meaning that it has? The answers that I want to propose come directly from the above-argued basic tenet of deflationism—that the equivalence schema grounds our use of the truth predicate—and don't depend on what I think that tenet implies about the meaning of "true" and the underlying nature of truth.

Clearly the issues of aboutness and meaning are intimately related to one another. For words derive their referential character from their meanings: e.g. any word meaning DOG is about dogs. Therefore the problem of aboutness may be rephrased as the question: what property constituting the meaning of a word could possibly account for its reference? Or, to put it another way, what constraint on the nature of meaning is implied by the fact that the meaning of term determines its referent? Evidently we must be able to answer this

---

[6] In so far as the source of our overall use of the truth predicate is our disposition to accept instances of the equivalence schema, then, given a use theory of meaning, it follows that the meaning of the truth predicate is fixed by that fact about it.

Strictly speaking we should distinguish between two factors that jointly determine our acceptance of the equivalence schema: (1) our decision to accept *some* schema of the form "The proposition *that p* is *K* iff *p*"; and (2) our decision to deploy the word "true" *if* we were to accept such a schema. Strictly speaking it is the second of these commitments that provides the fundamental regularity in our use of the truth predicate and that constitutes its meaning. For more on this complication, see Chapter 3 (response to Objection 17) and Chapter 6.

[7] The argument that truth does not have an underlying nature is based on two ideas (which can in turn be justified). First, the familiar facts about truth can all be explained on the basis of a theory whose axioms are instances of the equivalence schema (i.e. axioms such as "The proposition *that snow is white* is true iff snow is white"). And second, no theory from which this set of equivalence facts could itself be deduced would be simple enough to qualify as an *explanation* of them. For a defence of these claims, see *Truth*, 2nd edn., ch. 3.

question in order to be in a position to say what kinds of property constitute meanings.

The relevance of deflationism to these matters should be fairly obvious. For, as we have just said, one of the main difficulties in determining the nature of meaning has been the need to account for *aboutness*, i.e. *representation*, i.e. the fact that words refer to features of reality and that sentences can express objective truths. But to the extent that the phenomena of reference and truth are 'deflated', it is surely going to be easier to show how they are possible, and hence easier to devise a theory of meaning that can accommodate the representational power of language.

This presupposes, of course, that deflationism regarding the truth of propositions goes hand in hand with deflationism regarding the relations of *being true of* (holding between predicative concepts and sequences of objects) and *reference* (holding between singular concepts and objects). But this is very plausible. For not only are the pertinent considerations parallel to one another, but the three truth-theoretic notions are interdefinable. I will take it, therefore, that the conceptually fundamental principle governing our use of "is true of" is the schema

$$(y)[\text{Predicative concept } F \text{ is true of } y \text{ iff } f(y)],$$

rather than anything even roughly of the form

$$(x)(y)[x \text{ is true of } y \text{ iff } r(xy)];$$

and (as we shall see in detail in the next chapter) that the conceptually fundamental principle which explains our use of "refers" is

$$(y)[\text{Singular concept } N \text{ refers to } y \text{ iff } n = y],$$

rather than any principle or principles of the form

$$(x)(y)[x \text{ refers to } y \text{ iff } c(xy)].$$

Let me now be more concrete about the line of thought I am recommending—from deflationary truth to the analysis of meaning via a dissolution of the problem of aboutness. Consider the English word "dog". Which of its non-semantic properties (if any) is responsible for its having the particular meaning it has? Or to put it another way, which property '$u(x)$' satisfies the reductive theory

x means DOG = $u(x)$?

Now, as I have been emphasizing, it has been typically felt that the main difficulty in answering this question derives from the fact that the meaning of a predicate determines what it may correctly be applied to: in particular, that

x means DOG →
  x means something that is true of all and only dogs.

Or in other words—if we suppose, by definition, that an utterance is *true* (italicized) if and only if the proposition it expresses is true—the difficulty derives from the fact that

x means DOG →
  x is *true* of all and only dogs.

For it is taken for granted that this meaning-to-*truth* conditional places a very severe constraint on what '$u(x)$' might be.[8] But this presupposition, I want to suggest, stems from a misguided inflationism about truth-theoretic notions.

To see this, remember that from an inflationary point of view the basic principle governing "x is *true* of y" is not the equivalence schema but some conceptually more fundamental thesis. And notice that, depending on what that more fundamental thesis is taken to be, only certain reductive analyses of the meaning property (i.e. only certain choices of '$u(x)$') will be compatible with the meaning-to-

---

[8] I am assuming that the extension of a predicate is not context-sensitive; and in that case we can identify its meaning with the propositional constituent it expresses. If this is not so—if a certain predicate *is* context sensitive—then the appropriate conditional will be

x expresses the propositional constituent $\langle f \rangle$ → x is true of fs.

Moreover it can be supposed that the propositional constituent expressed by such a predicate is fixed by a combination of its meaning and the context in which it appears. Therefore, even if the assumption of context-insensitivity is incorrect, the extension of a predicate is determined, at least in part, by its meaning, and so the representational power of a word might seem to constrain how its meaning is constituted.

truth conditional. For example, given the common inflationary assumption that 'x is *true* of y' must reduce to some non-semantic relation, 'x bears r to y', we have

> x is *true* of all and only dogs =
> $(y)(r(xy) \leftrightarrow y$ is a dog$)$.

But then, in order for the meaning-to-*truth* conditional to hold, the property, '$u(x)$', to which the meaning property reduces, would have to imply the property to which the aboutness property reduces: it would have to be that

> $u(x) \rightarrow (y)[r(xy) \leftrightarrow y$ is a dog$]$.

And this could be so only if

> $u(x) = s(x) \& (y)[r(xy) \leftrightarrow y$ is a dog$]$.

Thus from the usual inflationary point of view the representational, referential power of the word "dog" imposes a substantive, *relational* constraint on what sort of non-semantic property might engender its meaning.

However, from a deflationary perspective the situation is quite different. For, *quite independently of what '$u(x)$' might turn out to be*, the meaning-to-*truth* conditional

> x means DOG $\rightarrow$
> x is *true* of all and only dogs

is trivially entailed by the equivalence schema (together with the definition of "*true*" for utterances in terms of "true" for propositions). Therefore, if (as deflationism dictates) we presuppose nothing about the nature of 'x is *true* of y' except those principles, then our need to accommodate the meaning-to-*truth* conditional can impose no constraint whatsoever on our choice of '$u(x)$'. In particular, there will be no need for the property in virtue of which "dog" possesses its particular meaning to be some sort of relation between that word and dogs. To put it another way: there can be no problematic conflict, in and of themselves, between the meaning-to-*truth* conditional and any theory of the form, 'x means DOG $= u(x)$'; but there *can* be a conflict between them given a further (inflationary) assumption of the form, '*x* is true of *y*= *r*(*x*,*y*)'; therefore deflationism does not enable the problem of aboutness to arise.

If this point of view is unrecognized then, given how difficult— perhaps impossible—it is to meet the constraint implied by inflation-ism, a likely outcome is a form of scepticism about meaning. A case in point is Kripke,[9] who has reasoned in effect that since the problem of aboutness is insoluble, there can be no 'genuine' facts about the meanings of words. More specifically, what Kripke has argued is that we cannot find underlying, non-semantic properties, $u(x)$, $v(x)$, $w(x)$, . . ., etc., of the words, "dog", "electron", "table", . . ., etc., which will satisfy the conditions

$u(x) \rightarrow (\,y)[r'(xy) \leftrightarrow y$ is a dog]
$v(x) \rightarrow (\,y)[r''(xy) \leftrightarrow y$ is an electron]
$w(x) \rightarrow (\,y)[r'''(xy) \leftrightarrow y$ is a table]
. . . and so on,

where the $r(xy)$ relations take something like the form 'There is a dis-position to apply *x* to *y* in ideal conditions *I*'. And on this basis he concludes that meaning properties have no underlying natures. But, as we have seen, this sort of constraint on a theory of meaning is motivated by an inflationary view of truth (whereby the meaning-to-*truth* conditionals must square with a prior analysis of the '*true* of' relation). Only from that point of view can it be argued that the prop-erty that constitutes the meaning of a predicate must entail a property of the form '$(\,y)[r(xy) \leftrightarrow f(x)]$'.

Thus, as deflationists about truth, we should not be insisting upon an account of predicate meaning along the lines of

$$x \text{ means } F = s(x) \,\&\, (\,y)[r(xy) \leftrightarrow f(y)]$$

(where *s* and *r* might somewhat depend on "*f*"). Nor, in that case, is there any reason to expect an account of the more general form

$$x \text{ means } F = T(x, f)$$

---

[9] See Kripke, *Wittgenstein on Rules and Private Language*. I elaborate the present critique of Kripke's argument in "Meaning, Use and Truth" and in Chapter 10 of this book.

(where *T* might depend on "*f*").[10] And this conclusion is quite liberating; for most of the theories of meaning in the literature *have* been crammed into one of these moulds and consequently don't work very well. To repeat our examples from Chapter 2, there is the theory that

> *x* means *F* = (*y*)(A tokening of *x* would, in appropriate circumstances, be caused by *y* ↔ *y* is *f*),

which, in different versions, has been proposed by Fodor, Stampe, and others; and

> *x* means *F* = the function of *x* is to indicate the presence of *f*s,

suggested, in one form or another, by Dretske, Papineau, Millikan, and Jacob.[11] The morals of the present discussion are: first, that the phenomenon of aboutness (representation, error, intentionality) does not provide a rationale for demanding such a theory; second, that the contrary assumption can stem from a misguided inflationism about truth; and third, that theories designed to accord with it are unsurprisingly unsuccessful.

The alternative, which becomes available and plausible once inflationism has been left behind, is to allow that

> *x* means DOG = *u*(*x*)
> *x* means ELECTRON = *v*(*x*)
> *x* means TABLE = *w*(*x*)
> . . . and so on,

where the non-semantic, meaning-constituting properties, '*u*(*x*)', '*v*(*x*)', '*w*(*x*)', . . . , may be non-relational: it is not assumed that, in

---

[10] The thought here is that in so far as the temptation to demand a non-semantic reduction of '*x* if *true* of *y*' has been undermined, then the analogous temptation to demand a non-semantic reduction of the schema '*x* means *F*' will also be undermined (a) because no such reduction would be required by the meaning-to-*truth* conditional, and (b) because the source of both temptations—namely the Constitution Fallacy—would have been exposed. See Chapter 2 (section 2) and Chapter 3 (responses to Objections 4 and 5).

[11] See Dretske, *Knowledge and the Flow of Information*; Stampe, "Toward a Causal Theory of Linguistic Representation"; Fodor, *Psychosemantics*; Papineau, *Reality and Representation*; Millikan, *Language, Thought and Other Biological Categories*; Jacob, *What Minds Can Do*.

order to mean *F*, a word must stand in some non-semantic relation
or other to *f*s. None the less it is quite possible, as we have seen, to
accommodate the phenomenon of aboutness, the determination of
extension by meaning.

The deflationary view of truth suggests that the truth of the
proposition that snow is white consists in nothing more than snow
being white, that the truth of the proposition that killing is wrong
consists in killing being wrong, . . ., and so on—which implies that
nothing in general constitutes the property of 'being true'. And, as I
have been arguing, this should lead us to acknowledge the possibility that '*x* means DOG' consists in something or other, '*x* means
ELECTRON' consists in something else, . . ., and so on—but that
there is no general account of the structure, '*x* means *F*'. We might
call such a view of meaning, "deflationary", both because it is *parallel to*, and because it is *justified by*, the deflationary view of truth.

A *use* theory of meaning would have this deflationary character—
i.e. the theory that each word's meaning is constituted by there being
a certain explanatorily basic regularity governing its overall deployment. For the basic use regularities of different words—like different
laws of nature—need have no common form; and they need not
relate the words they govern to the members of their extensions.
Elsewhere in this book (especially Chapter 3) I go into the reasons for
supposing that this is the right direction in which to look for the
nature of meaning. We can see how various familiar objections to the
use theory can be turned aside—e.g. its non-normativity, its alleged
implication of holism, and its alleged incompatibility with compositionality. And we can see how the primary, legitimate constraint on
a decent theory of meaning is very naturally satisfied—i.e. the need
to accommodate the explanatory relationship between the meaning
of a word and the ways in which we use it.

By itself, the deflationary view of truth does not motivate the use
theory of meaning. But it provides a vital part of the argument by
showing that a common reason for rejecting the theory was based on
a mistake. The line of thought, in a nutshell, is that in so far as the
conceptually fundamental principle about truth is the equivalence
schema—as it very plausibly is—then there is no reason to suppose
that what constitutes the meaning of a predicate is some sort of non-
semantic relation to the members of its extension; hence no reason
to insist that '*x* means *F*' reduces to something of the form '$T(x,f)$';
hence no reason, when all such theories prove inadequate, to have to

swallow the obscurities of anti-reductionism or non-factualism. A fair alternative is to embrace a more flexible, non-relational conception—one which is none the less naturalistic and none the less consonant with representation—namely, the use theory of meaning.[12]

[12] This chapter is a revised version of my "Deflationary Truth and the Problem of Aboutness", which appeared in E. Villanueva (ed.), *Philosophical Issues* 8 (Atascadero, Calif: Ridgeview, 1997). I would like to thank Brian Loar, Huw Price, Alberto Voltolini, Adam Kovach, and Scott Soames for their helpful comments on the original paper.

5

Reference

In the last twenty-five years or so discussion of reference has been focused on the relative merits of three alternative models. First, there is the *description* theory according to which x refers to y when x is associated with a description of y. This is the Frege–Russell view, championed these days by not many people.[1] Second, there is the *causal* theory according to which x refers to y when there exists a certain sort of causal chain linking x with y. This sort of view has been promoted in a variety of forms by Kripke, Evans, early Field, Devitt, and Loar.[2] Perhaps it deserves to be called the mainstream. And third, there is a relatively recent arrival on the scene, the *deflationary* theory (also known as 'minimalism' or 'disquotationalism') according to which x referring to y is roughly a matter of x being the *singular term "n"* (in quotes) and y being the *thing n* (out of quotes).[3] This is the view I will be trying to explain and defend in the present chapter.

Of any candidate account of reference, we should ask two distinct questions. Is it correct? And is it relevant—is it really an account of reference? It is important to keep this distinction in mind when assessing the description and causal theories; for in both of these cases it seems to me that, whatever may be the answer to the question

---

[1] See G. Frege, "On Sense and Reference", *Translations from the Philosophical Writings of Gottlob Frege*. ed. P. Geach and M. Black (Oxford: Blackwell, 1952); and B. Russell, "Knowledge by Acquaintance and Knowledge by Description", reprinted in his *Mysticism and Logic* (New York: Norton, 1929).

[2] See Kripke, *Naming and Necessity*; G. Evans, "The Causal Theory of Names", *Proceedings of the Aristotelian Society*, supp. vol. 47 (1973), 187–208; H. Field, "Tarski's Theory of Truth", *Journal of Philosophy* 69 (1972), 347–75; Devitt, *Coming To Our Senses*; and B. Loar, "Reference from the First Person Perspective", in E. Villanueva (ed.), *Philosophical Perspectives* 6: *Content* (Atascadero, Calif.: Ridgeview, 1995).

[3] See Leeds, "Theories of Reference and Truth"; Horwich, *Truth*.

of correctness, the answer to the question of relevance is pretty clearly No.

Thus the description theory in its pure form says that names are abbreviated definite descriptions. This claim may or may not be right; in light of Kripke's powerful objections, it probably is not. Right or wrong, however, it does not qualify as a theory of reference; for it does not so much as attempt to say what it is for a singular term to refer to an object, or even to specify which singular terms refer to which objects. Perhaps, in so far as it asserts the synonymy of each name with a definite description, we can draw the conclusion that the name refers to whatever the associated description refers to. But we are told nothing at all about the character of the relation between each of these two expressions and their common referent, and we are not even told what that referent is; so there is no theory of reference here. Nor is this problem remedied in more sophisticated versions of the description theory: e.g. the cluster theory, whereby a name is associated with a set of descriptions rather than a single one;[4] the metalinguistic theory, whereby the relevant description has the form 'the thing called "n" ';[5] or the causal description theory whereby the relevant description has the form 'the origin of such-and-such causal chain leading to our use of "n" '.[6] These varieties of description theory retain the fundamental defect of the pure version. They identify the referential properties of one type of singular term (names) with those of another type (descriptions), but say nothing about what we have in mind in supposing that a given singular term refers to (or is *about*, or *of*) a given object.

Similarly, what most people regard as the causal theory misses the main point. When we imagine the sort of causal chain Kripke gestured towards, we think of the process by which the use and reference of a name spreads in a linguistic community: the person I refer to by the name "Moses" is whoever was referred to by those who introduced me to the name, and the person they were referring to is who-

---

[4] See Wittgenstein, *Philosophical Investigations* esp. para. 87; and J. R. Searle, "Proper Names", *Mind* 67 (1958), 166–73.

[5] See W. Kneale, "Modality, De Dicto and De Re", in *Logic, Methodology and the Philosophy of Science: Prceedings of the 1960 International Congress*, 622–33 (Stanford, Calif.: Stanford University Press, 1962); and J. J. Katz, "Has the Description Theory of Names been Refuted?", in G. Boolos (ed.), *Meaning and Method: Essays in Honor of Hilary Putnam*, 31–61 (Cambridge: Cambridge University Press, 1990).

[6] According to Kripke, this idea was bruited by Robert Nozick. See n. 38 of Kripke's *Naming and Necessity*.

ever *their* teachers were talking about, and so on. Thus we have a causal chain whereby some people using a name cause others to use it, which causes others to use it, and so on. And Kripke's plausible thesis is that reference is preserved. It would be wrong, however, to think that this provides a causal theory of reference—even the crude outline of one. For in light of the subsequent anti-individualist work of Putnam and Burge we can see that what an individual means by *any* of his or her words—whether they be names, predicates, or even logical constants—is something inherited from members of the linguistic community, and not determined solely by what is going on in the speaker's mind.[7] Therefore one should distinguish between the facts in virtue of which a word has the meaning it does in a given language, and the facts in virtue of which a given member of the linguistic community understands the word in that way. But then it becomes clear that Kripke's remarks about the inheritance of reference pertain to the second issue, and that they have nothing specifically to do with singular terms. And as for the first issue—the issue of the facts that give a name its meaning and reference in the language—we haven't been given even so much as a first approximation of a causal theory. Indeed Kripke himself leaves it open that a name may enter a language by means of a description (e.g. 'Let us give the name "Vulcan" to the planet causing perturbations in the orbit of Mercury').

So the trouble with the description and causal theories is not so much that they are wrong, but that they are not what we are looking for; they are not really theories of reference. Properly understood, one of them gives a theory of the meanings of names, the other a theory of sociolinguistic deference; but neither makes any attempt to tell us about our conception of *x* referring to *y*.[8]

In order to rectify this situation, an uncontroversial starting-point is to acknowledge that "Aristotle" refers to Aristotle, "the capital of

---

[7] See H. Putnam, "The Meaning of 'Meaning'"; T. Burge, "Individualism and the Mental".

[8] Granted, one might try to concoct a more full-blooded causal theory—one that *would* propose a specific causal relation as the basis of reference. But no such theory is remotely plausible; consequently, very few have been advanced. One source of difficulty is the range of different kinds of primitive referring term (e.g. names of people, planets, places, postulates, properties, etc.), the breadth of which makes it unlikely that a unified account could be found. Another problem comes from names of abstract entities, such as numbers, which don't enter into causal relations. In addition, see the argument of section 3 below, to the effect that reference is not constituted by any non-semantic relation or relations.

Sicily" refers to the capital of Sicily, and so on. Anyone who has the concept of reference is able to recognize such facts. The question we must now address is whether these trivialities are not merely the start of the story, but the whole story. Does our conception of reference go beyond such beliefs, and does the nature of reference involve more than those trivial facts? Is there any reason to expect a theory which goes deeper than disquotation—a theory that provides some sort of reductive analysis of the reference relation, specifying what reference is?

The deflationist answer is No. Let me elaborate this position by sketching four interrelated aspects of it:

(1) an account of the meaning of "refers";
(2) an account of the utility of our concept of reference;
(3) an account of the underlying nature of reference—or rather, an account of how we know that reference has *no* underlying nature;
(4) an account of the meanings of names.

(1) *The Meaning of "Refers"*

The rough idea is that our meaning what we do by the word "refers" consists in our disposition to accept sentences such as

> Tokens of *London* refer to London,
> Tokens of *the highest mountain* refer to the highest mountain,

and so on. Since an *ambiguous* singular term, "n", when used as in these examples to designate a referent, must be understood in just one of its senses, it will not (in any sense of "n") be true to say that *every* token of "n" (individuated phonologically) refers to n. This is why the expression-types deployed in disquotational reference specifications are articulated using *star* quotation marks—indicating that they are individuated, not just phonologically, but also on the basis of meaning (as described at the beginning of Chapter 2).

Thus our meaning what we do by "refers" consists in our inclination to accept instances of the disquotational schema

> Tokens of *n* refer to n,

where what are substituted for the two occurrences of "*n*" are understood in the same way. But this won't do as it stands. In the first place, not all singular terms refer. It is false that *Atlantis* and *the largest prime number* refer to Atlantis and the largest prime number, because there are no such things to be referred to. So a more accurate rendering of what we accept would be

Tokens of *n* refer, if at all, to *n*

or, more formally,

(x)(Tokens of *n* refer to x iff $n = x$).

In the second place, even this improved schema cannot account for our attribution of reference to terms in foreign languages. But this deficiency can be dealt with by invoking a further principle, namely

v is the correct translation of $w \rightarrow$
    $(x)(w$ refers to x iff v refers to $x)$

which, combined with the home-language disquotation schema, gives us

n is the correct translation of w $\rightarrow$
    $(x)(w$ refers to x iff $x = n)$.

There is a further problem, however, which derives from context-sensitivity: for example, someone else's use of the word "me" does not refer to me. In order to handle this sort of phenomenon, we can invoke the concept of an *interpretation mapping*, Int, which, when applied to an expression token, first translates it (if necessary) into the home language, and then adjusts for the difference in context between speaker and interpreter. Thus, if w is a token of "me" then Int$(w) = $ *e*, where $e = $ the speaker; if w is a token of "now" then Int$(w) = $ *e*, where $e = $ the time of utterance, etc.[9] The schema constituting our concept of reference then becomes

---

[9] See the discussion of 'interpretation' in Chapter 3 (response to Objection 12). It might seem implausible that in order to possess the concept of reference we should have to possess such a sophisticated notion. But actually, the notion of interpretation is not especially recondite. It amounts to little more than '*what is said* by an utterance'.

$[\text{Int}(w) = *n*] \to (x)(w \text{ refers to } x \text{ iff } x = n)$.

Finally, one might suppose that, just as the concept of 'expressing a truth' (which applies to utterances) derives from the more basic concept, truth (which applies to propositions), so the concept, reference (which applies to singular terms), is derived from a more basic concept of reference (let us call it "reference*") which applies to the *de dicto* propositional constituents expressed by singular terms. And in that case the fundamental principles will be: (1) an *equivalence schema*

$(x)(\langle n \rangle \text{ refers* to } x \text{ iff } n = x)$

(where $\langle n \rangle$ is the propositional constituent expressed using the term "*n*"); and (2) a definition of "refers" in terms of "refers*"

$w \text{ refers to } x \text{ iff } (\exists k)(w \text{ expresses } k \ \& \ k \text{ refers* to } x)$.

Principles specifying which propositional constituents may be expressed by a given term are sketched in Chapter 3, in the response to Objection 12.

The deflationary thesis is that our meaning what we do by "refers" is constituted by our basing its overall use on either this pair of principles or the final disquotational schema.[10] Thus the concept of reference (for terms) may be explicitly defined in terms of reference* (for propositional constituents); but reference* is not grasped by our accepting anything of the form, '*x* refers to *y* iff *x* bears *r* to *y*'; so it is not explicitly definable.

---

[10] Keith Donellan famously argued (in "Reference and Definite Descriptions", *Philosophical Review* 75 (1966), 281–304) that we may use a definite description (e.g. "the man with the Martini") to refer to something that does not in fact satisfy that description (e.g. the man in the corner), as long as we believe that it satisfies it. One can suppose, nevertheless, that the descriptive expression *itself* refers only to what satisfies it. For the Donellan cases occur when a description manifests the deployment of a singular concept (e.g. THE MAN IN THE CORNER), which differs from the concept standardly and literally expressed, and which has a certain 'priority', in so far as it is the one the speaker will retain if he comes to recognize that the two concepts are not in fact co-referential. Thus one may use a singular term to refer to an object that is not the referent of that term.

(2) *The Utility of our Concept of Reference*

The second aspect of the deflationary perspective is a story about the function and utility of the concept of reference, together with a demonstration that the theory I have just sketched is capable of explaining that function and utility. Here a little caution is in order. For in ordinary language the term most often employed in connection with the above reference concepts is "about", rather than "refers". We tend to speak of *people* as referring to things, and of their doing so in virtue of their words or thoughts being *about* those things. Consequently, in looking for the utility of the above-characterized reference concepts it would be a mistake to focus on our ordinary use of the word "refers". The real issue is why we should need the notion of a certain thought being *about* (or *of*) a certain thing. Why, in other words, is it valuable for there to be a practice of characterizing the contents of thoughts and statements, *not* by alluding to how they are articulated by their subjects, but rather by alluding to the objects they are about? To put it in jargon terms, what is the point of *de re*, as opposed to *de dicto*, attributions of content?

The answer, I would suggest, is that this practice enables the acquisition of useful beliefs from other people. To be more specific, when a speaker expresses a discovery about his environment by means of some utterance u, the belief state of other people—to whom that discovery is reported—need not be the one those people would express with the same utterance, u, or even with a translation of it, but rather one that is adjusted to take account of the difference in knowledge and/or context between the speaker and those who are informed of what he said. In such a case they believe 'the same thing'—but only in the *de re* sense. For example, someone who comes out with "Those are poisonous" may be reported as having said that the mushrooms in such-and-such place are poisonous; someone who comes out with "Hesperus is red" may usefully be reported as having said that the evening star is red, etc.

Putting it schematically consider, first, a speaker S who asserts "a is f"; second, an ultimate recipient of information who does not understand the singular term "a" but who does understand "b"; and third, a reporter who knows all this and also knows that $a = b$. What can this reporter usefully communicate to the recipient about what S believes? Intuitively, what he wants to say is

S believes *that a is f*, and $a = b$

—but minus any information about S's singular term "a", since it does not mean anything to the recipient. But the proposition *that a is f* is identical to the result of applying the predicative propositional constituent expressed by "$f(\ )$"—namely $\langle f \rangle [\ ]$—to the singular propositional constituent expressed by "a"—namely $\langle a \rangle$. Thus, what the reporter would like to say (but minus any confusing information about S's singular term) is

S believes $\langle f \rangle [\langle a \rangle]$, and $a = b$,

where the term "$\langle a \rangle$" is in a referential, transparent position, open to objectual quantification. But now suppose the reporter accepts the equivalence schema

$(x)(\langle n \rangle$ refers* to $x \leftrightarrow n = x)$,

and, in particular,

$\langle a \rangle$ refers* to $b \leftrightarrow a = b$.

In that case, what he more or less wants to say is equivalent to

S believes $\langle f \rangle [\langle a \rangle]$, and $\langle a \rangle$ refers* to b.

And he is now in a position to leave out the useless and potentially confusing information about S's singular term by existentially generalizing into the position of "$\langle a \rangle$", arriving at

$(\exists x)(S$ believes $\langle f \rangle [x]$, and x refers* to b);

or, as he would phrase it colloquially,

S believes, about b, that it is f.

In this way, the notion of reference, simply in so far as it satisfies the equivalence schema, enables us to articulate *de re* attributions of content. Thus we have accounts of the concept of reference and of the utility of this concept that square well with one another, and thereby lend one another support. For it counts in favour of our deflationary account of the concept that we see how a concept conforming to that account would be worth having. And it counts in favour of our theory about the function of the concept that an otherwise plausible account of the nature of the concept turns out to be necessary and sufficient for explaining how it is able to perform that function.

(3) *The Underlying Nature of Reference*

Let us now turn to the third component of the deflationary view of reference: namely, that the reference relation has no underlying nature. Not only is the meaning of the term not given by some explicit definition of the form

"*x* refers to *y*" means "*x* bears non-semantic relation *r* to *y*",

but, in addition, we should expect no substantive discovery of the form

The relation of *x* referring to *y* *consists* (roughly speaking) in *x* bearing relation *r* to *y*.

This is certainly not to deny that there really is such a relation as reference. For one might well employ a liberal notion of property (and of relation) according to which every logically normal predicate expresses a property (or a relation). However, the question of whether or not this relation of reference is constituted by some underlying causal relation—or by some other non-semantic relation—is an entirely separate issue. And part of the deflationary position, as I see it, is that the reference relation is very unlikely to have any such underlying nature. For it is plausible that the explanatory basis for all facts regarding reference is a theory whose axioms are instances of the disquotational or equivalence schemata. This is because, on the one hand, such axioms appear to suffice to explain all other facts about reference; and, on the other hand, it is not likely that these facts will themselves be explained in terms of something more fundamental. After all, we are not here dealing with the sort of case, familiar in science, where a general characteristic of some type of system might well be expected to be explained *causally* in terms of the properties of the parts of such systems and the way those parts are combined. Thus the normal reason for anticipating an explanation is absent. Moreover, it is hard to see how the conditions for a deeper account of the disquotational or equivalence facts could possibly be satisfied. For a decent explanation would have to involve some unification, some gain in simplicity. But the disquotational and equivalence axioms are already very simple. Granted, there is one glaring respect in which those theories are complex: they each have infinitely many axioms. But we can see that no candidate explanatory account of their axioms could possibly make do with fewer than infinitely many axioms. For there are infinitely many possible names (and even infinitely many primitive propositional constituents that a name might express); and an adequate theory would have to say something different about each one of them. Thus the infinite aspect of the disquotation and equivalence theories cannot be improved on. Therefore there is not going to be a body of principles, from which those theories can be derived, and which is sufficiently simple to qualify as an explanation. Therefore we can conclude that the reference relations are not constituted by some more fundamental non-semantic relation.

(4) *The Meanings of Names*

Finally, let us switch focus from the character of the reference relation to the meanings of names. The first thing to be emphasized here is that the two issues are distinct. This needs emphasizing because proponents of the description theory and proponents of the causal theory tend to obscure the distinction. The description theorist does so by supposing that he gives an account of reference, when what he really offers is an account of the meanings of names. And the causal theorist does so by imagining that his account entails that names do not have meaning. But from the deflationary perspective on reference the two issues are not so intimately related. From our perspective, having fully explained the meaning of "refers", it still remains to deal with the meanings of names.

To that end we should start by reviewing the reasons for supposing that names do have meaning. These include various sorts of consideration. First, there is intuitive, ordinary language support. For we speak of someone's *understanding*, or failing to understand, a name;

and we speak of *translating* names from one language to another. Second, there is theoretical support. For the general role of a meaning property—namely, to explain the overall use of the words that possess it—will be no less required in the case of names than in the case of other types of word. Moreover, we have Frege's argument that the difference in 'cognitive value' between "*a* is *f*" and "*b* is *f*", which exists even when the names are co-referential, is best explained by attributing different meanings to them. And third, there is rhetorical support, which derives from seeing what is wrong with reasoning that has led people to infer that names *do not* have meaning. Specifically, no such conclusion follows from the fact that names are not synonymous with definite descriptions: they might well be unanalysable primitives. Nor, in that case, does it follow from the fact that they are rigid designators.

So let us take it that names *do* have meanings. The question then becomes: where do their meanings come from? Or more precisely: in virtue of which underlying non-semantic property of a name does it possess its particular meaning? In what does its meaning property consist?

Remember (from Chapter 3, response to Objection 10) the difference between this and the question: what is the meaning of a name? The latter question normally calls for an answer of the form

The name "*n*" has the same meaning as "so-and so",

or in other words

The name "*n*" means SO-AND-SO,

which presupposes that the name is *not* a primitive. Our question, on the other hand, leaves this open. It may be, if the name "*n*" is indeed non-primitive, that the answer takes the form

"*n*"'s meaning what it does consists in the fact that it is used as an abbreviation for "so-and-so",

or

"*n*"'s meaning what it does consists in the fact that the basic feature of its use is the holding *true* of "*n* = the so-and-so".

But perhaps "*n*" *is* primitive. In which case, it may be that

> "*n*"'s meaning what it does consists in the fact that the basic
> feature of its use is the holding *true* of "#*n*",

where "#*n*" is some collection of sentences formulated with the name
"*n*"; or

> "*n*"'s meaning what it does consists in the fact that the basic
> feature of its use is the holding *true* of "This is *n*" in
> circumstances *C*.

And there could very well be other possibilities.

This leads to the question: given a specific name, how are we to
decide what sort of property constitutes its meaning? What are the
adequacy conditions of a theory of the form:

> The name "*n*" means what it does in virtue of possessing
> property, $u(x)$?

To begin, it is worth noting some constraints one might be
wrongly tempted to impose—constraints which would make the
problem extremely hard, but which are in fact illegitimate.

First, it need not be assumed that all names have the very same
kind of meaning-constituting property. For look at the great variety
of kinds of name: of countries ("Italy"), numbers ("one"), historical
figures ("Aristotle"), theoretical entities ("spacetime"), fictional
characters ("Superman"), works of art ("La Bohème"), theories
("deflationism"), mistaken postulates ("Vulcan"), universals ("redness"), supernatural beings ("Zeus"), etc. These names have such different functions in our language that it would not be at all surprising
for them to have very different types of meaning-constituting property.

Second, the meaning of a name determines its referent. Therefore,
a name's meaning-constituting property also determines its referent.
But this implies merely that two names with the same meaning-constituting property must have the same referent. It does not imply that
the referent of a name is *explained* by its meaning-constituting property independently of what particular names possess the property. In
other words, it does not imply that from premises specifying

(1) the meaning-constituting property of a given name

and

(2) the character of reference

one can deduce which object, if any, is the referent of the name. This form of 'strong determination' of referent by meaning would obtain if and only if we had an *inflationary* (e.g. causal) theory of reference of the form

x refers to y iff x bears r to y.

For in that case, given that

x means what "n" means $\rightarrow$
x refers (if at all) to n,

or, in other words, given that

x means $N \rightarrow$
$(y)(x$ refers to y iff $n = y)$,

we could infer that the property constituting the antecedent, 'x means N', would have to entail whatever is the property that constitutes the consequent, '$(y)(x$ refers to y iff $n = y)$', and would therefore have to have the form

$s(x)$ and $(y)[x$ bears r to y iff $n = y]$.

And, given the inflationary theory of reference, any name with this meaning-constituting property would plainly refer (if at all) to the object n. Thus the referent of a name would be *explained* by its meaning-constituting property, independently of which names possess the property. However, there is no good reason to suppose that the meaning of a name must determine its referent in this strong, explanatory sense (rather than merely in the weak sense whereby 'same meaning' implies 'same referent'). Hence there is no reason to think that the meaning-constituting property of names should take the above form. These suppositions are motivated by an inflationary picture of reference. So, from our deflationary perspective they are not to be respected.[11]

Let us turn now from these tempting but illegitimate constraints to the real basis for specifying the meaning-constituting properties of names. For any type of word, our way of using it—the utterances in which it appears—is explained by a combination of various factors including, centrally, what we mean by the word. On this basis it can be argued (as we saw in Chapter 3) that the meaning-constituting property of a word is that property which, in combination with other factors, explains our overall use of the word. And from here it is a natural step to the conclusion that a word's meaning is constituted by the fact that a certain acceptance property governs its use. For example, arguably, the meaning-constituting property of the word "and" is that the fundamental feature of its use is our (conditional) disposition to accept "p and q" given "p" and "q", and vice versa— for an English speaker's overall deployment of "and" is best explained on the basis of that assumption.[12]

It seems reasonable to apply the same considerations to names. Given any name, there will exist a huge body of facts regarding its use; these facts will call for explanation by appeal to some *fundamental* fact about its deployment; and this fact—its possession of a certain basic acceptance property—will constitute its having the meaning it does.

As we have seen, there is no reason to expect that all names will have meaning-constituting properties of the very same type. For, in the first place, there is no need for a meaning-constituting property to *strongly* determine a referent; and in the second place, the various names mentioned above are used in very different ways and so we can anticipate a considerable variation in the kinds of basic acceptance property that explain these usages.

---

[11] See Chapter 2 (section 3) and Chapter 3 (response to Objection 5) for a parallel point about the relation 'x is true of y'. Granted, the possibility of *explaining* why anything with a given meaning-constituting property must have a given referent does not really require a *uniform* analysis of reference—it would suffice if there were a variety of different reference-constituting relations, $r_1, r_2, \ldots$, one for each different kind of name. But from the deflationary point of view, even this weaker assumption must be rejected.

[12] The relevant disposition is *conditional* for the reasons mentioned in Chapter 3 (in the response to Objection 17), and discussed at greater length in Chapter 6: namely, that meaning what we do by a word w requires merely that *if* some word were to be deployed in accordance with certain belief-forming regularities, it would be w.

More specifically, the following hypotheses seem to me to be not wildly implausible—at least as crude, first approximations:

> "Vulcan"'s meaning what it does consists in the fact that the
> basic feature of its use is the (conditional) holding *true* of
> "Vulcan = the planet (if any) causing such-and-such per-
> turbations in the orbit of Mercury";

> "one"'s meaning what it does consists in the fact that the
> basic feature of its use is the (conditional) holding *true* of
> the Peano axioms of arithmetic;

> "Aristotle"'s meaning what it does consists in the fact that the
> basic feature of its use is the (conditional) holding *true* of
> "This is Aristotle" when pointing at Aristotle.

It might be objected to the last of these proposals that one can understand the word "Aristotle" perfectly well without having the disposition to say "That is Aristotle" in the presence of the right guy. In response, we can appeal to the above-mentioned phenomenon— known variously as 'deference to experts', 'the causal transmission of reference', 'the division of linguistic labour', and 'semantic anti-individualism'—which has been characterized by Kripke, Putnam, and Burge. In light of this phenomenon, we have seen that we must distinguish between the fact in virtue of which a word has a certain meaning in the language, and the fact in virtue of which a given individual uses the word with that meaning. From the use-theoretic point of view, the former fact is to be located by focusing on so-called 'experts' in the use of the word and finding the regularity that best explains their overall deployment of it. And the latter fact will then be the fact of standing in something like a Kripkean 'causal relation' to experts who conform to that regularity.

In the case of the name of a person, the 'experts', to whom the rest of us defer, are those who are (or were) acquainted with the person, and who are (or were) in a position to say "This is n" when n is present. That is the fact about the name's use that gives it its mean-ing in the language, and the rest of us inherit this meaning via the Kripkean causal chain even though we do not exhibit expert usage of the name.[13]

---

[13] Tyler Burge (in "Reference and Proper Names", *Journal of Philosophy* 50, (1973), 425–39) has argued in favour of the assimilation of proper names to predicates,

Needless to say, these remarks offer no more than a very rough, preliminary idea about how to identify the properties in virtue of which names have their meanings. A complete account—covering each of the many different kinds of name—would no doubt be extremely complicated and difficult to provide. But I hope to have made it plausible that an account along use-theoretic lines can in principle be given. Though the details will be messy, the overall conception of name meaning, and the associated deflationary account of reference, are nice and simple.[14]

on the grounds that we say such things as "There are three Pauls in the room". But this issue is orthogonal to the present discussion. For, in the first place, even if Burge is right, the question will still arise as to when a given name applies to a given object; alternative answers—alternative accounts of 'x is true of y'—may be offered in terms of either a description theory, a causal theory, or a deflationary theory; and the grounds for preferring deflationism will be equally strong. In the second place, there will remain the question of how a name can be used (as in "Paul is here" or "That Paul is English") to refer to a unique person; and again, any of the three frameworks might be invoked. (Note that from our perspective, "That n" is simply one of the types whose substitution in the equivalence schema constitutes the notion of singular reference.) And in the third place—regarding the *meanings* of names if they are indeed predicative—they might none the less be constituted along the various use-theoretic lines indicated in the text.

[14] Thanks to Emma Borg, Brian Loar, Daniel Noonan, and Stephen Schiffer for helpful discussion of the material in this chapter, which is a rewritten and expanded version of my "Disquotation and Cause in the Theory of Reference", in E. Villanueva (ed.), *Philosophical Issues* 6: *Content* (Atascadero, Calif.: Ridgeview, 1995).

6

Implicit Definition, Analytic Truth, and A Priori Knowledge

Given how hard it is to find *explicit* definitions of interesting notions, it has been common to look instead for *implicit* definitions—to suppose that terms may ƀe provided with their meanings by the assertion of statements containing them. It has been often said, for example, that the postulates of a geometry implicitly fix what is meant by the words "line" and "point", that the basic laws of classical logic define the logical constants, including "or", "not", and "every", and that Peano's axioms of arithmetic specify the meanings of "zero", "successor", and "number". Moreover, there has been a tendency to draw epistemological conclusions from such semantic theses. It is frequently supposed, not merely that certain sets of postulates define some of their constituent terms, but also that those postulates are bound to be correct since they are mere definitions; so there can be no question that we are justified in maintaining them; thus implicit definition provides analytic truth which yields a priori knowledge.

In this way, what we might call "the strategy of implicit definition" promises to be an invaluable technique both in semantics and epistemology. Certainly this is how things seemed to the positivists and logical empiricists (notably, Poincaré, Carnap, Reichenbach, and Ayer),[1] and, as we shall see in the work of Christopher Peacocke and Paul Boghossian, similar ideas are very much alive today. On the other hand, the strategy can seem almost too good to be true; and indeed there has been no shortage of philosophers who have

[1] See H. Poincaré, *Science and Hypothesis* (London: Walter Scott Publishing, 1905); H. Reichenbach, *The Philosophy of Space and Time* (New York: Dover, 1968); R. Carnap, "Empiricism, Semantics and Ontology" (1950), in his *Meaning and Necessity*, 2nd edn. (Chicago, Ill.: University of Chicago Press, 1956); A. J. Ayer, *Language, Truth and Logic* (1936) (New York: Dover, 1952).

expressed misgivings about the feasibility and epistemological utility of implicit definition—including, for example, Frege (in the course of his well-known dispute with Hilbert) and, more recently, Prior, Quine, and Dummett.[2] In this chapter I want to address these issues by attempting to answer the following four questions:

(a) How might it be possible for implicit definitions to do what they are intended to do? How could they succeed in providing words with meaning?

(b) What would be their epistemological import? If a postulate is an implicit definition, does it thereby become *true a priori*? Need it be *true* at all?

(c) Are there any such things? Given Quine's sceptical attack on meaning, can there in fact be any implicit definitions?

(d) Could a sentence be '*true* in virtue of its meaning alone', or *analytic* in any other philosophically important sense?

1. *The Nature of Implicit Definition*

To begin at the beginning: an implicit definition of a word is supposed to work by our deciding that certain sentences (or rules) containing it are correct, and by our presuming that this decision fixes the word's meaning. But what is the justification for that presumption? How exactly could it come about that our regarding a certain (perhaps conjunctive) sentence "#*f*" as *true* would provide the constituent "*f*" with a meaning, and what exactly is the meaning that "*f*" would acquire? This question has a widely accepted answer: namely, that the decision to regard "#*f*" as *true* is, implicitly, a decision to give

---

[2] See the correspondence between Frege and Hilbert in Frege's *Philosophical and Mathematical Correspondence* (Chicago, Ill.: University of Chicago Press, 1986), 31–52; G. Frege, "On the Foundations of Geometry", First Series (1903) and Second Series (1906), in his *Collected Papers on Mathematical Logic and Philosophy*, ed. Brian McGuiness (Oxford: Blackwell, 1983); W. V. Quine, "Two Dogmas of Empiricism", in his *From a Logical Point of View* (Cambridge, Mass.: Harvard University Press, 1953); A. N. Prior, "The Runabout Inference-Ticket", *Analysis* 21 (1960), 38–9; and Dummett, *Elements of Intuitionism*.

"*f*" the meaning it would need to have in order that "#*f*" be *true*.[3] But this standard answer is subject to some powerful objections, as a consequence of which the prospects for implicit definition are put into considerable doubt.

One commonly cited difficulty is the 'existence problem': the problem of whether there is *any* meaning that "*f*" could have which would render "#*f*" *true*. For it is being assumed that the rest of the sentence "#—" somehow already has a meaning. But given that meaning, there may then be nothing that could be meant by "*f*" that would make *true* the combination "#*f*". For it may be that, in virtue of the meaning of "#—" alone, and regardless of "*f*", "#*f*" would entail something false (for example, if "#—" were the expression "Snow is green and the moon is ——"). And, in that case, any attempt to give "*f*" the meaning needed to make "#*f*" *true* is doomed. Thus we can be sure to have implicitly defined "*f*", in accordance with the standard conception of implicit definition, only if we can be sure that there exists a meaning for "*f*" relative to which "#*f*" would be *true*.

This problem was articulated forcefully by Arthur Prior as an objection to the idea that the logical terms, "not", "or", and so on, are implicitly defined by the rules of inference in which they participate.[4] Tongue in cheek, he proposed to introduce a new connective "tonk" by means of the rules

$$\frac{p}{\therefore \quad p \text{ tonk } q} \qquad\qquad \frac{p \text{ tonk } q}{\therefore \qquad q}$$

which, taken together, would allow the deduction of any conclusion from any premise. So there is evidently no meaning that "tonk" might have that would make these rules valid. This vividly illustrates the need, when purporting to specify a meaning as 'that which would make such-and-such sentences *true* (or such-and-such rules valid)', to be justified in the assumption that the sentences (or rules) *could* be made *true* (or valid). But where might that justification come from?

---

[3] For simplicity I am focusing on the case in which implicit definition proceeds by regarding a *sentence* (which could be a long conjunction) as *true*. But this discussion carries over in an obvious way to the case of implicit definition in which certain *rules of inference* are regarded as *valid*. As in previous chapters, I use the term "*true*" (italicized) to mean "expresses a true proposition".

[4] Prior, "The Runabout Inference-Ticket".

There is a simple answer to this question: namely, that the existence of a meaning for "f" that would make "$\#f$" *true* follows from the *truth* of "$\#f$"; so that we will be justified in thinking that there is such a meaning in so far as we have reason to accept "$\#f$". Moreover, in appropriate evidential circumstances, we may well have such reason; for in light of acknowledged epistemological standards, "$\#f$" might qualify as a plausible theory.[5]

Notice, however, that this answer, though correct in itself, has devastating consequences for the epistemological import of implicit definition. For in so far as our confidence that we have succeeded in defining our terms rests upon our reason to think that the containing sentences are *true*, we cannot, on pain of circularity, suppose that this reason derives from the status of these sentences as implicit definitions. Nevertheless it must be acknowledged that, to the extent that no such epistemological payoff is desired or envisaged, the existence problem is far from insuperable: we can easily have reason to believe that there exists a meaning for "f" that would render "$\#f$" *true*.

A second and more stubborn difficulty (stressed in Nuel Belnap's response to Prior's article)[6] is that when we speak of '*the* meaning "f" would need to have in order that "$\#f$" be *true*', we presume, not only that there exists such a meaning, but that there is exactly one of them. If there is more than one meaning that "f" might have that would result in the truth of "$\#f$", then "f" is not *defined* by the requirement that "$\#f$" be *true*. And, once again, there is a problem of justifying a presupposition of the alleged definition; for it is not at all clear how such uniqueness can be established. In this case it does not help to note that we may have some independent reason to accept "$\#f$".

Besides the existence and uniqueness problems, which are fairly well known, there are, it seems to me, two further difficulties with the standard model of implicit definition: that is, with the idea that "f" is given whatever meaning it needs to have for "$\#f$" to be *true*. Even if there does exist one and only one such meaning, can we be sure that "f" comes to possess it? And, supposing it does come to possess it, what would explain how this happens? I call these the *possession* problem and the *explanation* problem. Let me elaborate.

In general, if you want to give a particular object a particular

---

[5] Thanks to David Lewis for bringing this response to my attention.
[6] Nuel D. Belnap, "Tonk, Plonk and Plink", *Analysis* 22 (1962), 130–3.

property it will not be enough to say "Let it have that property": rather (or, in addition), you have to *do* something. You can't make a wall red just by saying "Let it be red"—you have to paint it. Well, this point applies to meaning properties too. You cannot give a word a certain meaning simply by declaring, however earnestly or passionately, that it has that meaning. Something more must be done. So even if, having somehow solved the existence and uniqueness problems, we can be reasonably confident that a single meaning is indeed specified by

> The meaning "*f*" would need to have in order that "*#f*" be *true*

we will neither ensure nor bring it about that "*f*" has that meaning merely by saying "Let it be so".

Focus, to begin with, on the possession problem. It is obvious how to ensure that "*f*" does come to possess that meaning: we must make it certain that "*#f*" is *true*. The trouble is that this is not always what we do. There are cases of implicit definition—notably, the definition of theoretical terms in science—in which we regard the containing sentence (a theory formulation) as *true*, but *not* as certainly *true*: we acknowledge some probability of its being *false*. And in such a case, even though we are sure that our tentative endorsement of that theory formulation has bestowed a meaning on "*f*", we cannot be sure that the meaning bestowed is the one that would make the theory formulation *true*. Moreover, it may later turn out to be certainly *false*—it may turn out to make incorrect predictions. This is how we regard supplanted theories: not merely as no longer useful—but *false*. None the less, the theoretical terms were meaningful and were given their meanings by implicit definition. Therefore the meaning given to "*f*" by accepting "*#f*" need not be the meaning needed for "*#f*" to be *true*. This is the possession problem.[7]

One can deal with this objection by denying that scientific theoretical terms are *directly* implicitly defined by the less than perfectly

---

[7] This difficulty is not removed by supposing that the real implicit definition of a theoretical term is provided by some subset of the theory's postulates—or perhaps the disjunction of all conjunctions of most of them (as suggested by David Lewis in his "Psychological and Theoretical Identifications", *Australasian Journal of Philosophy* 50 (1972), 249–58). For these alternatives may equally well turn out to be false.

certain theories in which they appear, and by following Carnap, Russell, Ramsey, and Lewis in the thought that one can factor such a theory into two independent components: an a posteriori, existential generalization, '$\exists x(\#x)$', which says that there exists a property with certain characteristics, #——; and an a priori conditional, '$\exists x(\#x) \to \#f$', which says that if there is such a property then it is f-ness. There is nothing tentative about the second of these commitments; and so this conditional (rather than "$\#f$") might be held to be the real implicit definition of "f".[8] Note, however, the following points. First, the existential generalizations invoked here are of dubious coherence in so far as they invoke quantification into predicate positions.[9] Second, if such conditionals do give the proper form for an implicit definition of a scientific term, then it would seem natural to suppose that *all* implicit definitions have something like this form, including those of arithmetical, geometrical, and logical terms (although new terminological devices, including variables ranging over quantifiers, would have to be introduced in order to express the two components of a logical theory). And if that is so, then implicit definition would be epistemologically impotent. It could not be argued, for example, that the fundamental principles of logic, since they implicitly define the logical constants, are known a priori. Thus the negative epistemological moral of the existence problem is reinforced. And third, the explanation problem is left untouched. It remains unclear how our regarding a sentence (that is, the appropriate conditional) as *true* could result in our giving meaning to one of the terms it contains. Let me stress that in airing these questions I am not rejecting the idea that when a term "f" is implicitly defined by the theory "$\#f$", this occurs in virtue of the implicit commitment to what I will call the Carnap conditional, "$\exists x(\#x) \to \#f$". On the contrary, for reasons we shall encounter later on, the idea strikes me as very attractive. My point here is that it stands in need of clarification, that

    [8] See Russell, *The Analysis of Matter*; Carnap, *Der Logische Aufbau der Welt*; Ramsey, "Theories"; and Lewis, "How to Define Theoretical Terms". Thanks to Philip Percival for reminding me of this strategy. But I should not have needed reminding, since I adopt it myself in "How to Choose amongst Empirically Indistinguishable Theories", and in "A Defense of Conventionalism".

    [9] The problem is that, unless "$\exists x(\#x)$" entails a false observation sentence, there is bound to be some 'property'—perhaps highly contrived and 'grue-like'—which satisfies it; therefore we appear to lose the intuitive distinction between truth and empirical adequacy. One may want to respond by restricting the domain of quantification to 'natural properties'; but it is by no means clear how this class is to be demarcated.

it counts against the epistemological interest of implicit definition, and that it does nothing to resolve the explanation problem.

To elaborate the last of these problems, even if we grant that the meaning given to "*f*" *is* that which would make "*#f*" (or "∃*x*(*#x*) → *#f*") *true*, we should be puzzled about *how* that meaning comes to be associated with "*f*". Grant that it does, and that this somehow happens as a result of our decision to regard a certain thing as *true*. But how could this process work? What we lack is some account of *what meaning is* that would enable us to understand how it could happen that our assertion of a sentence containing "*f*" manages to provide it with a meaning. This is what I am calling the explanation problem, and it arises no matter whether the implicit definitions are taken to be substantive postulates, or merely to be Carnap conditionals of the form "∃*x*(*#x*) → *#f*".

Thus the standard model of implicit definition (namely, that in regarding "*#f*" as *true* we give "*f*" the meaning it would need to have for "*#f*" to be *true*) faces four difficulties. The first concerns whether there exists anything that meets the description, 'the meaning "*f*" would need to have in order that "*#f*" be *true*'. This worry can be assuaged (by inferring the existence of that meaning from the truth of "*#f*"), but at the cost of depriving implicit definition of epistemological import. The second difficulty concerns whether that description is *uniquely* satisfied. This remains unresolved. The third concerns whether, if there is one such meaning, "*f*" comes to possesss it (given that "*#f*" could turn out later to be *false*). This might be handled by supposing that the real implicit definition is not "*#f*" but "∃*x*(*#x*) → *#f*". But it is unclear that this idea can be made intelligible; and even if it can, it would reinforce the epistemological feebleness of implicit definition. And the fourth problem concerns the possibility of explaining how "*f*" comes to acquire a meaning. This is also unresolved. In view of our inability to overcome these difficulties—especially the uniqueness and explanation problems—and in so far as we do not want to abandon the desirable prospect of implicit definition, it is well worth looking for an alternative to the standard model of how the decision to regard "*#f*" as *true* can provide "*f*" with a meaning.

I think we should begin by focusing on the last of the problems I mentioned—the explanation problem—for it seems to me that if we accept the most straightforward solution to it, we will thereby put ourselves in a position to deal with the other problems as well. The most straightforward solution to the explanation problem involves our friend the use theory of meaning—the view, roughly speaking, that the meaning of a word is engendered by there being a certain regularity governing its use. From this perspective, when we introduce a new term "*f*" by deciding to regard "*#f*" as *true*, we are instigating a particular way of using "*f*". And that practice—whereby all uses of the word stem from our acceptance of "*#f*"—will constitute its having a certain meaning. Thus what I am proposing is that we regard the meaning that is implicitly specified, not, in the way we have been imagining so far, as

> The meaning "*f*" would need to have in order that "*#f*" *be true*,

but rather as

> The meaning constituted by *regarding* "*#f*" as *true*.

This use-theoretic model of implicit definition not only provides a trivial solution to the explanation problem, but avoids all the other difficulties that afflict the standard, truth-theoretic model.

Consider the *existence* problem. As we have seen, this is by no means a fatal objection to the standard truth-theoretic model, as long as one abandons any hope of getting epistemological mileage out of implicit definition. For if we can find reason to believe that "*#f*" is *true*, then we must have at least as good a reason to believe what is entailed by that claim—namely, that "*f*" means what it needs to mean for "*#f*" to be *true*. But the use-theoretic model offers a different solution to the existence problem. According to the use theory of meaning, all that needs to be done to show that a given set of alleged regularities of use constitutes a possible meaning is to show that those regularities *can* be satisfied—that is, to show that they characterize a *possible* use. It is one thing to write down an alleged set of regularities, and another thing for it to be logically possible that they be satisfied; and an implicit definition can be successful only if it specifies a regularity that can be satisfied.

For example, it is pretty easy to see that the "tonk" rules of inference violate this condition. Not only can they not *be* valid, but they cannot even be *regarded* as valid (i.e. cannot be *followed*) because the regularities of use that would constitute following these rules of inference cannot be satisfied; so they do not characterize a possible use for the word "tonk". For in order to follow them a person would have to be disposed to infer and to accept any arbitrarily specified declarative sentence, including, for any sentence, both it and its negation. But it is plausible that amongst the facts of use that constitute the meaning of "not" is that one not tend simultaneously to assert "*p*" and "not *p*". Thus the "tonk" rules cannot be followed by a community that has a term meaning negation. And that is why they fail as an implicit definition.[10]

If this analysis is right, then the "tonk" example provides no reason to suspect that the meanings of *our* logical constants are not fixed by *our* basic rules of inference. For the problem with "tonk" is that the proposed regularities for its use cannot be satisfied. But evidently no such difficulty can attach to the regularities governing the actual logical constants, "and", "every", and so on. There may of course be a question as to exactly *which* basic regularities govern their use—e.g. as to whether they are those implicit in classical logic. But there can be no question that we are *able* to satisfy the regularities we are *actually* satisfying. So, given the use theory of meaning, there can be no question that these regularities constitute the meanings of the logical constants.[11]

So much for the existence problem: if a meaning is given by a possible use then the existence of a meaning associated with a certain alleged regularity is guaranteed by showing that this regularity can be satisfied. Similarly the *uniqueness* problem is easily dissolved in the context of a use theory of meaning. For if each meaning property is

[10] Even if there were no sign for negation in the language, the "tonk" rules would still be unfollowable. For following them would imply a disposition to believe every proposition expressible in the language; and, given the nature of belief, that is impossible. For one of the characteristic features of belief states is that they enter into deliberations resulting in action. A person's actions depend on his desires and beliefs, so that, given a fixed body of desires, different actions will be the expression of different beliefs. Consequently, in so far as only one of several possible actions, in a given situation, is actually performed, it must be (in so far as this outcome was the result of deliberation) that the agent possessed the beliefs that would lead, given his desires, to that action, and did *not* possess any of the combinations of belief that would have dictated some other action. Therefore it is necessary that the regularities in the use of certain expressions specify circumstances in which certain things are *not* to be believed. Consequently it is impossible for the "tonk" rules to be followed in a thoroughgoing way.

[11] It might be doubted whether *every* possible pattern of use for a word constitutes a meaning. Such doubts are addressed in Chapter 3, specifically in the responses to Objections 5, 8, and 20.

constituted by a certain basic regularity of use, then once we have specified a basic regularity for the use of "*f*"—e.g. that all uses of it stem from our regarding "#*f*" as *true*—we must have specified a definite meaning.

Notice that although it is possible for words with distinct meanings to share *some* of their regularities of use, if they were to be governed by the same basic regularity, then their total uses would be indistinguishable and it would be quite natural to say, as the use theory predicts, that they are synonyms. Thus it is indeed plausible that a specification of the basic regularity for the use of a term determines a single meaning. Here is an example. It can be argued that the basic fact about our use of the word "true" is our disposition to accept instances of the schema

The proposition that *p* is true if and only if *p*.

Thus it might be said that this schema provides an implicit definition of the word "true". However, one might worry about how this could be so since, given our knowledge of arithmetic, we would equally well accept instances of

The proposition that *p* is true and $1 + 1 = 2$ if and only if *p*.

For "is true" and "is true and $1 + 1 = 2$" do not have the same meaning; therefore a unique meaning for "*f*" is not determined by the schema

The proposition that *p* is *f* if and only if *p*.

But the answer to this worry is that in the case of the word "true" our acceptance of this schema is arguably the *sole* acceptance property from which all uses of the word derive; whereas in order to account fully for the uses of the other predicate, we will need to postulate a further basic acceptance property (namely, that given the assumption that something satisfies it, we accept "$1 + 1 = 2$"). This illustrates the idea that expressions with different meanings—i.e. with different overall uses—will conform to different (although perhaps overlapping) basic regularities of use.

Finally, there was the *possession* problem: how can we be sure that the term actually possesses the meaning specified in its implicit definition? Given the standard, truth-theoretic model (whereby the meaning to be assigned to "f" is that which would make "$\#f$" *true*) the difficulty is that, in order for "f" to get that meaning, "$\#f$" must be *true*; but arguably there are implicit definitions in which "$\#f$" turns out not to be *true*. However, given the use-theoretic conception of implicit definition no such problem can arise. For in so far as the meaning we are specifying is

> The meaning "f" will get if the explanatorily basic fact about its use is our acceptance of "$\#f$",

we know that "f" acquires the meaning simply by being aware that we are conforming to the regularity that constitutes it—i.e. that all our uses of "f" are explained by our acceptance of "$\#f$".

Notice that although the meaning of "f" derives, according to this view, from its theoretical role, and although it will be given that role (hence that meaning) if the theory, "$\#f$", is accepted, this theoretical commitment is not a *necessary* condition of "f"'s being given that meaning. For we may know the theoretical role of "f" without having any inclination to believe the theory. So, for example, we can mean CALORIC by the word "caloric" even though we do not believe the theory of heat which fixes its meaning. Similarly, it would seem that an intuitionistic logician might know what we mean by our logical constants despite rejecting the classical principles that we accept.

In order to accommodate this point we must distinguish two relationships that a word can bear to the belief-forming regularity of use that constitutes its meaning. One possibility is that the word is actually used in accordance with that regularity—i.e. the specified patterns of belief-formation are actually displayed. But another possibility is that "f" is merely assigned a certain *potential* use—i.e. there is a conditional commitment to use "f" in accordance with that regularity if it were ever to be displayed. In this second case, the meaning is *possessed* by "f" but not *deployed*, whereas in the first case it is both possessed and deployed. More formally, these two possibilities may be expressed on the one hand as a commitment to the substantive theory "$\#f$", and on the other hand as a commitment merely to the Carnap conditional implicit in that theory, "$\exists x(\#x) \rightarrow \#f$".

Henceforth I shall employ the following terminology. I shall say that a sentence S is the *direct* implicit definition of a term, when our basic acceptance of S is necessary, as well as sufficient, for the term to mean what it does. And, more broadly, I shall say that any stronger sentence will (indirectly) implicitly define the term, in so far as it entails the direct implicit definition. The acceptance of those stronger sentences will be sufficient, but not necessary, for the term to mean what it does. Thus if "$\exists x(\#x) \to \#f$" is the direct implicit definition of "f", then "$\#f$" will be an implicit definition of it.

What has emerged so far is that if we suppose that the meaning conferred on "f" by an implicit definition is that constituted by regarding a certain sentence as *true*, rather than that which "f" must have to make it *true*, then the four difficulties are eliminated. The *existence* of that meaning is guaranteed by the satisfiability of the regularity—that all uses of the word stem from regarding the sentence as *true*; the *uniqueness* of the meaning is guaranteed by the uniqueness of the basic regularity governing the use of "f"; the word's *possession* of that meaning is guaranteed by the fact that our use of "f" is governed by that regularity; and the fact that "f" does, in virtue of that usage, acquire a meaning, is *explained* by the very nature of meaning.[12]

2. *The Epistemological Import of Implicit Definition*

Armed with this use-theoretic conception of implicit definition, I want now to move on to the second of my initial questions and con-

---

[12] In the case of *explicit* definition—when one says "Let word "f" have the meaning that "g" already has"—only the fourth of these questions arises: namely, how does it come about that "f" acquires the meaning it does? For merely saying "Let it be so" obviously is not enough. The natural solution to this problem, as in the case of implicit definition, invokes the use theory of meaning. We can suppose that what gives "f" the meaning it has is our using it in accordance with certain regularities—and that this is achieved by our adoption of the rules of inference

$$\therefore \quad \frac{\ldots g \ldots}{\ldots f \ldots} \qquad\qquad \frac{\ldots f \ldots}{\ldots g \ldots} ,$$

allowing us to go from any sentence containing "f" to the sentence obtained from it by replacing "f" with "g", and vice versa. Notice that "f" will not thereby obtain *exactly* the same meaning as "g"; for the above rule provides the basic regularity for the use of the word "f", but not for the expression "g", which may be a complex whose use is determined by the regularities governing its constituents. For further discussion, see Chapter 7, response to Objection 3.

sider the epistemological import of implicit definition. If, by asserting a sentence S, we implicitly define one of its constituents and thereby help to fix the meaning of the whole sentence, what then can be inferred about the truth of S and about the way in which its truth might be known?

The first thing to be emphasized is that it is consistent with the sentence S being *taken* to be *true* (by definition), that it is in fact false. (Similarly, it is consistent with certain rules of inference being *regarded* as valid (by definition) that they are in fact invalid.) In other words, it is conceivable that, although it be constitutive of the meaning of sentence S that we accept it (i.e. regard it as *true*), it is nevertheless not *true*. And this point applies just as well whether S is a substantive theory, "$\#f$", or merely a Carnap conditional, "$\exists x(\#x) \rightarrow \#f$". To put the matter somewhat paradoxically: 'truth by definition' (i.e. truth *according to* definition) does not imply truth.[13]

The second thing to be borne in mind is that it is consistent with S being taken to be *true* (by definition) that it is so regarded for *empirical* reasons. It may be, for example, that we decide to hold *true* certain sentences, containing novel terms, because this will provide us with a good explanation of observed phenomena. Thus an evidently empirical theory might (indirectly) implicitly define its theoretical terms.[14]

In the third place, not only, as we have just seen, are implicit definitions not *all* a priori, but, in light of epistemological holism, it could well be that *none* are a priori (at least, within science). Epistemological holism is the far from implausible idea that the credibility of any scientific hypothesis is judged by assessing the credibility of a whole collection of hypotheses to which it belongs. And this idea leads naturally to Quine's web-of-belief model of theoretical development, according to which the evolution of our total system of scientific beliefs is governed by nothing more than the constraints of empirical adequacy, conservativism, and global simplicity. But if this model is correct then nothing is a priori—not even sentences that

[13] Paul Boghossian makes this point in his "Does an Inferential Role Semantics Rest upon a Mistake?", *Mind and Language* 8 (1993), 1–27.

[14] Admittedly, while one recognizes something as an implicit definition, it cannot be rational to deny it. For if a sentence S is regarded as *true* then (no matter whether this is or is not meaning constitutive) it should not simultaneously be thought false. However, this conditional can have no epistemological import: it obviously cannot be what *justifies* our acceptance of S. For even if the assertion of S were *un*justified, one might none the less define one of its terms by asserting it.

suffice to provide our terms with their meanings. Rather, every sentential element in our total theory formulation earns its keep by contributing to the best way of accommodating experience.[15] (This is not to deny that some of the elements may have been *acquired* independently of experience—perhaps present at birth. But, if the model is correct, then even these innate elements may be *retained* only because they help to compose the best overall theory formulation.)

Nor is this situation essentially changed if we shift attention from theory formulations to theories themselves, i.e. from the *expressions* of belief to *what* is believed. For let us suppose that each meaningful, declarative sentence expresses a *proposition*—an entity correlated with an equivalence class of synonymous sentences. Then it may be that the transition from theory formulation *S* to some *apparently* incompatible formulation *S** might, given the changes in meanings occasioned by that transition, not constitute the adoption of a genuinely incompatible theory. None the less, the old theory was abandoned and the new one adopted with an eye to the best way of accommodating experience. Thus our beliefs themselves—and not merely their formulations—are a posteriori.

An inclination to suppose that the content of an implicit definition must be known a priori can derive from the idea that implicit definitions involve nothing more than trivial linguistic convention. But this impression is quickly dispelled once we appreciate the difference between an *indirect* implicit definition and a conventional decision to convey a certain meaning in one way rather than another. As we have seen, an indirect implicit definition, in which we decide to assert a certain body of postulates, may be regarded (à la Carnap *et al.*) as the product of two intertwined commitments: first, to believe a certain set of propositions (of logic, geometry, arith-

---

[15] It might be argued that some of our logical commitments are fixed by the mechanism of the web—implicit in the constraints governing its evolution—and therefore not revisable through the operation of those constraints. More specifically, it might be argued that the constraint of empirical adequacy (namely, that whatever is derivable from beliefs in the interior of the web should not conflict with the beliefs keyed directly to experience) presupposes a commitment to (at least) the laws of modus ponens and non-contradiction—which, consequently, are unrevisable, hence a priori. In response, however, it can be said that although the constraint of empirical adequacy requires that the web employ *some* principles of belief derivation and belief conflict, it is non-committal on exactly what they are. It says merely that the combination of (a) theoretical postulates, (b) observational beliefs, (c) criteria of conflict, and (d) inference rules must remain in mutual harmony. For the sake of simplicity, any of the contents of either (a), (b), (c), or (d) might be modified in accord with that constraint.

metic, or whatever), and second, to express them in one way rather than another. Only the second of these could plausibly be regarded as an arbitrary linguistic convention. The former—the decision about what to believe (which constitutes the decision about which concepts to deploy)—precedes any decision about how to label those concepts. This could be a priori only if (a) there were some source of a prioricity other than linguistic convention, and (b) the web-of-belief model were incorrect.

Now it may well be that the web-of-belief model is *not* generally correct. For outside the context of science there is no reason to suppose that our beliefs are governed by the Quinean constraints of empirical adequacy, global simplicity, and conservatism. Thus *non-*scientific a priori knowledge may well exist. However, for the reasons we have just been developing, such a priori knowledge could not be the result of linguistic stipulation. Even in the case of a non-empirical belief, there remains the distinction between the content of the belief and the words in which it is expressed. And direct implicit definition can bear only on the second of these things.

But what about this second commitment—the decision to express our beliefs in one way rather than another? Is this not itself a belief—a belief whose content may be articulated, as we have seen, as the Carnap conditional, "$\exists x(\#x) \rightarrow \#f$"? And surely this is a priori? However, as we noted above, there is reason to doubt that such commitments are really *beliefs* properly so called; for their articulation involves non-standard quantification (into predicate positions) of the sort that perhaps only logicians understand. Nevertheless, insisting that those commitments are not genuine beliefs is not, it seems to me, the crucial thing. For they may be regarded as 'implicit beliefs', which would not require the believer to have the notions deployed in their articulation. The crucial thing, rather, is that these 'beliefs', even if they exist and *are* a priori, are very far removed from what philosophers have wanted to justify as a priori by virtue of implicit definition: namely, the explicit commitment to principles of logic, arithmetic, etc. What the web-of-belief model implies is that none of these is a priori.

Thus, no matter whether we are regarding sentences or propositions as the objects of belief, it is not implausible that every explicit, scientific belief is justified by its contribution to the quality of our total theory. No belief is justified merely by observing that it fixes meaning (or that it is expressed by something that does). For, from the fact that our acceptance of *S* suffices to fix the meaning of a constituent term, it does not follow that it is a good idea to believe it; nor that if we do believe it we will not eventually be led, for empirical reasons, to abandon that belief; nor even that the belief is true.[16]

Let me further clarify this point of view by contrasting it with two discussions of definition and apriority which, though recent, have a striking affinity with the logical empiricist model which I have been criticizing. Christopher Peacocke has argued that it may be a condition of possessing a certain concept that one believe a certain proposition which contains it.[17] In other words, it may be constitutive of the concept expressed by "*f*" that it plays a specific role in the cognitive economy of those who possess it—a role that includes believing the proposition that #*f*. This idea is intimately related to the use theory of meaning, and I wholeheartedly endorse it. However, Peacocke claims in addition that all such 'concept-constituting' propositions must be true, and hence are known a priori—and both of these theses run counter to what I have been suggesting.

Let us grant, for the sake of argument, that it is necessary for being a 'legitimate' possession condition for a concept that the beliefs it

---

[16] Of course, these points apply only to *scientific* assertions. As mentioned above, there may well be cases of non-scientific a priori knowledge. Consider some of the standard alleged examples of what is known a priori:

> All bachelors are unmarried.
> If John is taller than Mary, then Mary is not taller than John.
> If John persuaded Mary to go, then Mary intended to go.
> "Snow is white" is *true* iff snow is white.
> The chess bishop moves diagonally.

Since these are not scientific hypotheses, we need not suppose that their credibility is hostage to Quinean empirical considerations.

Where does this leave logic, arithmetic, and geometry—which are deployed both inside and outside science? My own inclination is to say that within science such beliefs are subject to Quine's empirical revisability argument: quantum logic may turn out to be needed in the best overall theory; so the logic, arithmetic, and geometry of science are a posteriori. However, regardless of what science comes up with, it seems likely that in ordinary life, in legal contexts, in game-playing, and in other non-scientific areas, we will continue to rely on classical logic, on standard arithmetic, and on Euclidean geometry. They are a priori. Thus we might end up with two logics: an a priori one involving our familiar logical concepts, and an a posteriori one deploying technical versions of "and", "not", "every", etc.

[17] Peacocke, *A Study of Concepts*, and "How are A Priori Truths Possible?", *European Journal of Philosophy* 1 (1993), 175–99. Peacocke's views have now somewhat evolved—see his "Implicit Conceptions" in E. Villanueva (ed.), *Philosophical Issues*, vol. 9: *Concepts* (Atascadero, Calif.: Ridgeview, 1997)—but he continues to maintain that a priori knowledge derives from the nature of concepts.

requires be rendered true by the semantic value of the concept. That is to say, suppose that 'believing that #*f*' can be a 'legitimate' possession condition for the concept expressed by "*f*" only if the semantic value of that concept is such as to make it true that #*f*. In that case there is indeed a valid inference from the fact that 'believing that #*f*' is a 'legitimate' possession condition, to the conclusion that it is true that #*f*. However, this argument could constitute an explanation of our knowledge that #*f* only if there were some independent account of how we know (1) that the possession conditions for the concept include the requirement to believe that #*f*, and (2) that this possession condition is 'legitimate'. But we are given no explanation of how these things could be known. And in the case of (2), this is especially problematic. For what basis can we have for thinking that the possession condition 'believing that #*f*' is 'legitimate' (i.e. that the semantic value of the concept renders it true that #*f*) other than some independent reason to think that this proposition *is* true? But in that case we cannot explain our justification for believing in the truth of that proposition on the basis of the fact that this belief is required by a 'legitimate' possession condition. Nor can we rule out the possibility that both the proposition that #*f*, and the thesis that believing it is a 'legitimate' possession condition, are a posteriori and false.

Moreover, not only does Peacocke's second thesis (regarding the apriority of possession-condition propositions) fail to follow from the first (regarding their truth), but the first thesis is also dubious. For why should the possession conditions of a concept have to be 'legitimate'? Why should the beliefs they require have to be true? For consider the question of what renders some method of deploying the concept its *possession condition*. Peacocke's plausible answer is that a possession condition should be identified as that method of deployment of a concept which is 'primitively compelling'—or, as I would put it, which offers the best explanation (when combined with other psychological laws) of the total use of the concept, including all the beliefs in which it appears. But either way, there is no reason to think that the possession condition of a concept could not require us to believe propositions that happen to be false. There is no motivation, either semantic or epistemological, for the assumption that the commitments required by possession conditions must be correct.

Peacocke writes as though possession conditions will require *substantive* commitments—the adoption of particular logical, arithmetical, geometrical, and scientific theories. But in so far as this is right, then we have already seen how possession conditions could well be mistaken; for any such theory might come to be regarded as false. A better strategy, I have suggested above, would be to distinguish between the *possession* of a concept and its *deployment*: i.e. between the association of a concept with a potential, belief-forming regularity, and its actually being deployed in that way to form beliefs. Supposing we can articulate the content of the former commitment as something along the lines of '$\exists x(\#x) \rightarrow \#f$', then it becomes harder to see how beliefs required by *possession*-conditions could fail to be a priori. But in that case the possession conditions of concepts will not require us to believe anything whose justification has been regarded as philosophically problematic—we will not be required to believe any particular logical, arithmetical, geometrical, or physical theories—and so the significance of the a priori correctness of possession conditions will be extremely limited.

Paul Boghossian's explanation of a priori knowledge is also reminiscent of the logical empiricist strategy.[18] The essence of it is as follows. An attempt at implicit definition will fail if it is impossible to deploy a term in the way the definition prescribes (as in the case of "tonk"). But suppose "*f*" is *purportedly* implicitly defined by "*#f*". Then, according to Boghossian, we know a priori

> *If* "*f*" has a meaning, then "*#f*" is *true,*

since this follows from the very nature of implicit definition; and we know a priori

> "*f*" has a meaning

(at least in certain cases). Moreover the argument from these premises to the conclusion, "*#f*" is *true*, is valid. Therefore "*#f*" is known a priori.

However, this line of thought is susceptible to more or less the

[18] P. Boghossian, "Analyticity Reconsidered", *Nous* 30 (1996), 360–91; and "Analyticity", in C. Wright and R. Hale (eds.), *A Companion to the Philosophy of Language* (Oxford: Blackwell, 1997). As my criticism will indicate, it seems to me that the account of aprioricity that Boghossian develops in these essays conflicts with the above-mentioned insight in his earlier paper (see n. 13 above): namely, that what is meaning constitutive need not be *true*.

same criticism as Peacocke's. Granting for the sake of argument that we do know a priori that "*f*" is meaningful, why should we accept the first, conditional premise? One possibility is that we have stipulated that we have a 'legitimate' implicit definition only if "*f*" has acquired the meaning that is necessary and sufficient for "#*f*" to be *true*. But in that case it looks as though our knowledge that we have a 'legitimate' implicit definition must be inferred from an independently motivated belief in the truth of "#*f*". On the other hand, in so far as we are prepared (as I think we should be) to countenance implicit definition merely on the basis that "#*f*" is *regarded* as *true*, then it simply does not follow that "#*f*" *is true*. Indeed there are cases (in science) where it is not.[19]

Of course this critique is based on the presumption (which Boghossian endorses) that an implicit definition, "#*f*", is something substantive—like a principle of logic, arithmetic, or geometry—something, as it happens, whose justification has been generally found problematic. If we abandon this presumption and move towards the Carnapian view that conditionals of the form "∃*x*(#*x*) → #*f*" give the general form of a direct implicit definition, then it is immediately apparent that implicit definition cannot help with these long-standing epistemological problems.

It is perhaps worth stressing that the conditional which, according to Boghossian, is a priori in virtue of implicit definition—namely,

If "*f*" has a meaning, then "#*f*" is *true*,

is quite different from the Carnap conditional

If ∃*x*(#*x*), then "#*f*" is *true*.

The Carnap conditional is indeed very plausibly a priori, for it merely expresses the linguistic decision to articulate our belief in one way

---

[19] It might be thought that one could *stipulate* that "*f*" is to have whatever meaning (if any) would make "#*f*" *true*, and that one could thereby vindicate Boghossian's premise (that if "*f*" has a meaning then "#*f*" is *true*). But this does not work. For even if we went through some such stipulational ceremony, we would have no reason to think that it succeeded in bestowing the meaning it describes. It may well be that, quite independently of the stipulation, our regarding "#*f*" as *true* bestows a quite different meaning on "*f*".

rather than another. But, as we have seen, it goes no distance at all towards showing the a prioricity of that belief itself—of the belief that "#*f*" is *true*. Boghossian's conditional, on the other hand, although it might easily take us (and by a priori means) to the truth of "#*f*", is not itself generally a priori. As long as we may coherently *regard* "$\exists x(\#x)$" as *true*, then tonk-like possibilities will be excluded, the implicit definition will succeed, and "*f*" will acquire a meaning. But it is none the less possible that "#*f*" (and hence the whole conditional) is a posteriori and false. And even if it is a priori and *true*, its a priori truth is not explained by its status as an implicit definition. Thus there is an enormous difference between Boghossian's *slight* weakening of the original implicit definition strategy which is designed to handle tonk-like problems, and Carnap's *extreme* weakening, which concedes that only the conditional component of a theory is a priori. The latter is what is called for. But no interesting a priori knowledge can emerge from it.

3. *Quine's Challenge*

I have been arguing that there is no decent route from meaning constitution (or concept constitution) to interesting a priori knowledge. Indeed, I suggested earlier not only that implicit definitions (of the usual, substantive form) *need not* be a priori, but that they *cannot* be, at least within science, since nothing of that form is a priori. In coming to the latter conclusion I assumed the correctness of Quine's epistemological holism and of the web-of-belief model to which it leads. But I am simultaneously maintaining the anti-Quinean view that terms have non-holistic meanings which are given by specific regularities of use for them. I think, in other words, that it is possible to distinguish, from amongst all the things we say, a subclass of utterances and inference patterns that are meaning constitutive. Thus I am inclined to endorse epistemological holism, but to reject meaning holism and meaning nihilism. And the question arises as to whether this is a tenable combination of commitments. For does not epistemological holism imply either meaning holism or meaning nihilism? Was that not what Quine showed us in "Two Dogmas of Empiricism"?

I think not. What Quine showed was: first, that synonymy, hence meaning itself, is not easy to characterize objectively; second, that,

given the adequacy of the web-of-belief model, these semantic concepts have no explanatory role in epistemology and therefore do not,
as far as *epistemology* is concerned, stand in any need of objective
characterization; and third, that the misconceived move to identify
the meaning of a sentence with the set of circumstances in which it
should be accepted (which is the *verificationist* theory of meaning)
would indeed imply, given epistemological holism, either that the
meaning of each sentence depends on which other sentences are
accepted, or that sentences do not have meanings. Evidently these
considerations fall far short of a demonstration that epistemological
holism *per se* implies either meaning holism or meaning nihilism,
and, as Quine himself subsequently acknowledged,[20] they leave open
the prospect of a non-epistemological conception of meaning.

None the less, the question must be faced as to what, after all, *is*
the basis for dividing the things we say with a word into those utterances and inference patterns that constitute its meaning and those
that do not. The answer I am inclined to give (which was spelled out
in Chapter 3, and which has been implicit in much of the above discussion) is based on *explanation* rather than *justification*. It is common sense to suppose—indeed this seems central to our concept of
meaning—that our acceptance of the sentences we accept is to some
extent *explained* by what we mean by them. For example, it is because
of what I mean by "table" that I am induced to call *this* a table; and
it is given what I mean by "1", "2", "3", "+" and "=" that I feel that
I have to accept "1 + 2 = 3". Thus meaning is what (in part) explains
usage. This suggests that we attempt to divide the entire usage of a
word into those patterns (or regularities) of its use that are *explanatorily basic* (judged by the usual criteria of simplicity and unification)
and those uses that are mere consequences of these patterns (together
with other factors), and that we then identify the explanatorily basic
patterns with those that provide the meaning of the word. In the case
of the logical constants, in so far as we believe that our total use of
them is best explained by our (conditional) adherence to the axioms
and basic rules of classical logic, then we may conclude that it

---

[20] W. V. Quine, "Reply to Hellman", in L. Hahn and P. Schillp (eds.), *The
Philosophy of W. V. O. Quine* (La Salle, Ill.: Open Court, 1986). For further discussion
see my "Chomsky versus Quine on the Analytic–Synthetic Distinction", *Proceedings
of the Aristotelian Society* 92 (1991–2), 95–108; "Scientific Conceptions of Language
and Their Philosophical Import", in E. Villanueva (ed.), *Science and Knowledge*
(Atascadero, Calif.: Ridgeview, 1993), 123–33.

is this fact which constitutes our meaning what we do by those symbols.

Thus, in relation to the Quine of "Two Dogmas" and *Word and Object*, the position taken in this discussion is mixed: I am in accord with his scepticism about a priori scientific knowledge, but opposed to his scepticism about synonymy, translation, and meaning. With respect to his third famous scepticism in this area—that regarding *analytic truth*—my reaction is equivocal, although more sympathetic than not. The difficulty with being categorical on this point is, first, that Quine discusses various conceptions of analyticity, of which the most important are

> (1) *true* in virtue of meaning alone
> (2) synonymous with a logical truth
> (3) a priori *true*
> (4) meaning constitutive,

but without adequately distinguishing them;[21] and second, that, at least as I see it, his sceptical conclusions are generally correct even when the considerations on which they are based are not. In particular, his critique of notions (1), (2), and (4) depends on his scepticism about meaning, which I am rejecting; none the less, one might argue that these notions are indeed defective. In a nutshell, notion (1), although intelligible, cannot be satisfied, since the *truth* of any sentence will inevitably depend, not merely on what it means—on what proposition it expresses—but also on whether that proposition is true; and notions (2) and (4), though both intelligible and satisfied, are of little philosophical interest, since they don't entail aprioricity—which was, after all, the main point of analyticity. Thus there is indeed no useful distinction between the analytic and the synthetic.

My overall conclusion is that there can be non-holistic, implicit definitions. These will constitute the meanings of terms by mandating the assertion of specific sentences containing them. But implicit definition is not the easy path to substantive knowledge (in, for example, logic, arithmetic, and geometry) that many have supposed it to be. For meaning-constituting assertions merely specify how cer-

---

[21] See Boghossian's "Analyticity Reconsidered" for a valuable discussion of these issues.

tain substantive commitments would be expressed were they adopted. Moreover, it suffices for their meaning-constituting role that these conditionals are *regarded* as *true*; in fact they may well not be.[22]

[22] This chapter is a slightly rewritten version of my paper of the same name, which appeared in *Nous* 31 (1997), 423–40. For helpful comments on the material in that paper I would like to thank Ned Block, Paul Boghossian, Tim Crane, Ernie LePore, David Lewis, David Papineau, Christopher Peacocke, Philip Percival, and Gabriele Usberti.

7

The Composition of Meanings

The title of this chapter is intended to suggest a pair of related problems: first, the issue of how the meanings of sentences are built out
of the meanings of their constituent words; and second, the issue of
what sort of stuff meaning is, how it is created, which of an expression's underlying properties give it the particular meaning it has. My
focus here is going to be on the connection between these two issues:
on the question, roughly speaking, of what meanings must be like in
order to be compositional. Or, more precisely, what constraint is
placed on an account of the underlying nature of meaning properties
by acknowledging that the meanings of complex expressions are typically engendered by the meanings of their parts? My aim will be to
answer this question, first, by giving a general, deflationary account
of what it is to understand a *sentence*; second, by showing how this
account yields an exceedingly simple explanation of how such understanding arises; and third, by concluding that the compositionality
of meaning imposes no constraint at all on how the meaning properties of *words* are constituted.

Let me start with an example. Presumably our understanding of
the sentence "dogs bark" arises somehow from our understanding of
its components and our appreciation of how they are combined.
That is to say, "dogs bark" somehow gets its meaning (or, at least, *one*
of its meanings) from the meanings of the two words "dog" and
"bark", from the meaning of the generalization schema "*ns v*", and
from the fact that the sentence results from placing those words in
that schema in a certain order. However, as Davidson was the first to
emphasize, it is not possible to produce a strict logical deduction of
what "dogs bark" means from these more basic facts alone.[1] So a

[1] D. Davidson, "Truth and Meaning", in his *Inquiries into Truth and Interpre-tation*.

question arises as to which further premises are required. What assumptions about the character of meaning should be added in order to obtain an explanation of the meaning of the sentence on the basis of the meanings of its words?

The answer that I would like to suggest derives from the following simple idea, which is the basic thesis of this chapter: namely, that understanding one of one's own complex expressions (non-idiomatically) is, by definition, nothing over and above understanding its parts and knowing how they are combined. In other words, once one has worked out how a certain sentence is constructed from primitive elements, and provided one knows the meanings of those elements, then, automatically and without further ado, one qualifies as understanding the sentence. No further work is required; no further process needs to be involved, leading from those initial conditions to the state of understanding the sentence. For all we have in mind when we speak of understanding a complex expression of our own language is that those conditions (of understanding its words and being aware of their mode of combination) are satisfied.

If this is correct, then the fact that "dogs bark" means what it does—or, as I will put it (maintaining the convention of capitalizing an English expression to obtain a name of its meaning), the fact that "dogs bark" means DOGS BARK—is constituted by whatever is the complex fact regarding its mode of construction and the meanings of its constituents.[2] This turns out to be the fact that the sentence

---

[2] Let me be more explicit about the route from my assumption about what it is to understand a complex expression to my conclusion about how its meaning is constituted. Suppose that understanding a complex of one's own language is (as I assume) identified with the state of understanding its parts and appreciating how they are put together. Then, understanding "dogs bark" (i.e. knowing what it means) is constituted by knowing both what its parts mean and how they are combined. But (as we saw in Chapter 2, section 1, and shall see again in the response to Objection 8) these items of knowledge are *implicit*: someone knows (fully) what an expression means when what it means in his idiolect is the same as what it means in the community language. Therefore, the fact that "dogs bark" means what it does (in language L) is constituted by the facts regarding how it is composed from primitives and what those primitives mean (in language L).

Jim Higginbotham has argued (in conversation) that the mode of construction of a sentence may itself have a meaning which contributes to the meaning of the whole sentence; in which case our understanding the sentence would require more than simply understanding the words in it and seeing how they have been combined. It seems to me, however, that any so-called 'method of combination' which intuitively has a meaning (for example, predication or conjunction or "*ns v*") can be regarded as a schematic *constituent* of the sentence. Thus we can make it a matter of stipulation that no meaning attaches to the procedures by which these and other constituents may be

results from putting words meaning what "dog" and "bark" mean, into a schema meaning what "*ns v*" means: that is (employing my convention for referring to meanings), the fact that it results from putting words whose meanings are DOG and BARK into a schema whose meaning is $NS\ V$. Thus the meaning property

x means DOGS BARK

consists in what I shall call the 'construction property'

x results from putting terms whose meanings are DOG and BARK, in that order, into a schema whose meaning is $NS\ V$.

Just as being water consists in being made of H_2O, and just as redness consists in reflecting certain wavelengths of light, so the meaning property of "dogs bark" consists in its construction property.[3]

This constitution thesis, I would like to suggest, provides the answer to our initial question: it is the missing premise that we need in order to show how the meaning of "dogs bark" is engendered. And whatever its defects may turn out to be, it has at least the virtue that it does indeed allow the meaning of "dogs bark" to be deduced from, and explained by, the meanings of its parts and its method of construction. For, given that

"dog" means DOG,
"bark" means BARK,
"*ns v*" means NSV,[4]

combined. Note, moreover, that even if Higginbotham's suggestion were correct, this would not have a substantial effect on the deflationary position advanced here. Our constitution thesis would have to be revised slightly to say that the meaning of a sentence consists in its mode of construction having a certain meaning and its constituents having certain meanings. But the explanation of compositionality would then be no less trivial. And it would be equally clear that compositionality cannot constrain how the meaning properties of words are constituted.

[3] As indicated, the general idea of 'property *S being constituted by* property *U*' is a very familiar one. It obtains, roughly speaking, when *S* and *U* are coextensional, and when facts about *S* are explained by this coextensionality. I think it best not to equate the relation of property *constitution* with that of property *identity*, but nothing here hinges on preserving this distinction. For further discussion, see Chapter 2, section 2, and the response (in the present chapter) to Objection 11.

[4] Strictly speaking, meaning facts have the form, "*S*'s expression *k* means *E*"— since one and the same sound type, *k*, may be meant differently by different people,

and

> "dogs bark" results from putting the terms "dog" and "bark"
> in the schema "*ns v*",

it logically follows that

> "dogs bark" results from putting terms meaning DOG and
> BARK in a schema meaning *NS V*;

which, given our extra premise, then yields

> "dogs bark" means DOGS BARK

—just what we wanted to explain.[5]

Moreover, it seems fairly clear how to generalize this example.

---

depending on their language. However, since I am concerned with what is meant by the expressions of a single, arbitrarily selected speaker S, explicit reference to the speaker is suppressed for the sake of ease of exposision. Thus I write ""dog" means DOG" instead of "S's word "dog" means DOG"; and I ask which property '$u(x)$' constitutes the meaning property 'x means E', rather than asking which property '$u(S, x)$' constitutes the meaning property 'S's expression x means E'.

[5] One might suspect that

> "dogs bark" means DOGS BARK

cannot really be what we want to explain because, given our convention for naming meanings, it amounts to little more than

> "dogs bark" means what "dogs bark" means,

which seems too obvious to be the item of knowledge that constitutes understanding. In order to assuage this concern, note the following points. First, although it is obvious, the fact at issue is none the less subject to substantive explanation; for we can show how "dogs bark" comes to have the property that constitutes 'x means DOGS BARK'. Second, it is far from unusual to give substantive explanations of facts which exhibit the same appearance of triviality: e.g. that the man elected was the man elected, that the colour of blood is the colour of blood, and so on. Third, despite its obviousness, this may well be the fact about "dogs bark" whose knowledge coincides with understanding that sentence. No doubt *explicit* knowledge of it is irrelevant—neither necessary nor sufficient for understanding; but we might suppose that when that fact holds of a given speaker (in virtue of his expression "dogs bark" having the appropriate construction property), then it qualifies as *implicitly known* by that speaker, and it is such implicit knowledge that constitutes understanding. (See the response to Objection 8 for more on this point.) And fourth, even the more familiar formulations of what needs to be explained—e.g. that "dogs bark" expresses the proposition that dogs bark, or that "dogs bark" is true if and only if dogs bark—focus on facts that are no less obvious.

Consider an arbitrary complex expression "*e*", and suppose that it is constructed by combining certain primitive terms (some of which are schemata) in a certain order. That is,

> "*e*" is the result of applying combinatorial procedure P to the primitives $\langle$"w_1", . . ., "w_n"$\rangle$

My proposal is that the meaning property of "*e*"—namely, '*x* means E'—is constituted by the construction property

> *x* results from applying procedure P to primitives whose meanings are $\langle W_1, \ldots, W_n \rangle$

(where W_1 is the meaning of "w_1", etc.). Assuming this constitution thesis, it is clear how, paralleling the reasoning for "dogs bark", we can explain why "*e*" means what it does from the facts about what its primitive constituents mean and from the fact about how it is constructed from those primitives. The great simplicity of such an account is what justifies the constitution thesis (by 'inference to the best explanation').

This strategy deserves to be called "deflationary", for it shows that the compositionality of meaning is much easier to explain than we have often been led to believe. It would not seem to be the case, as contended by Davidson and his many followers, that compositionality dictates an explication of meaning properties in terms of *reference* and *truth conditions*. Indeed, since our explanation did not involve *any* assumptions about how the meaning properties of the primitives are constituted, it would seem that compositionality *per se* provides absolutely *no* constraint upon, or insight into, the underlying nature of meaning.

It is important not to confuse the present proposal with various further theses associated with compositionality. I am merely claiming to have indicated how the facts about what complex expressions mean are explained by the facts about what their parts mean. I have not yet claimed to have provided a finite set of axioms from which it is possible to infer the meaning (or the truth condition) of each sentence of a language. Indeed I shall argue that, in so far as our goal is an explanation of facts of the form ' "*e*" means E ', then finite axiomatization should not be required. Moreover, I have not yet focused on the composition of *meanings themselves*—of the entities, *y*, that stand in the relation 'x means y' to linguistic expressions: I have not yet addressed the question of how such meaning entities are 'built up' out of their parts. My reason for postponing discussion of this issue is rhetorical. For it is much less controversial to suppose that sentences mean what they do because of what their words mean, than to suppose that sentences are associated with meaning entities which are constructed out of the meaning entities associated with words. Especially for the sake of anyone who would baulk at such compositional meaning entities, it is important to see that our capacity to understand all the sentences in a language can be explained without invoking them. However, I myself am happy to countenance compositional meaning entities, and toward the end of the chapter I will show how the deflationary picture can be developed in a very natural way in order to yield an account of them.

In what follows I would like to further clarify and defend the deflationary view of compositionality by considering a variety of likely objections to it. They will be organized around four alleged failings of the strategy: first, its not appreciating how substantive a constraint on theories of meaning is really entailed by compositionality; second, its not engaging any of the issues of interest to those who work in semantics; third, its ignoring the essential role of knowledge and inference in the understanding of a language; and fourth, its not respecting the relational structure of meaning properties and not articulating the compositional structure of meanings themselves.

Objection 1. It is surely false that compositionality imposes no constraint at all on the nature of meaning. For there are many proposals—e.g. that the meaning property of a sentence consists in its having a certain assertibility condition, or that the meaning property of an expression consists in its having a certain use, or conceptual role, or associated prototype structure—which are recognized as unsatisfactory precisely because they do not square with compositionality.

Correct. But I am not maintaining that compositionality is so trivial that *no* view about meaning could be in tension with it. My claim is the more modest one that compositionality imposes no constraint on how the meaning properties of the *primitives* are constituted. For whatever their underlying nature may turn out to be, there are bound to be construction properties (of the form 'x results from applying procedure P to primitives whose meanings are $\langle W_1, \ldots, W_n \rangle$'). Hence (given the deflationary proposal about how the meaning properties of complex expressions are constituted) it is bound to be the case that the facts regarding the meanings of the complex expressions are derived from facts about the meanings of the primitives.

However, if complex meanings are *not* analysed in this way—if we instead postulate a general and uniform account of meaning (an account intended to apply to all complex expressions as well as to primitives)—then there will indeed arise a real question as to whether compositionality can be accommodated. Suppose, for example, we hold that the meaning of an expression (every non-connective expression) is engendered by its truth or reference condition (depending on whether the expression is a sentence or not). In that case, since it is not obvious that the truth or reference condition of every complex expression may be derived, by means of simple rules associated with the connectives, from the reference conditions of the primitives, it is not obvious that compositionality can be respected. Similarly, if we are inclined to suppose that the meaning of a sentence comes from its assertibility condition (the condition in which it should be assigned a high probability), then compositionality causes problems. For example, the assertibility condition of a conjunction 'p and q' is not determined, via a simple rule governing "and", by the assertibility conditions of the two conjuncts.[6]

So my thesis is certainly not that *all* theories of meaning are compatible with compositionality. It is rather that all theories regarding

---

[6] This is because

$$P((A \; \& \; B)/x) = P(A/x) + P(B/x) - P((A \lor B)/x),$$

i.e. the probability of a conjunction (relative to any condition x) depends not merely on the probabilities of its conjuncts but also on the probability of their disjunction. For example, let x = The car won't start, A = There is no petrol in the tank, and B = It has a broken starter; and suppose that $P(A/x) = 0.8$ and $P(B/x) = 0.2$. The problem is that these facts (which, on the proposed theory, help fix the meanings of "A" and of "B") do not determine the value of $P((A \; \& \; B)/x)$ (and therefore don't enable us to determine the meaning of "$A \; \& \; B$"). We would also need to know whether non-starting is, or is not, almost invariably the result either of A or of B. If it is, then $P((A \; \& \; B)/x)$ is low; if not, then $P((A \; \& \; B)/x)$ might well be high. But this further fact is not something provided by our knowledge of the meanings of "A" and "B".

the meaning-constituting properties of primitive terms are compatible with compositionality; so that compositionality *per se* puts no constraint on the basic nature of meaning. For if we analyse the meaning properties of complexes in the deflationary way suggested, then compositionality is guaranteed and cannot be jeopardized no matter what we go on to say about how the words get their meanings.[7]

Objection 2. But is it not implausible to deny that meaning has a *uniform* underlying nature of some sort the same for both primitives and complexes? Surely, if "dog" possesses its particular meaning in virtue of exemplifying some property of a given kind *K*—perhaps a reference condition, or a use, or a causal relation to the world—then "dogs bark" possesses *its* meaning in virtue of some property of roughly the *same* kind.

Actually, I see no good reason to make this uniformity assumption—to think that what provide complex expressions with their meanings are analogous to what provide words with their meanings. None the less, the deflationist proposal is not in conflict with such an assumption. True, the proposal is that we take the meaning property of a complex to be constituted by a property of the form

$$x \text{ results from applying } P \text{ to terms meaning } \langle W_1, \ldots, W_n \rangle.$$

---

[7] Jerry Fodor and Ernie LePore have argued that the meaning of a term cannot be constituted from its stereotypical exemplars, because this would be inconsistent with the compositionality of meaning: for example, from knowledge of the stereotypical pets and stereotypical fish, one cannot infer what would count as a stereotypical pet fish. But this line of thought is flawed, because it unjustifiably presumes that if the meanings of the primitive terms are given by stereotypes then so must the meanings of the complexes in which those terms appear. The alternative I am suggesting is that the meaning property of "pet fish" might consist in some property of the form, 'x is the result of applying the schema "*a n*" to words whose stereotypes are S_1 and S_2'. See their "The Pet Fish and the Red Herring". For parallel arguments—questionable in the same way—against constituting word meanings from conceptual roles or recognitional capacities, see their "Why Meaning (Probably) Isn't Conceptual Role"; and see Fodor's "There are no Recognitional Concepts; Not Even RED". A response to the last of these papers is given in my "Concept Constitution", in E. Villanueva (ed.), *Philosophical Issues* 9 (Atascadero, Calif.: Ridgeview, 1998).

However, it is quite consistent with this policy to go on to argue, first, that there is a certain kind, *K*, of underlying property whose instances provide *words* with their meanings, and second, that the construction property is itself constituted from a property of just that kind. Admittedly, no such further reduction is *required* by the deflationist proposal. But this is a good thing, since it is by no means obvious that the meaning properties of complexes are constituted by the same kind of underlying thing as the meaning properties of words. But the possibility of some such uniform account is certainly not precluded.

Consider, for example, the idea that the meaning property of an expression is constituted by some aspect of its *use*. In particular, let us imagine that the following relations of constitution hold between specific meaning properties and specific regularities of use:

'*x* means DOG' consists in '*x* has use U_1'
'*x* means BARK' consists in '*x* has use U_2'
'*x* means *NS V*' consists in '*x* has use U_3'.

Therefore the property which constitutes the meaning property of "dogs bark", namely

x results from putting words meaning DOG and BARK in a schema meaning *NS V*,

itself reduces to

x results from putting words whose use properties are U_1 and U_2 into a schema whose use property is U_3.

Now suppose that we are able to find a further use property, '*x* has use U_4', that is equivalent to this reduced construction property. Imagine, moreover, that this could be done for every such construction property. We could in that case conclude for all expressions, including both primitives and complexes, that their meaning properties are constituted by their uses; so we would end up with a uniform account.[8]

---

[8] Let me stress that we have no good reason to expect a uniform account. A superficially appealing rationale for one might derive from supposing that any reduc-

Objection 3. It is possible for expressions constructed in different ways to have the same meaning: for example, "bachelor" and "unmarrried man", and "Brutus assassinated Caesar" and "Caesar was assassinated by Brutus". But such relations of synonymy are precluded by the deflationary proposal, which reduces the meaning property of an expression to its mode of construction.

The kind of meaning that is supposed to be preserved under translation between languages is relatively *fine-grained*: we translate "celibataire" as "bachelor" not as "unmarried man", and we translate "Brutus a assassiné Caesar" as "Brutus assassinated Caesar" not as "Caesar was assassinated by Brutus". Thus we do have a conception of meaning relative to which "bachelor" and "unmarried man" differ in meaning, as do active and passive versions of the same sentence. And it is such fine-grained meaning properties that I suggest are analysable as construction properties.

However, we are certainly not prevented from recognizing, in addition, a coarser-grained kind of meaning, characterized in terms of some similarity relation between fine-grained meanings, and relative to which there would be no difference in meaning between "bachelor" and "unmarried man" or between active and passive. One way of implementing this idea would be to distinguish between the syntactic and semantic structure of an expression (perhaps identifying the latter with 'logical form') and to attribute the same semantic structure to certain expressions whose syntactic structures are different. We could then suppose that the coarse-grained meaning property of an expression is constituted by its *semantic* construction property. Of course, it remains to specify the circumstances in which different expressions are to be assigned the same semantic structure.

---

tive analysis of a meaning property whose form is 'x means F' must contain a reductive analysis of the constituent 'x means y', and concluding that there must be a general theory of meaning whose form is "x means $F = T(x, f)$"—where T is independent of whether "f" is simple or complex. But this line of thought presupposes what I have been calling the Constitution Fallacy: it wrongly assumes that reductive analysis preserves logical form—i.e. that if a fact has a certain constituent, then any reductive analysis of that fact must contain either that constituent or something to which it reduces. This point is taken up again in the response to Objection 11. For more see Chapter 2 (section 2), Chapter 3 (response to Objection 4), and my "Concept Constitution".

But we do not need to answer that question in order to see how the compositionality of coarse-grained meaning will be explained.

A related objection derives from the intuition that the link between expressions and their meanings is arbitrary, depending on nothing but our linguistic stipulations—so that it would be perfectly possible for us to decide to give, for example, the meaning DOGS BARK to the word "glub" (or even to a non-verbal gesture). And if this is so, it would seem to refute my claim that the meaning property, '*x* means DOGS BARK', is constituted by the construction property, '*x* results from putting terms meaning DOG and BARK into a schema meaning *N S V*'. For this constitution thesis would imply that only complex expressions could have the same meaning as "dogs bark".

Again, however, what we can say is that the constitution thesis concerns the fine-grained conception of meaning and that it is only in some more coarse-grained sense that a primitive term (or gesture) can be given the same 'meaning' as a complex. The intuition that any expression "*e*" can be given any meaning *F*—i.e. that it can be given the same meaning as any other expression "*f*"—is based on the correct idea that one can always decide to give "*e*" a use whereby it is interchangeable with "*f*", by accepting the rules of inference

$$\frac{\ldots e \ldots}{\therefore \quad \ldots f \ldots} \qquad \frac{\ldots f \ldots}{\therefore \quad \ldots e \ldots}$$

And we can acknowledge that this sort of practice does indeed characterize a legitimate, actually deployed conception of 'sameness of meaning'. But notice that such a practice cannot explain how a complex expression comes to acquire its normal meaning. Nor can it accommodate the notion of meaning that is relevant to translation. The deflationary constitution thesis does both of these things—and with no counterintuitive consequences, as long as the distinction between fine-grained and coarse-grained meaning is borne in mind.[9]

---

[9] The difficulties to which I am responding in this section were impressed upon me by Stephen Schiffer. I would like to thank him for helping me to clarify and strengthen my position both here and in many other parts of this chapter.

Objection 4. Meaning is not as trivially compositional as the deflationary proposal would imply. For suppose that a certain type of use theory of meaning is correct: suppose the meaning of a word consists in the tendency to assert certain sentences containing it. In that case our understanding of that word would depend on our understanding of those sentences. Therefore we surely could not hold (on pain of circularity) that our understanding of those sentences is based on our understanding of their constituents. Thus, whether the meanings of the parts do or do not explain the meanings of the wholes depends on what the meanings of the parts consist in—it depends on its not being the case that their meanings consist in the use of wholes containing them.

Not at all. It is a mistake to think that a use theory of meaning, no matter how holistic it is, would preclude compositionality, or detract from it to any degree. After all, we are familiar, in general, with systems whose elements are characterizable *functionally*—i.e. by reference to the behaviour of certain complexes that they form. And clearly the characterization of elements in this way does not conflict with the possibility of identifying the complexes in terms of how they are composed out of these functionally identified elements. In particular, in maintaining that the meaning of a word is constituted by the *behaviour* of certain sentences containing it we are not implying that the word's meaning is constituted by the *meanings* of those sentences, and so we are free to identify each sentence meaning in terms of the functionally identified meanings of the words.

The contrary impression arises from the temptation to reason as follows: if a word derives its meaning from its deployment within certain asserted sentences then, since those sentences must be understood in order to be asserted, our understanding of them is *necessary* for our understanding of the word. And this is correct as far as it goes. But it does not follow that our understanding of the sentences is *explanatorily prior* to our understanding of the word. Just as a substance qualifies as 'carcinogenic' only in virtue of its effects, so a condition necessary for making an 'assertion' (namely, that one understand what one is saying) may be explanatorily posterior to the act of asserting. Thus even though assertion requires understanding,

it is none the less possible that the direction of explanation be from
(1) asserting certain sentences containing a word, to (2) understanding that word, to (3) understanding those sentences.

Suppose, for example, that the meaning of "true" is constituted by
our inclination to accept instances of "The proposition *that p* is true
if and only if *p*". This implies that we must understand certain
instances of that schema (e.g. the one obtained by replacing "*p*" with
"snow is white") in order to be able to understand the word "true".
But it does not follow that we understand "true" on the basis of
already having understood "The proposition *that snow is white* is true
if and only if snow is white". Thus the deflationary account of compositionality is not in any tension with the use theory of meaning—
not even with a highly holistic use theory.[10]

> **Objection 5.** But surely meaning could not be *necessarily*
> compositional. For compositionality is what explains the
> *contingent* fact that we are able to understand such a huge
> number of entirely new sentences; so it must itself be
> contingent.

However, what really explains our quasi-infinite ability to understand
a language is *not* the compositionality of meaning, but rather the fact
that we are able to learn the meanings of its words and to identify the
structures of its sentences. Neither of these skills is trivial; neither is

[10] It might be felt that the meaning of a word can vary depending on the complex
expression within which it occurs, and that consequently the meanings of these complexes are not explained via the meanings of their parts. For example, arguably, the
meaning of "sad" varies, depending on whether it is occurring in "sad woman" or "sad
story"—and similarly for "red" in "red hair", "red wine", "red alert", etc., and for
"dog" in "big dog", "wooden dog", etc. However, such examples do not really illus-
trate any failure of compositionality. Rather, they may be taken to reveal a holistic
interdependence of the meanings of words: i.e. that the meaning of "sad" derives from
a regularity of use that characterizes the various inferential roles of various complexes
in which it appears. And this does not imply that this meaning depends on the *meanings* of those complexes. Alternatively, it may be conceded that the word "sad" really
is ambiguous. In that case we can also concede that the meaning of "sad" in "sad *f*"
may be inferred from the meaning of "*f*" on the basis of restrictions (either gram-
matical or pragmatic) on what "sad" may sensibly be combined with. But again it
would not follow that the meaning of "sad" is *explained* by either the meaning of "*f*"
or the meaning of "sad *f*".

possessed by us as a matter of necessity. As Wittgenstein emphasized, it is a contingent fact about human beings that certain patterns of generalization, constituting particular linguistic practices, come naturally to us, whereas others—though perhaps imaginable—could not (as a matter of psychological law) be engaged in. Thus certain meanings—those tied to unnatural regularities of use—are not graspable by human beings. Moreover, the ability to hear (or read) a sequence of words and figure out its syntactic and semantic structures (if any) is far from trivial. One might well have trouble with "The dog the cat scratched barked"; clearly the length and complexity of the expressions whose structures we are able to discern are constrained by psychological factors. Thus some of the conditions governing our impressive (but limited) capacity for understanding a language are indeed non-trivial and contingent—namely, the ability to understand its words and appreciate how they are combined; but the compositionality of meaning is not amongst those conditions.

So far we have been examining objections to the deflationary approach which accuse it of blindness to how substantive a constraint on the nature of meaning is imposed by compositionality. A related cluster of likely complaints about it, to which I now turn, concerns the apparent uselessness of the approach, its alleged failure to address any of the problems with which those in the field of semantics have been occupied.

Objection 6. The deflationary thesis doesn't begin to *solve* the problem of compositionality, but merely restates it. For it is granted on (nearly) all sides that an expression's meaning derives from the fact that it is constructed in a certain way from elements with certain meanings. What we want to know is *how* this happens, whereas the deflationary account does no more than reiterate *that* it happens.

But this complaint is unfair. The only thing granted on just about all sides is that the meaning of a complex is *somehow* explained by the meanings of its parts. In supposing that there is simply nothing more to understanding an expression than understanding its elements and appreciating the way they are combined with one another, and in concluding that the construction property of an expression is what *constitutes* its meaning property, we give a particular answer to the question of how this happens, of the nature of the explanatory connection.

Objection 7. The problems of compositionality with which philosophers, linguists, and psychologists have been occupied are substantive and difficult ones. So we can only conclude that the deflationary approach, which would trivialize the whole issue, fails to engage any of the interesting questions about it.

But what are the problems on which people have been working so hard? One is the Davidsonian project of giving a Tarski-style truth theory for a natural language: that is, of showing how the truth conditions of the various kinds of sentence (including counterfactual conditionals, belief reports, etc.) are derivable from the reference conditions of the elements of the language. This is indeed a substantive and difficult project. But its bearing on the problem of compositionality is called into question by the deflationary proposal.

As Davidson originally posed this problem, it is provoked by the observation that we are each able to understand a virtually limitless array of complex expressions of our language, including things we have never encountered before. This phenomenon is to be explained by the supposition that our understanding of each such complex is determined by our understanding of the relatively small number of primitives. So we are left with the question of how this determination is possible—to which Davidson's answer was that, as far as he could tell, it is possible if, and only if, knowledge of sentence meanings is constituted by knowledge of their truth conditions. For in that case we can piggy-back on Tarski: each Tarskian derivation of the truth condition of a sentence on the basis of the referents of its parts can be seen as an explanation of how the sentence is understood.[11] This

---

[11] Davidson's position on the relationship between meanings and truth is not entirely clear. In some of his earlier writings he does appear to maintain that the truth condition of a sentence is what constitutes its meaning. This has the virtue of enabling one to see how Tarski-style derivations of the truth conditions of our sentences would

answer has been widely accepted, and is presupposed in the widespread efforts to force natural language into the framework of a Tarski-style truth theory. But my proposal entails that Davidson's answer is wrong. Compositionality can be explained, I have been arguing, without analysing meaning in terms of reference and truth. And if this is so, then one cannot insist that the Davidsonian research programme *defines* the problem of compositionality except by changing the subject and forgetting about what we were originally puzzled by.

Notice that my point here is not to deny the existence of an intimate relationship between the meanings of sentences and their truth conditions. On the contrary, from the deflationary perspective we are well placed to appreciate the *real* character of this relationship. We can see, in particular, that there is no need to suppose that the meaning property of a sentence *consists in* its truth condition. And this is a good thing, since there are well-known difficulties (possibly insuperable) in articulating a conception of '*s* is *true* iff *p*' which is strong enough to constitute '*s* means that *p*'.[12] Abandoning this idea, we can be open to the arguments in favour of *inverting* its order of explanation, and of saying instead that the truth condition of a sentence is a consequence of its meaning together with the disquotational property of truth. Thus Davidson is wrong to dismiss the deflationary proposal (a form of which he briefly considers at the beginning of his "Truth and Meaning") on the grounds that the construction property of a sentence would not even explain how its truth condition is determined, let alone its meaning. For consider what he could have in mind by 'explaining the truth condition of a sentence'. If it is stipulated that only a Tarski-style derivation will qualify, then Davidson's complaint begs the question against the deflationary

---

provide an explanation of our capacity to understand them. However it turns out to be difficult to find a construal of 'truth condition' in which that simple constitution thesis could be made plausible. (For, given a 'material' reading of the conditional, the sentence "snow is white" is *true* if and only if grass is green, but it does not mean GRASS IS GREEN.) In later writings (and presumably in reaction to this difficulty) Davidson appears to retreat from this straightforward reduction of meaning properties to truth conditions. However, it is unclear (a) what exactly the weakened position is; and (b) whether anything less than the original, stronger position can help to explain, in the way Davidson wants, how our understanding of complex expressions depends upon our understanding of their parts.

[12] These difficulties, briefly articulated in the previous footnote, are discussed in Chapter 3, response to Objection 6.

alternative. But if not, we can perfectly well explain the truth condition of a sentence by first explaining its meaning and then citing the schema, '*s* means that $p \rightarrow s$ is *true* iff *p*'.

Nor is it my intention to deny the importance for semantics of *certain* aspects of Davidson's programme. We can appreciate that it uncovers logical forms which provide evidence regarding the semantic and syntactic structures of complex expressions. But this concession lends no support whatsoever to the further Davidsonian thesis that compositionality can be explained only by explicating meanings as truth conditions. Nor, therefore, does it imply that the semantic structures we postulate must be of the kind governed by a Tarski-style truth theory. And since it is by no means obvious that there exists a Tarski-style truth theory for all of the multifarious departments of a natural language, it is just as well that compositionality can be explained without presupposing that some such theory can be devised.

Moreover there is no justice in the complaint that deflationism leaves little room for serious research in connection with compositional semantics. It calls for us to characterize the syntactic/semantic structure of the language: to identify the primitives, and possible modes of combination, out of which all the complex expressions may be constructed. And it calls for us to discover, for each primitive term, the properties that explain its overall use and thereby provide it with the meaning it has.[13] These are tough problems on which a great deal of work has been done and still remains to be done. Until they are solved we will not have a complete understanding of what the meanings of particular complex expressions consist in. But the general explanation of how compositionality works is another matter, and much simpler. To this question the deflationary perspective provides a complete answer that is independent of whatever may be the solutions to the substantive problems.

Moving on now from concerns about the triviality of deflationism, some will feel that this approach goes wrong right at the outset in not treating understanding as a species of knowledge produced by inference. That is:

---

[13] In Chapter 3 it is argued (a) that the meaning-constituting property of a word is the characteristic which provides the explanatory basis of its overall use. And (b) that this characteristic is itself a regularity of use—something like 'the fundamental law' governing the behaviour of the word.

Objection 8. The deflationary account fails to do justice to the intuition that we *figure out* the meanings of complex expressions on the basis of our knowledge of what their parts mean and how they are constructed. For the situation is surely not just that the *facts* about the meanings of primitives determine the *facts* about the meanings of the complexes. It is rather that our *knowledge* of the basic facts must lead by some inferential process to our *knowledge* of what the complexes mean.

This is indeed a tempting intuition; but it cannot be correct, and so the deflationary attitude should not be faulted for failing to respect it. Let me explain. The intuition is tempting because, typically, when someone's knowledge *that p* is based on his knowledge *that q* this is because he has inferred *p* from *q*. Therefore, since we are supposing that our understanding of complexes is based on our understanding of primitives, and since understanding an expression is surely a matter of knowing what it means, we are inclined to conclude that our understanding of complex expressions *must* be the result of inference. But this reasoning is flawed. Granted, in *typical* cases in which one item of knowledge engenders another, we begin with a representation of the first fact—an explicit belief state—and from this representation is deduced (or otherwise inferred) a representation of the second one. But transitions between states of understanding do not work in this way, because the beliefs involved in knowledge of meanings are *implicit*.

To see this, remember (from Chapter 2, section 1) that explicit knowledge of what something means (e.g. the knowledge that "dogs bark" means DOGS BARK) can be acquired trivially (from the capitalizing convention by which the meaning designator "DOGS BARK" was defined), and is certainly not sufficient for understanding. Rather, in order for a person, S, to understand an expression, e, it suffices that the meaning of e in S's idiolect be more or less the same as its meaning in the community. And for this to be so it suffices that whatever property provides e with its meaning in S's idiolect (e.g. the basic regularities governing his use of e's constituent words, together with his method of constructing e from those words) resembles the property that provides e with its meaning in the rest of the community. If this is so, then S will qualify as implicitly knowing what e means—regardless of what he may explicitly maintain. Thus

> *S*'s believing that his expression *e* means DOGS BARK

is the same thing as

> *S*'s expression *e* having the meaning DOGS BARK in his
> own idiolect.

So the point is not to deny that for *S* to understand *e* he must *believe* that it has a certain meaning. The point is rather that this belief is not articulated: it is nothing over and above his giving that meaning to the expression. Therefore an explanation of how someone comes to understand a complex expression does indeed involve an explanation of how he comes to believe that the expression has a certain meaning. But since that belief is implicit—consisting in no more than the fact that the expression means a certain thing in his idiolect—its explanation should not be expected to involve inferential processes.[14]

Thus we can see both why the inferential model of understanding is tempting, and also how that temptation can be resisted. But, in addition, it is clear that the intuition cannot be *generally* correct, on pain of infinite regress. For although there may be *some* language whose complex expressions are understood as a product of explicit inference, such inferences would have to take place in a more basic language whose complexes would themselves already have to have some content or meaning; and if inferences are required for this, then a yet more basic language would be needed in which to conduct them . . . and so on. So there must be a way of coming to understand complex expressions (of *some* language) that does not involve explicitly inferring what they mean. According to the way that I am suggesting, once the syntactic/semantic structure of a complex has been worked out, and given that the meanings of its parts are known, then nothing more needs to happen; for the satisfaction of these conditions already constitutes our understanding of that complex.

If this is how the complex expressions of our most fundamental language of thought are understood, then it is plausible that the complex expressions of our spoken language (supposing it to be different) are understood in the same way. An appreciation of their

---

[14] With respect to one's own idiolect, if an expression possesses a certain meaning then one qualifies as implicitly believing it has that meaning and (since error is impossible) as implicitly knowing it has that meaning. Thus meaning entails understanding.

syntactic/semantic structure may well involve computational processes. But there is no *conceptual* need for any further mechanism to take us from the results of such processes (and from premises about the meanings of words) to conclusions about the meanings of sentences. For our knowledge of the meaning of a sentence will consist in the fact that we have computed its structure and know the meanings of its constituents.

This conceptual analysis of what it is to understand the complexes of one's spoken language does not preclude the possibility, or diminish the probability, of there being further psychological processes that enter, as a matter of empirical fact, into communication and thought. In particular, it is a not unreasonable empirical speculation that the understanding of a spoken sentence brings about its translation into Mentalese, a universal language of thought. If there is such a process, it presumably appeals to some internalized correlation between spoken words and Mentalese terms, and it presumably consists in taking the identified structure of the spoken sentence and imposing it on the corresponding Mentalese terms. Nothing at all would be explained by supposing that the mind goes through explicit deductions, in Mentalese, of what the complex spoken expressions mean—e.g. from the premise (amongst others) that "dog" means DOG to the conclusion that "dogs bark" means DOGS BARK.

Objection 9. There can be no threat of infinite regress, because the language in which we infer the meanings of complex natural-language expressions is Mentalese and the elements of this language do not need to be understood. Indeed they cannot be understood; for they don't *have* meanings, they *are* meanings.

It is all very well to refuse to speak of 'understanding' and 'possession' of meaning in connection with the language of thought, and thereby to hope to retain the idea that when a complex is, properly speaking, 'understood', inference is invariably involved. But this strategy is of no real help in explaining compositionality. It merely obscures the fact that the same issues arise with respect to Mentalese, but in a slightly different formulation. Thus, in exact parallel to the questions we encountered at the beginning, we have:

(1) How does the fact that a complex expression of Mentalese has (or is) a certain meaning, depend on the fact that the primitives have (or are) certain meanings?

(2) In virtue of which of its underlying properties does an expression of Mentalese come to have (or be) the meaning it has (or is)?

(3) How does the way we answer question (1) constrain our answer to question (2)?

Not only are the issues essentially the same, but so are the deflationary answers. In a nutshell: a complex expression of Mentalese comes to have (or be) the meaning it has (or is) in virtue of its possessing a certain construction property; and this explains compositionality without implying anything about the underlying nature of meaning properties, about the facts in virtue of which the elements of Mentalese come to possess (or embody) the particular meanings they do.

Thus whether or not one chooses to say that Mentalese is 'understood' and that its expressions 'have' meaning, the fact remains that, at the fundamental level, compositionality is not explained in terms of inference.

Objection 10. The fact that meaning is compositional is supposed to explain how we are able to attribute meanings to the unlimited number of complex expressions in our language; for compositionality implies that all the facts about what complexes mean derive from a tractable number of facts about what the primitives mean. But if this is what compositionality implies, then it would seem that the deflationary account does not square with it. For in deriving the meanings of the various complex expressions, we have had to invoke, in addition to the finitely many explanatory premises regarding the meanings of the primitives, an unlimited number of further premises specifying how each of the complex meaning properties are constituted. Thus the deflationary story is not finitely axiomatizable, and hence defective.

Admittedly the set of deflationary explanations of meaning facts such as "dogs bark" means DOGS BARK

is not first-order finitely axiomatizable: assuming that our back-ground logic is the first-order predicate calculus (where there is no substitutional or second-order quantification), each such explana-tion requires a separate premise specifying how the relevant meaning property is constituted. However, in so far as a meaning theory is supposed to prove all the facts of the form '"*e*" means *E*', it is unrea-sonable to impose a first-order finite axiomatization requirement upon it, because no such condition could possibly be satisfied. This is in part because the terms denoting meanings (terms such as "DOGS BARK") are, from the point of view of the predicate calcu-lus, unanalysable primitives. Therefore, since there are infinitely many such primitives, infinitely many premises are needed to deduce facts about all of them. Moreover, a similar problem is engendered by the terms that designate sentences—terms such as "dogs bark". These also are primitives of the predicate calculus, and so infinitely many axioms are needed to characterize all of their meanings. So we have ample reason to conclude that a requirement of first-order finite axiomatization is unreasonable.

Nor is it reasonable to weaken the requirement by dropping the ban on substitutional and second-order quantification. For although some such weakened condition would no longer be unsatisfiable, it is questionable what motive there could be for imposing a requirement of this sort. One cause of mistakenly thinking that finite axiomat-ization should be expected of a decent meaning theory is the already criticized assumption that we must arrive by *deduction* at our know-ledge of what complex expressions mean. If this were so, then we would have to be capable of knowing all the premises; so (one might be tempted to think) there could be no more than finitely many of them. But understanding a complex expression need not be the prod-uct of an inference based on the meanings of the premises. As we saw in the response to Objection 8, the assumption that it does need to be, though tempting, is ill-founded and necessarily false.

The real issue is not how we could *infer* the meanings of sentences from the meanings of their words, but rather, how the meanings of sentences could be *explained* by the meanings of their words. And what the deflationist proposes is a possible answer to this question, even though the deductive arguments that formulate the proposed explanations are not finitely axiomatizable. It is certainly conceivable that—whether finitely axiomatizable or not—the meaning properties of the complex expressions consist in their construction properties. And if they do, then the compositionality of meaning is explained.

Perhaps an analogy will help here. Suppose we were to designate the *sound* of an expression by putting vertical lines around it. We could then say

> "dog" sounds |dog|,
> "dogs bark" sounds |dogs bark|,

and so on. And suppose we wished to explain why complex expressions sound the way they do on the basis of the order of words in them and how those words sound. We would need to assume that the property

> x sounds |dogs bark|

consists in the property

> x is composed of a word sounding |dogs| followed by a word sounding |bark|.

But this assumption, together with analogous premises for the infinitely many other cases, could not be deduced from a finite number of axioms (since expressions like "|dogs bark|" are primitives). Rather, we would have to invoke the schema: the property

> x sounds $|w_1, w_2, \ldots, w_n|$

consists in the property

> x is composed of a word sounding $|w_1|$ followed by a word sounding $|w_2| \ldots$ followed by a word sounding $|w_n|$.

But the fact that each instance of this schema is a separate explanatory premise in no way impugns our ability, with the help of its instances, to explain why each complex expression sounds the way it does. And the same goes for meaning. In so far as our aim is to explain such facts as that "dogs bark" means DOGS BARK, then finite axiomatization is neither possible nor necessary.

In order to open the door to finite axiomatization it is often allowed that the meaning theory deploy *structural descriptions* of sentences rather than their quote-names. Similarly one might drop the requirement that meaning properties be expressed in the form '*x* means *E*', and allow that they also be specified descriptively. Relative to these liberalizations, it does appear to be possible to give a deflationary meaning theory that is finitely axiomatized. The central axiom would be

> The meaning property of the complex expression that results
> from applying the combinatorial procedure *P* to the
> sequence of terms *S* = the property of 'resulting from
> applying *P* to a sequence of terms whose meaning prop-
> erties are those of the terms in *S*'.

From this we could deduce, for example, that

> The meaning property of the result of substituting "dog" and
> "bark" in "*n*s *v*" = the property of 'resulting from the sub-
> stitution of a word with the meaning property of "dog"
> and a word with the meaning property of "bark" into a
> schema with the meaning property of "*n*s *v*" '.

And given further premises specifying the meaning properties of the three constituents, this will entail

> The meaning property of the result of substituting "dog" and
> "bark" in "*n*s *v*" = the property of 'resulting from the sub-
> stitution of a word with the meaning property '*x* means
> DOG' and a word with the meaning property '*x* means
> BARK' into a schema with the meaning property '*x* means
> *NS V*',

which in some sense specifies the meaning of "dogs bark". Thus a kind of first-order finitely axiomatized meaning theory is possible. But as I emphasize above, the possibility of providing such an account is of no great significance.

This response prepares the ground for a fourth and final class of objections, having to do with the relational structure of meaning facts and the compositional structure of meanings themselves:

Objection 11. The complex meaning property '*x* means DOGS BARK' is evidently *relational*: it consists in the holding of the meaning *relation*, '*x* means *y*', between an expression, *x*, and a certain meaning *entity*, namely, DOGS BARK. Therefore a satisfactory analysis of the meaning property must reflect that relational structure: it must consist in an analysis of the relation, '*x* means *y*', appended to an analysis of the entity, DOGS BARK. But the deflationary proposal violates this condition. It would analyse '*x* means DOGS BARK' as '*x* results from putting terms meaning DOG and BARK into a schema meaning *N*S *V*'. And it is impossible to divide this construction property into an analysis of '*x* means *y*' and an analysis of the entity, DOGS BARK; so it can't be the property in which '*x* means DOGS BARK' consists.

But (as we saw in Chapters 2 and 3) it is wrong to think that one property may constitute another only if they have the same logical structure. In particular, it is wrong to think that a relational property cannot be reducible to a monadic property. For example, one might well reduce the relation

x exemplifies f-ness

to the monadic property

$f(x)$.

Or one might take the fact that

The proposition that dogs bark is true

to consist in the fact that

Dogs bark.

In general, the content of the claim that the relatively superficial property, 'being f', *consists in* the underlying property, 'being g', is to assert a fundamental explanatory relation between them. It is to say not merely that all *f*s are *g*s and vice versa, but also that this bicon-ditional explains various facts about the superficial property. Thus, when we suppose that 'being water' is constituted by 'being made of H_2O molecules', we are supposing that the biconditional

$$(x)(x \text{ is water} \leftrightarrow x \text{ is made of } H_2O)$$

is the explanatorily fundamental principle that accounts for the prop-erties of water (e.g. that it is colourless, boils at $100°C$, etc.). Similarly, in maintaining that 'meaning DOGS BARK' consists in 'being con-structed in such-and-such a way', it is being claimed that the exten-sional equivalence of these properties is what explains the characteristics of the meaning properties of complex expressions (e.g. the circumstances in which they are attributed). There is no reason why the explanatory relation between superficial and consti-tuting (underlying) properties should not exist even when they have different logical forms; and this impression is confirmed by the rela-tively uncontroversial above-mentioned examples of propositional truth and property exemplification.

Therefore the deflationary reduction cannot be disqualified on the basis of its form. Nor can it be rejected for not telling us anything about the meaning entity, DOGS BARK. For it does provide a char-acterization of it, though admittedly in a somewhat incomplete and roundabout way. It identifies DOGS BARK as what is meant by any expression which possesses a certain construction property. Thus in reducing '*x* means DOGS BARK' to the construction property, we are characterizing the entity DOGS BARK relative to our as yet unanalysed understanding of the relation, '*x* means *y*'.[15]

---

[15] Though nothing in this chapter depends on it, I argue in Chapters 2 and 3 that *meanings* are *concepts* (the constituents of belief states), and that "*x* means *y*" should be analysed (roughly) as "Occurrences of *x* provide reason to expect the presence of *y*". Thus, ""chien" means DOG" amounts to "Occurrences of "chien" provide reason to expect the presence (in the mind of the speaker) of the concept DOG". This strat-egy goes against the popular Gricean idea that one must distinguish between the notion of 'meaning' deployed within semantics and the one deployed elsewhere—for example, when we say "Smoke means fire".

Objection 12. We have not yet managed to capture the idea that 'big' meanings are made of 'little' ones. For even though the deflationary analysis might enable us to see how facts such as '"dogs bark" means DOGS BARK' are determined by facts about what "dog" and "bark" mean, this doesn't show how the meaning itself—the entity, DOGS BARK—is produced by the constituent meanings, DOG and BARK.

True. But it is not hard to accommodate this further intuition by adding extra material to the deflationary proposal. It is enough to suppose (with Frege) that the meaning of the schema "*ns v*" is a *function* which, when applied to the meanings of "dog" and "bark", yields the meaning of "dogs bark". Or, in other words, that

$$NS \ V(\text{DOG, BARK}) = \text{DOGS BARK}.$$

This supplement preserves the virtues of our earlier analysis but, in addition, shows how the meaning of "dogs bark" is the product of its constituents' meanings.

Generalizing, what I am suggesting is that we conduct the explanations of complex meaning facts using the Fregean principle

The meaning of the result of applying combinatorial procedure *P* to a sequence of primitives = The result of applying *P* to the sequence of the meanings of those primitives.[16]

This principle allows an explanation of the fact that a complex has the meaning it has in terms of facts about the meanings of its constituents and facts about how it is constructed. Moreover, this explanation, unlike what we had before, proceeds *via* the fact that the

[16] Note that a combinatorial procedure, *P*, acts on any sequence of functions and objects—it may say, for example, 'Apply the second member to the result of applying the third member to the first member'. Therefore *P* can perfectly well act both on a sequence of words (including schemata) and on the sequence of their meanings. The only requirement is that if a given expression can coherently be the argument of a given functional expression, then the meaning of the first expression can coherently be an argument of the meaning of the functional expression.

meanings of the complexes are generated by their constituents' meanings.

So, for example, the basic meaning facts would, as before, take us from

> "dogs bark" results from putting the terms "dog" and "bark" in the schema "*ns v*"

to

> "dogs bark" results from putting terms meaning DOG and BARK in a schema meaning *NS V*.

Then, given the Fregean principle, we would explain why it is that

> "dogs bark" means *NS V* (DOG, BARK).

Thus what "dogs bark" means (i.e. DOGS BARK) is identical to *NS V* (DOG, BARK). So in explaining the above fact, we are explaining why

> "dogs bark" means DOGS BARK.

Thus although, as Davidson maintains, there is no real need to invoke meaning entities in order to explain how the understanding of sentences arises from the understanding of their component words, we should not suppose that compositionality precludes a recognition of such entities and of their compositional character. For, as we see, it is not hard to add these further ideas to the picture, and thereby to vindicate our naive way of thinking about meaning.[17]

---

[17] In so far as we are allowed to pick out sentences and meanings by means of descriptions, then the present approach yields a first-order finitely axiomatized meaning theory. For example, the Fregean axiom entails

> (The result of applying "*ns v*" to "dog" and "bark") means (the result of applying the meaning of "*ns v*" to the meaning of "dog" and the meaning of "bark"),

which, together with the axioms specifying the meanings of "*ns v*", "dog", and "bark", entails

> (The result of applying "*ns v*" to "dog" and "bark") means (the result of applying *NS V* to DOG and BARK),

which would be the theorem specifying the meaning of "dogs bark".

Objection 13. But how can this conclusion be reconciled with the argument against compositionality which has been given by Stephen Schiffer:[18] namely, that (1) the referents of that-clauses are not determined by the referents of their constituent words; therefore (2) there is no Davidsonian, Tarski-style account of compositionality (for a language containing that-clauses); therefore (3) meaning is not compositional?

The answer is that Schiffer's line of thought can be resisted at various points. First, his case in favour of (1)—that there is no compositional reference theory for that-clauses—depends upon the assumption that the referents of the constituents of that-clauses must be non-semantic entities (for example, physical objects or ways of thinking about objects). But this sort of nominalistic–reductionist presupposition may well be rejected (and it does not square with Schiffer's own *anti*-reductionism regarding the referents of *entire* that-clauses). Second, the inference from (1) to (2)—that there can be no truth-conditional account of compositionality—may well be questioned. After all, *quotation* does not preclude such an account, even though the referent of a quote-name is not determined by the referents of parts (since there aren't any parts). Moreover, that-clause sentences might turn out to be reducible to quotation sentences: it might be, for example, that "*S* believes that *p*" amounts to something like "*S* believes what is expressed by '*p*'". And third, the move from (2) to (3)—that meaning is not compositional—need not be accepted. Schiffer argues that since the meaning of a sentence determines its truth condition, then, if there is no Tarski-style explanation of a sentence's truth condition, there can be no explanation of its meaning either. But notice that although we can indeed explain the truth condition of a sentence on the basis of an explanation of its meaning (simply by citing the schema, "*s* means that $p \rightarrow s$ is true iff p") we do not thereby obtain a *Tarski-style* explanation of that truth condition. For such a thing would have to proceed on the basis of

---

[18] S. Schiffer, "A Paradox of Meaning", *Nous* 28 (1994), 279–324. In subsequent writings Schiffer argues (along lines that are similar to those developed here) that it is possible to give a trivial account of compositionality—what he calls a "pleonastic compositional meaning theory". See his "Meanings and Concepts", *Lingua e Style* 33 (1998).

premises regarding the *referents* of the primitives. Consequently the impossibility of a Tarski-style theory would not preclude an explanation of the meanings of complexes on the basis of the *meanings* of their words—which is precisely what is provided in the deflationary strategy.

The thirteen points just discussed comprise the difficulties most seriously threatening the approach to compositionality that I sketched at the outset of this chapter; but none of them succeeds in undermining it. Thus we are left with the following deflationary position. The compositionality of meaning is *very* easy to explain: one needs merely to suppose that in order to count as understanding a complex expression it suffices to understand its elements and structure—hence that the meaning property of a complex expression consists in the property characterizing its construction. It follows that nothing need be assumed about the underlying nature of meaning: as far as compositionality is concerned, the meaning property of a word could derive from its reference, an internal conceptual role, a construct out of possible worlds, some relation to a communal use, or anything else. *A fortiori*, there is no need to assume that meanings consist in truth conditions; and since this assumption, though frequently made, is far from unproblematic, it is just as well that we can get along without it. In so far as we would like to be able to say positively what a meaning property is, it might seem that the deflationary approach to compositionality takes us in the wrong direction—by expanding, rather than narrowing down, the range of live options. But, on reflection, this liberalization is a helpful step. Showing how small a constraint is provided by compositionality makes it easier for us to find something that can satisfy the remaining conditions on a decent account of meaning.[19]

[19] This chapter is a slightly modified version of my paper of the same title which appeared in the *Philosophical Review* 106 (1997), 503–31. I would like to thank Ned Block, Jerry Fodor, Pierre Jacob, Jean-Yves Pollock, Stephen Schiffer, and Zoltan Szabo for their criticism of earlier drafts of that paper. These drafts were a development of ideas presented in my "What Is It Like to Be a Deflationary Theory of Meaning?", in E. Villanueva (ed.), *Philosophical Issues*, 5: *Truth and Rationality*, (Atascadero, Calif.: Ridgeview, 1994), 133–54. Other work tending in a similar direction includes Martin Davies, *Meaning, Quantification, Necessity* (London: Routledge & Kegan Paul, 1981) (see pp. 37–44); and Terence Parsons, "Fregean Theories of Truth and Meaning", in M. Schirn (ed.), *Frege: Importance and Legacy* (Berlin: Walter de Gruyter, 1996), and Parsons, "Theories of Meaning and Truth" (unpublished).

8

Norms of Language

It is often maintained that the normative aspects of language put a substantial constraint on acceptable theories of meaning and truth—to the extent, some would say, of altogether precluding purely 'naturalistic' or 'descriptive' accounts of them. My goal in this chapter is to try to establish that this is not so. I shall not be denying that language is pervaded with normativity—with oughts and ought nots. But I think these phenomena can be explained without having to suppose that truth and meaning are *intrinsically* normative notions. What I shall be arguing, in other words, is that the evident normativity of language can give no reason to reject wholly non-normative accounts of those notions—accounts such as the deflationary theory of truth and the use theory of meaning.

Let us begin by looking at a couple of the authors who have drawn anti-naturalistic conclusions from linguistic normativity. One prominent example is Michael Dummett, who has complained that the deflationary theory of truth is inadequate—too weak—on the grounds that it leaves out the *value* we attach to truth. In his famous paper, "Truth",[1] he compares the making of true statements to the winning of a game such as chess. He points out that we could describe the rules for how to move the various pieces and we could specify which positions count as winning the game—but still something vital to the concept of winning would have been left out: namely, that one *tries* to win. And according to Dummett the same goes for truth: the deflationary theory merely identifies the circumstances in which things are true; it tells us, for example, that the proposition *that dogs bark* is true if and only if dogs bark; but it leaves out the vital fact that we want our statements to be true.[2]

[1] M. Dummett, "Truth", *Proceedings of the Aristotelian Society* 59 (1958–9), 141–62.
[2] Something like this position has been reiterated recently by Crispin Wright in his book *Truth and Objectivity* (Cambridge, Mass.: Harvard University Press, 1992). He

Another philosopher who has made much of the normative character of language is Saul Kripke in his *Wittgenstein on Rules and Private Language*.[3] Kripke emphasizes that, for example,

"+" means PLUS →
    one ought to apply "+" to the triple ⟨68, 57, 125⟩

and maintains that any account of the underlying nature of this meaning property—any reductive theory of the form

x means PLUS = $p(x)$

—must accommodate that normative implication. But he goes on to argue that no behaviouristic or mentalistic account can meet this constraint, so no such account can be correct. For example, one might be tempted to suppose that meaning PLUS by a symbol is simply a matter of being disposed to apply it to certain triples of numbers (including ⟨68, 57, 125⟩) and not others. But that cannot be right, Kripke says; for how could the existence of any such brute, *factual* disposition determine what I *ought* to say? How could it provide the requisite justification? How could it guide me to my answer? How could it be that I answer in light of what "+" means?

My plan is to scrutinize this pair of considerations in order to see whether they really do preclude the deflationary theory of truth and the use theory of meaning. But before engaging this task it will be

maintains that deflationism is wrong on the grounds that truth is a goal, hence a genuine property, not merely a device of generalization. See the Postscript of my *Truth* (2nd edn.) for further discussion of Wright's argument. Bernard Williams is another philosopher who has expressed sympathy for the view that redundancy-style accounts of truth cannot do justice to its value. See his "Truth in Ethics", *Ratio* 8 (1996), 227–42. Hilary Putnam agrees, suggesting that when deflationism is combined (as it naturally is) with a use theory of meaning, it leaves us with "methodological solipsism of the present instant" or, even worse, with the conclusion that "the very idea of thinking is a myth". See "Does the Disquotational Theory of Truth Solve All Philosophical Problems?" and "On Truth", both in his *Words and Life*, ed. J. Conant (Cambridge, Mass.: Harvard University Press, 1995).

[3] Kripke, *Wittgenstein on Rules and Private Language*, especially pp. 11, 21, 24, and 87. Some other philosophers sympathetic to the intrinsic normativity of meaning are John McDowell ("Wittgenstein on Following a Rule", *Synthese* 58 (1984), 325–63); Allan Gibbard ("Meaning and Normativity", in E. Villanueva (ed.), *Philosophical Issues* 5: *Truth and Rationality* (Atascadero, Calif.: Ridgeview, 1994), 95–115); and Robert Brandom (*Making it Explicit*, Cambridge, Mass.: Harvard University Press, 1994), and Putnam, as just mentioned.

helpful to give a preliminary sketch of various interrelated respects in which language engenders facts about what we ought and ought not to say.

One way in which norms arise in connection with language is manifested when we teach it to children; we require them to obey certain rules of grammar and to associate certain meanings with the words. So, for example, one of the rules of English is that the word "dog" means DOG. Thus one might say, making the normativity explicit,

Oscar ought to mean DOG by "dog".

But notice that this in no way suggests that the property '*s* means DOG by "dog"', is *itself* normative; the only evidently normative property here is '*s* ought to mean DOG by "dog"'. Nor is there any reason to think that the *explanation* of the normative fact will somehow show that the meaning property itself is intrinsically normative. For the explanation of that fact is plainly pragmatic: it is good for Oscar to give words their English meanings because that is what the members of his community do, and he will not be able to communicate and live well unless he means what everyone else means. Just as the property of 'taking an umbrella' is itself blatantly non-normative despite the fact that Oscar ought sometimes to exemplify it, so the meaning property could perfectly well be purely 'naturalistic' (whatever exactly that might be) despite its participation in the above normative fact. So the norms regarding what to mean do not at all suggest that meaning properties are intrinsically normative. Nor are these norms what either Dummett or Kripke have in mind.

A second normative aspect of language is that one ought not deliberately to make false statements—one ought not to lie. This is an ethical norm: it says that a certain way of using language is morally wrong. And we might wonder whether it has implications about the nature of meaning. In particular, does it imply that meaning a certain thing by a word is itself something normative? In order to answer this question we must consider the basis for the norm. *Why* is lying wrong? And the answer is fairly obvious. Lying is wrong because it engenders false belief and thereby does some *harm* to the person lied to. Thus the wrongness of lying is explained by the undesirability of having false beliefs: that is, the undesirability of applying "dog" to things that are not dogs, and so on.

Thus we have identified a third, more fundamental, normative aspect of language, namely, that one ought to think what is true; in particular

> *x* means DOG →
> *x* ought to be applied to dogs and only to dogs.

For the sake of simplicity I will focus here on the desirability of believing *only* what is true, rather than the desirability of believing something *because* it is true. Although these two norms are intimately related to one another, the latter requires a more complicated formulation, since the vast majority of true propositions are of no concern to us and no value attaches to believing them. Notice that, besides being the ground of the prohibition against lying, the truth norm also plays a substantial role in accounting for the above-mentioned norms specifying which meanings a child ought to attach to his words. For a good part of the value of using the same language as everyone else in one's community is being able to acquire true beliefs from them.

In addition, the truth norm is surely what lies behind our norms of epistemic rationality or justification. In that sense of "ought" it might be, very roughly speaking, that

> *x* means DOG →
> *x* ought to be applied to friendly, long-haired, four-legged animals that lick and bark.

But it could plausibly be said that this normative implication is a consequence of the norm of truth speaking—a recommendation about how to satisfy it.[4] Thus the basic norm of language is the truth norm. Moreover this is precisely the phenomenon with which both Dummett and Kripke are concerned. Dummett thinks it implies that the deflationary theory of truth is inadequate; and Kripke thinks that it implies that meaning properties are not reducible to non-semantic use properties.

---

[4] Strictly speaking it might be that what we *ought* to do is not *actually* to avoid false belief, but rather to *aim* to avoid it, by conforming to the canons of epistemic justification. In other words it may be that, in so far as we have no direct control over our conformity with the norms of truth, they should not be thought to specify what we *ought* to do. I shall ignore this complication in what follows.

In assessing these claims it is vital to keep in mind a point made earlier: that a property may have normative implications without itself being normative. For example, killing is *prima facie* wrong; none the less one can presumably characterize '*x* kills *y*' in entirely non-normative terms. Therefore the normative import of truth and meaning does not immediately entail that they are normative notions. So Dummett and Kripke are not vindicated merely by the fact that truth and meaning have certain normative implications. Rather, the issue hinges on how this fact is explained. *Why* is it that

> *x* means DOG →
> > *x* ought to be applied only to dogs

and

> *x* ought to be applied to *y* only if *x* is *true* of *y*.

(Note that I am continuing to follow the convention of using "*true*", rather than "true", when speaking of *utterances* rather than the propositions they express). Are such norms consistent with the deflationary theory of truth and the use theory of meaning; or does their explanation reveal that meaning and truth are intrinsically normative?

We can simplify matters by asking ourselves what exactly is the relationship between Dummett's concern and Kripke's. On the face of it they are quite different: one focuses on truth and the other on meaning. But on reflection it becomes clear that they amount to exactly the same thing. Moreover, it becomes clear that we have here a perfect example of how truth is deployed as a generalizing device, and of the temptation, when this is not recognized, to suppose that the resulting generalization states a fundamental property of truth itself. For consider the normative import of each meaning property

> *x* means DOG →
> > *x* ought to be applied only to dogs,
> *x* means ELECTRON →
> > *x* ought to be applied only to electrons,
> . . . and so on.

Or, more formally,

x means DOG →
  (y)(x ought to be applied to y → y is a dog),
x means ELECTRON →
  (y)(x ought to be applied to y → y is an electron),
. . . and so on.

What is the general principle of which these claims are instances? Well, this is one of those cases (discussed in Chapter 4) in which the normal method of arriving at a generalization does not work. Unless non-standard quantifiers (not found in ordinary language) are introduced and explained, it will not do to say

$(x)(F)[x$ means $F →$
  (y)(x ought to be applied to y → y is f)].

For we can quantify neither into predicate positions, nor into capitalized positions (whose significance has been explained in terms of quotation, via the schema 'F is the meaning of "f"'). The real solution is provided by our conception of 'being *true* of', in virtue of the fact that it is governed by the schema

x means $F → (y)(x$ is *true* of $y ↔ y$ is f).

For this enables us to recast our initial 'infinite list' of instances into a form that *is* susceptible to generalization in the normal way. For example, given the instances of the '*true* of' schema

x means DOG →
  (y)(x is *true* of $y ↔ y$ is a dog),
x means ELECTRON →
  (y)(x is *true* of $y ↔ y$ is an electron),
. . . and so on,

the items on our list of Kripkean conditionals imply

x means DOG →
  (y)(x ought to be applied to $y → x$ is *true* of y),
x means ELECTRON →
  (y)(x ought to be applied to $y → x$ is *true* of y),
. . . and so on.

Consequently, whatever the antecedent (i.e. whatever x means), we arrive at the same consequent, namely

> $(y)(x$ ought to be applied to $y \to x$ is *true* of $y)$.

This provides the general norm we were looking for.[5] Thus we may conclude that there is a single norm here, an example of which is

> x means DOG $\to$
> $(y)(x$ ought to be applied to $y \to y$ is a dog),

and that the concept of truth enters the picture only as a way of generalizing such examples. Therefore Dummett could not be more mistaken: not only does the norm of truth acceptance reveal no inadequacy in the deflationary conception of truth; but, on the contrary, that norm provides a paradigm for the deflationist's view of truth as merely a device of generalization.

There remains, however, the claim of Kripke's: that this norm implies the impossibility of any factual, non-normative reduction of meaning properties. But, as I said earlier, given the distinction between normative import and intrinsic normativity, that claim is by no means self-evidently correct: to address it we must look at how exactly the norm is to be explained. *Why* is it a good thing to *hold* true only what *is* true?

In order to answer this question we must first acknowledge that there are two distinct ways of construing the norm of truth acceptance. One is pragmatic: on this construal it says that it is a good idea from the practical point of view to have true beliefs. The other is not pragmatic: it reflects the idea that we value knowledge for its own sake, independently of any practical benefits that it might bring.

The practical desire for truth is explained and justified by our conviction that true beliefs facilitate successful behaviour; that actions based on true beliefs are more likely to lead to the achievement of the agent's goals than actions based on false ones. To see why we should think this consider, to begin with, action-guiding beliefs of the form

> If I perform action A, then X will occur.

---

[5] It is a *generalization* of Kripke's particular conditionals in the sense that, relative to the '*true* of' schema, it logically entails each one of them.

Suppose one has such a belief in a context where X is desired. As a matter of psychological fact, that particular combination of belief and desire will tend to lead to the action A being performed.[6] Moreover, if the belief is true—if it is indeed the case that

If A is performed, then X will occur

—then X *will* occur: i.e. the desire will be satisfied. Thus we see why we should want our action-guiding beliefs to be true. But such beliefs are inferred from other beliefs; and the rules of inference we employ tend (we assume) to preserve truth. Consequently it is reasonable to want any belief that might occur as a premise in such an inference to be true. But it is hard, if not impossible, to find a belief of which one can be sure that it could never participate in this sort of inference. Therefore it is reasonable for us to want all of our beliefs to be true.[7] Thus we can explain the pragmatic norm of truth acceptance without making any assumptions about the nature of meaning. And on this basis we can explain why any word meaning DOG should be applied only to dogs, and, in general, why words should be applied only to those things of which they are *true*. For, given that

We ought (from a pragmatic point of view) to apply DOG
only to dogs,

and given the necessary correlation between applying a word and applying the concept it expresses—in particular

x means DOG →
(y)(We apply x to y → we apply DOG to y)

—it follows that

x means DOG →
x ought (from a pragmatic point of view) to be applied
only to dogs.

---

[6] Arguably, the tendency to perform those actions one believes will realize one's goals is not merely a contingent, empirical fact, but an essential property of desire, knowable a priori. But my argument assumes only that this tendency exists and that we recognize its existence. The argument does not depend on further assumptions regarding the modal and epistemological status of the tendency.

[7] For a more elaborate version of this explanation, see my *Truth*, ch. 3.

This explanation of the normative import of '*x* means DOG' makes no assumptions at all about how that meaning property is constituted. And the same goes for other such properties. Therefore their normative import can give us no reason to doubt that they are reducible to entirely non-normative use properties.

But what about the idea that truth is valuable for its own sake? Are we not compelled, on this basis, to concede that truth is intrinsically normative? Not at all. In the first place, it is by no means evident that this idea is correct. No doubt some people want their beliefs to be true regardless of any practical benefits. However, there are also people who do not care about 'pure knowledge'; and it is not obvious that these people are deluded. In other words, if someone applies the word "dog" to a cat, he is certainly saying something false, and he is in a state that might well lead to effects that are bad for him— but whether, independently of these practical matters, he is doing something he should not do is not at all obvious.[8]

In the second place, even if true belief *is* intrinsically valuable, it is possible that the explanation of this fact lies ultimately in the pragmatic utility of true belief. For it may be that 'being good' (in the relevant sense) is analysable as something roughly along the lines of 'being *normally* conducive to human welfare'. And in that case the above explanation of truth's pragmatic value might well be developed into an account of its intrinsic value. Note that the pragmatic character of such an account need not be taken to undermine the *intrinsicality* of the value. For to recognize the value of truth 'for its own sake'—i.e. to suppose that truth is good even in those cases where it will not have (and cannot be expected to have) any practical benefits—is not to deny that the explanation of that value may hinge on the *normal* advantages of truth.

And in the third place, even if no such pragmatic account of the norm is satisfactory, this still gives no reason to conclude that properties like '*x* means DOG' are intrinsically normative. As I illustrated with the example, "Killing is wrong", it might be possible for our most basic normative principles to have the form

$$(x)(Dx \to Nx),$$

---

[8] See Judith Jarvis Thomson's "The Right and the Good", *Journal of Philosophy* 94 (1997), 273–98, for a critique of the notion of 'intrinsic value'.

where "*D*" describes some state of the world and "*N*" specifies what ought or ought not to be done in that situation. Thus the normative implications of a meaning property leave it entirely open that its nature is completely non-normative.

Before ending, there is a further point raised by Kripke that should be addressed. As he notes, one might well feel that the property, '*x* means PLUS', cannot be constituted by dispositions to use *x* in a certain way (i.e. dispositions to apply it to some things but not others), because this would not accommodate the feeling we have that what we mean by a word *guides* our use of it and provides a *reason* for deploying it as we do. Thus it is not merely that

> *x* means PLUS →
>> *x* ought to be applied in such-and-such a way,

but also that

> *x* means PLUS →
>> one is, in some sense, 'directed' to apply *x* in such-and-such a way.

As he puts it:

So it does seem that a dispositional account misconceives the sceptic's problem—to find a past fact that *justifies* my present response. As a candidate for a 'fact' that determines what I mean, it fails to satisfy the basic condition on such a candidate . . . that it should *tell* me what I ought to do in each new instance. (p. 24)

Notice that the assumption here is not merely that what one means *explains* what one says; but that it does so in a special way—namely, by providing 'directions' or 'instructions' that we can follow if we want. But is it really true that meaning properties have this 'guiding' character? I don't think so; and, despite what I have just quoted, Kripke doesn't really think so either. For him, it is only an imagined sceptic about meaning who insists that any adequate reduction of meaning properties must square with this apparent fact about them, and who is confronted with the problem of not being able to find any account that does so. Kripke himself would resolve this 'paradox' by pointing out that the 'guidance' constraint is misconceived. Thus he says:

Almost all of us unhesitatingly produce the answer '125' when asked for the sum of 68 and 57 . . . And we do so without justification. Of course, if asked why we said '125', most of us will say that we added 8 and 7 to get 15, that we put down 5 and carried 1, and so on. But then, what will we say if asked why we carried as we do? . . . The entire point of the sceptical argument is that ultimately we reach a level where we act without any reason in terms of which we can justify our action. We act unhesitatingly but *blindly*. This . . . is an important case of what Wittgenstein calls speaking without 'justification' ('Rechtfertigung') but not 'wrongfully' ('zu Unrecht'). (p. 87)

This assessment of the situation seems to me entirely just. It implies, however, that candidate meaning-constituting properties cannot be disqualified on the basis of failing to explain how what we mean *justifies* what we say.

But is it not none the less the case that meaning what we do is a matter of following certain *unarticulated* rules of usage, and that the very idea that we are *following rules* involves *intrinsically* some sort of normative pressure or 'obligation' to conform to them? In other words, is it not plausible that our meaning what we do by "dog" is constituted by our following certain rules for the use of that word— not for the sake of truth or rationality, but simply as a necessary condition of having that meaning—and that in so far as we are following those rules then we 'ought' (in some sense) to comply with them? The point is not supposed to be that, since meaning is rule following, then, if one wants to mean a certain thing, one had better follow the appropriate rules. The point is rather that the very notion of 'following rule R' entails that anyone who is doing so is making some sort of mistake when he does not conform, and *ought* therefore to conform; so he cannot count as meaning DOG unless he has a certain normative characteristic.

In response, however, one might say that the only norm automatically associated with following a rule is a *sui generis* 'obligation' which is stipulatively deduced *from* the fact of rule following and in no way constitutive of it. In other words, we are at liberty to construct a special notion of 'ought' by means of the convention that

S follows rule $R \rightarrow S$ 'ought' to conform with R,

without putting any constraint whatsoever on which facts underlie the antecedent. In that case the automatic 'normative' import of meaning would be explained along the following lines:

S means *F* by *w*,

∴ *S*'s use of word *w* has non-normative property *P*,

∴ *S* follows rule *R* for the use of *w*,

∴ *S*'s use of *w* 'ought' to fit *R*.

Therefore we would have no reason to suppose that meaning properties are constitutionally normative.[9]

On the basis of our examination of the various respects in which language is normative, I believe we can conclude that Dummett and Kripke and their followers are mistaken: it is quite consistent with our proclivity for truth that meaning properties are constituted by intrinsically non-normative regularities of use, and that our conception of truth is fully captured by the deflationary equivalence schema.

---

[9] For a more thorough discussion of Kripke's sceptical view of meaning and rule following, see Chapter 10 below.

9

Quelling Quine's Qualms

How is it possible for a word or a sentence to be meaningful and yet not to have a meaning? That this is not merely possible but generally true is the startling conclusion of the considerations advanced by Quine in chapter 2 of *Word and Object* and which he has refined in subsequent writings, notably "Ontological Relativity" and *Pursuit of Truth*. In this chapter I will hazard a reconstruction of Quine's argument—a reconstruction which I hope does justice to it, but which reveals, I believe, a serious defect: namely, that although its main assumptions are indeed correct, the shocking conclusion cannot really be derived from them. More specifically, I will argue that we should welcome Quine's sceptical scrutiny of the naive conception of meaning, which he calls "the museum myth", and in addition that we should endorse a qualified form of his behaviourism regarding semantics; but I will suggest that these ideas ought to have led him, and ought to lead us, to a use theory of meanings rather than to a denial of meanings. Thus Quine's basic assumptions turn out not to undermine the main contention of this book: on the contrary, they provide support for it.

Quine's line of thought begins—at least in my formulation of it— by his calling to our attention our tendency to take for granted, without justification, a picture of meaning containing the following elements: (1) that there is a set of entities, known as *meanings* or *concepts*, with which we are immediately acquainted; (2) that each term of a language is associated with ('possesses') one of these entities, and thereby becomes meaningful; (3) that we construct our conceptions of sameness of meaning—that is, of synonymy within a language and translation between languages—on the basis of the prior conception we have of these meaning entities; and (4) that we are able thereby to rationalize the procedures we employ for trying to arrive at correct manuals of translation, and to explain why it is useful to be in possession of manuals that are correct.

Quine's critique of this naive picture may be divided into two parts: a methodological prologue and a constructive analysis. In the first part, the methodological prologue, he objects to the series of conceptual priorities to which the picture is committed: namely, that we derive explanations of the conditions of justification for our manuals of (i.e. beliefs about) translation, and for the utility of such manuals, from some prior conception of their content, which stems in turn from our immediate grasp of the meaning entities. According to Quine, this order of explanation should be reversed. We must begin with the idea that certain translation manuals are useful, facilitating foreign travel. This is what explains why some are taken to be 'better' than others—they enable more accurate predictions, hence more successful negotiations. Therefore this is what determines the basis on which we select manuals of translation: i.e. it determines what is taken to be evidence for 'a correct translation'. Thus we arrive at our conception of the facts of translation. Then, finally, we may obtain our notion of meaning in terms of this conception of translation: meaning is that which is preserved in correct translation. To put it another way, our conception of what it is for a foreigner to have certain beliefs derives from our procedures (which include methods of arriving at translation manuals) for deciding when they have those beliefs; and these procedures are adopted on the basis of the pragmatic, predictive benefits that they engender. Thus the first component of Quine's critique is the claim that our only route to *meaning* is via *translation* which is itself reached from the *pragmatic function of translation manuals*.

In the second component of his critique Quine proceeds to implement this methodological proposal. His constructive analysis has three stages. First, beginning with plausible assumptions about the pragmatic point of translation, he derives a certain conclusion about the properties of an adequate translation manual: namely that a translation scheme is adequate if it preserves all dispositions to assent and dissent (i.e. manual T adequately translates A's language into B's if, whenever A is disposed to assent to, or dissent from, an utterance, then B is disposed to assent to, or dissent from, the translation under T of that utterance, and vice versa). Second, on this basis he argues that there will be many nonequivalent, yet perfectly adequate, translations into our language of just about any foreign expression. And third, he thereby obtains the conclusion that there can be no such entities as meanings. Thus the naive picture—the museum myth—is shown to be not merely unwarranted but false.

This, I take it, is the structure of Quine's critique of meaning. In what follows I plan to go over the three steps in his constructive analysis, filling in some of the details and explaining where I have reservations. Instead of beginning at the beginning I am going to consider the steps in reverse order, looking progressively more deeply into his rationale for meaning scepticism. So I will start by considering how one gets from the existence of multiple translations to the nonexistence of meanings. Next I will examine the main premise of this argument and show how Quine derives it from his thesis about the conditions sufficient for adequate translations: that is, how he gets to the lemma that many nonequivalent translation manuals will exist from the thesis that any good predictor of assent/dissent dispositions will be an adequate translation manual. And then I will consider the first stage in Quine's constructive analysis (which is the one I think most debatable): his derivation of the adequacy of any assertibility-preserving manual from the pragmatic *raison d'être* of translation. At the end of the chapter I will attempt to rectify what I believe is the main defect in this reasoning and I will suggest that the proper standards of adequacy will leave us with unique translations and with a use theory of meaning.

To begin, then, at Quine's final step, let us imagine that we have established an 'indeterminacy' thesis (I):

(I)   There are two adequate manuals of translation between language J and English such that according to one of them the translation of foreign word v is "e" and according to the other the translation is "$e*$"—where "e" and "$e*$" are not regarded as coreferential by English speakers (i.e. we do not accept 'Something is e if and only if it is $e*$').

And let us also assume thesis (M):

(M)   If a word has a meaning then an adequate translation of that word must have the same meaning,

and thesis (S):

(S) If two English (context-insensitive) referring expressions
have the same meaning then they are regarded as coreferential by speakers of English.

It follows from these theses that *v* does not have a meaning. For if it
did then, given (M), any adequate translation of *v* would have the
same meaning. Therefore, given (I), both "*e*" and "*e**" would have
that meaning, hence the same meaning as one another. And therefore, given (S), "*e*" and "*e**" would be regarded as coreferential,
which, given (I), they are not. Therefore *v* does not have a meaning;
so, given (M) and (I), neither does "*e*" or "*e**". Thus if premises (I),
(M), and (S) can be shown to be typically correct, then Quine's
renunciation of meanings will be quite justified.

Of these premises the most controversial has been thesis (I) concerning the multiplicity of translations, and we shall be considering
in a moment how Quine attempts to support it. It is worth noting,
however, that even if (I) is accepted it is none the less possible to resist
the sceptical conclusion, since one well might choose to deny thesis
(M). The rationale for so doing would not simply be an unreasonable
attachment to the 'museum myth', but rather a quite general and
plausible anti-verificationist view about the relationship between
truth and justification: namely, that one should be prepared to countenance some space between them—even space that is in principle
ineliminable. Therefore, in so far as "adequate" is taken to mean
"useful" or "justified", one might hold that even if there are many
adequate translations, only one of them is *true*, and only that one
need preserve meaning; therefore (M) is incorrect, and so the case
against meanings collapses. To amplify a little, one might distinguish
between *determinate* truth, which requires decidability on the basis
of underlying facts, and truth *simpliciter*, which does not. In that case
one could say that although many of the truths of translation are
indeterminate (since the underlying facts of verbal behaviour do not
fix them), they none the less exist.[1] And in this way one would be able
to hang on to meanings as those entities that are preserved in
correct (not merely *adequate*, and not necessarily *determinate*)

---

[1] The idea that just one of the various adequate manuals of translation is true is
analogous to the view, regarding vague predicates, that there is some fact of the matter—admittedly indeterminate—about exactly where its boundaries lie. For a defence
of this position see my *Truth*, ch. 5.

translation, correlated with equivalence classes under the translation relation.

The plausibility of this sceptical attitude towards thesis (M) is enhanced by consideration of an analogous thesis (R) regarding reference: namely,

(R) If a word has a referent, then any adequate translation of that word must have the same referent.

For it is constitutive of what we mean by "refers" to accept instances of the disquotational schema, '"n" refers (if at all) to n'. Therefore, even in the face of a plurality of nonequivalent, adequate translations of a foreign term v (including one into "e" and another into "$e*$"), we will be inclined to regard it as perfectly determinate that "e" refers to e and "$e*$" refers to $e*$. But we cannot suppose that v refers to the same thing as both "e" and "$e*$", since they are not coreferential. Therefore (R) must be denied. But having taken this somewhat counterintuitive step, it is not additionally counterintuitive to deny (M) as well. These principles stand or fall together; and (R) must go; therefore it is natural to give up (M) too, and to apply to translation manuals the familiar distinction between the true and the merely justified.

Thus the step from indeterminacy of translation to meaning scepticism is questionable. However, let us now put this issue aside and begin to descend deeper into Quine's line of thought by examining the basis for the indeterminacy of translation thesis (I). As we have just seen, it is possible to resist his meaning scepticism even if one concedes that there exists a plurality of adequate translations. But should we make that concession? Why suppose that there are bound to be several adequate translations of virtually any expression?

For the case of words (as opposed to sentences) Quine provides us with a simple and ingenious argument, which turns on what he calls "proxy-functions". Let f be any 1–1 function: for example, the function that takes each physical object into its 'cosmic complement', which is everything in the universe outside that object. Thus it takes this table into the scattered entity that consists in everything but this table; and it takes that scattered entity into everything but that entity—namely, back to the original table. Now let us introduce, corresponding to each name "a", an additional singular term "$a*$", by means of the stipulation

$$a* = f(a),$$

and let us introduce, for each primitive predicate "G", an additional predicate "$G*$" such that

$$\{x\}\{G*[f(x)] \leftrightarrow G(x)\},$$

and similarly for relational predicates. (Thus, in the case where f is the 'cosmic complement' function, we would introduce the term "Socrates*" to name the cosmic complement of Socrates, and the term "red*" to apply to anything that is the cosmic complement of something red, etc.) In that case it is not hard to see that, for every atomic sentence,

$$G(a) \leftrightarrow G*(a*).$$

And it follows that every (extensional) sentence "p" is definitionally equivalent to the sentence "$p*$" which is derived from "p" by replacing every primitive term in it by the corresponding 'star' term. Therefore, if we assume that such equivalences are recognized by speakers of the language, it follows that "p" and "$p*$" are co-assertible: that in circumstances in which there is a disposition to assent to (or to dissent from) "p", if asked, there will also be a disposition to assent to (or to dissent from) "$p*$", and vice versa. Now suppose that the holistic totality of assertibility facts for a certain English speaker, s, is

$$Ds(\text{"}p\text{"}, \text{"}p*\text{"}, \text{"}q\text{"}, \text{"}q*\text{"}, \ldots).$$

That is to say, Ds specifies, for each sentence, the circumstances in which s is disposed to assent to it and to dissent from it. Given the co-assertibility of each sentence with its 'star', it must be that

$$Ds(\text{"}p\text{"}, \text{"}p*\text{"}, \text{"}q\text{"}, \text{"}q*\text{"}, \ldots) = Ds(\text{"}p*\text{"}, \text{"}p\text{"}, \text{"}q*\text{"}, \text{"}q\text{"}, \ldots).$$

Consequently, if we transform the body of facts regarding the speaker's assent/dissent dispositions Ds by means of the function $T*$ which takes each term into the star of that term, then what results is the same as the body of facts with which we started.

Now in order to be able to go from this result to thesis (I) regarding the multiplicity of adequate translation manuals it is necessary (and sufficient) to embrace the following assumption (A):

(A)   Any manual of translation that preserves assertibility is adequate.

Or more precisely: suppose that language H has sentences $h_1, h_2, \ldots$, that language J has sentences $j_1, j_2, \ldots$, that the totality of assertibility facts for a certain speaker of H is $D(h_1, h_2, \ldots)$, and that the totality of assertibility facts for a certain speaker of J is $D(j_1, j_2, \ldots)$ (i.e. the assent/dissent dispositions of the two speakers are the same, modulo substitution of H-sentences for J-sentences). In that case, according to thesis (A), the translation schema that matches h_1 with j_1, h_2 with j_2, \ldots, and so on, is adequate.

On the basis of this assumption together with the proxy-function considerations we can prove thesis (I): that there are many adequate translations of virtually every term. For let H be my language and J be the language of a person (e.g. my doppelgänger on a completely twin earth) who has exactly the same verbal dispositions as I have. Consider any proxy function f, and the corresponding translation mapping T^* which matches the terms in my language with the star (relative to f) of those terms in J. Any such scheme—of which there are many—will preserve all the assertibility facts. Therefore, given thesis (A), any such scheme will provide an adequate manual of translation.

Thus if thesis (A) is correct—if any assertibility-preserving mapping is an adequate translation manual—then, given the proxy-function considerations, it follows that thesis (I) is correct—each of our words is adequately translatable in many nonequivalent ways. And from thesis (I) it can then be argued at stage three (*pace* the reservations I expressed earlier about this move) that there are no such things as meanings. So everything boils down to the plausibility of thesis (A), and hence to the first stage in Quine's constructive analysis where he attempts to show that this thesis may be derived from the pragmatic function of translation manuals. Let us examine this reasoning.

Before proceeding, however, it is important to recognize a severe limitation of the proxy-function considerations—a limitation emphasized by Quine himself. They purport to provide us with alternative, nonequivalent translations of *words*. Hence they threaten the very idea of *word* meanings. But they do not offer uncontroversially nonequivalent translations of *whole sentences*. So they can pose no threat to *sentence* meanings. For although they imply that a foreign sentence, *j*, might be translated equally well as either *h* or *h**, these alternatives are definitionally equivalent to one another and it is far from obvious that they differ in meaning. Therefore one might respond to the proxy-function considerations by conceding that words do not have meanings, but at the same time continuing to maintain that sentences do have them. Thus the thoroughgoing scepticism about meanings to which Quine subscribes requires a thesis stronger than (I); it requires a thesis which would refer to expressions in general, and not merely to words. And the justification for that strengthened version of (I) will not come out of the proxy-function considerations. Now, neither Quine nor anyone else has offered a *demonstration* of the stronger indeterminacy thesis. And although Quine says that he finds it plausible, he admits that he not only has no proof of it, but despairs of finding even a single clear-cut example. As he would put it: whereas the 'inscrutability of reference' (which concerns the translation of *words*) is proved by proxy-function considerations, the 'indeterminacy of translation' (which concerns *sentences*), though likely to be true, is not demonstrable.

Let us therefore return to our scrutiny of the supposedly easier Quinean case against *word* meanings. Our critique of this argument will suggest, I believe, that there is in fact no indeterminacy of word translation—which will imply that there is no indeterminacy of sentence translation either.

In order to derive conditions of adequacy for translation manuals from the requirement that they be useful one must make some assumptions about how such manuals are used and what makes them valuable. On the first point we may suppose that an *H*-speaker, interacting with *J*-speakers, will use manual *T* as follows: instead of saying what he would have said if he were interacting with fellow *H*-speakers he substitutes the translation of what he would have said (i.e. he substitutes the sentence $T(h)$ for the sentence *h*); and when a *J*-speaker makes an utterance he responds as if it were an *H*-speaker making the translation of that utterance (i.e. he imagines that $T(j)$ was uttered rather than *j*). In other words, for an *H*-speaker to adopt manual *T* in his interactions with *J*-speakers is for his expectations regarding a foreign utterance, *j*, to be the same as the expectations he has, when dealing with *H*-speakers, regarding the utterance $T(j)$. As for the question of what it is for such a policy to be successful, i.e. for the manual to be useful, the answer is pretty obvious. A manual is pragmatically adequate if it in fact gives the same sort of ability to operate in the foreign context that we normally enjoy within our own linguistic community. Thus, we are often able to predict, on the basis of someone's utterance, some feature of the environment, or something about what the speaker will do or say. So an adequate translation scheme would provide us with exactly the same ability in dealing with foreigners. Similarly, in our own community we are often able to predict the effects on others of what we say; therefore an adequate translation should also provide that ability in the foreign community.

Now let us see what conclusions about the conditions of adequacy for translation schemes can be drawn from these observations about their use and utility. In the first place, we can see that the facts about which scheme is being used and whether it is working properly are open to ordinary observation. They are entirely determined by observable relations between what is said, the environment, and other behaviour. Such behavioural facts are the only data relevant to the assessment of a translation scheme, because, as we have seen, an adequate manual is one that converts reliable patterns of expectation in the home context into reliable expectations abroad. And whether this is so is a matter of behaviour alone. Thus Quine's behaviourism in this domain is vindicated.

In the second place, we must consider whether it is possible to justify thesis (A): that any assertibility-preserving mapping is adequate. This is the burden of the first stage in Quine's constructive analysis. If (A) does follow from our assumptions about the way manuals are used and about what constitutes successful use, then his proxy-function argument (at the second stage) will show that there are indeed multiple, nonequivalent, adequate translation manuals. And (at the third stage) this lemma will imply (arguably) that word meanings do not exist. But how can principle (A) be supported?

Actually I don't think it can be. The best that can be done to support it, as far as I can see, would go something like this. Consider a translation mapping T that preserves all facts of assertibility. More specifically, suppose that the entire complex of assertibility facts concerning a typical J-speaker consists in $D(j_1, j_2, \ldots)$, and that all the facts concerning what I am disposed to assert are given by $D(h_1, h_2, \ldots)$, and that T matches h_n with j_n. Now suppose I deploy T as a translation manual in my dealings with J speakers. In that case my assertibility dispositions, in those dealings, will exactly match those of the J speakers, and my expectations will be just as reliable as they are at home. Therefore any mapping that preserves all assertibility dispositions is functionally adequate, hence correct.

The flaw in this argument, it seems to me, is that there is too much emphasis on what a person would be disposed to accept under questioning, and not enough on what is actually accepted and on how those conclusions are reached. We can grant that a non-standard manual of translation, T^*, which preserves all the facts of assertibility, will be adequate as far as *some* expectations are concerned— expectations of what the foreigner will be *disposed* to accept (under questioning) in various circumstances, and expectations, given what he is disposed to say, of certain environmental conditions. But it does not follow—and nor would it seem to be true—that such a manual will be perfectly adequate with respect to *all* the predictions that we might want to make: specifically, predictions about what will be spontaneously accepted and predictions about how those commitments will be arrived at.

For people do not produce strings of obviously equivalent sentences; typically, one of them alone is maintained. Thus, in appropriate circumstances I think and say "That is a rabbit"; but I will not think "The cosmic complement of that is the cosmic complement of a rabbit"—even though I might be disposed to work it out and assent to it if queried. Consequently, if we use such facts about *actual* usage, together with a translation scheme, to generate expectations about what foreigners will say under similar circumstances, then only one of the various assertibility-preserving schemes will be right. For remember, in general, how a translation scheme is deployed to generate predictions: we are to have exactly the expectations we would have had if we were dealing with members of our own linguistic community—modulo the substitution of the corresponding foreign sentence for our own. Thus if a foreign speaker makes a certain utterance we are to have the expectations that we would have had if one of our own people had said whatever, according to our translation scheme, translates that utterance. Similarly, if the circumstances are such as to lead us to expect that one of our speakers would make a certain utterance, then we are to expect the foreigner to come out with whatever is the translation of that utterance.

Thus T^* is likely to engender incorrect expectations about what the foreigner will say. In addition, it will fail to predict the foreigner's *inferential* behaviour. For we infer h^* from h, not the other way round. We first observe (or in some other way discover) that "That's a rabbit" is true, and then, given the definition of h^* in terms of h, we reason that "The cosmic complement of *that* is the cosmic complement of a rabbit" must also be true. Moreover, the fact that we reason in this way is a behavioural fact about us—a fact about our behaviour with respect to h and h^*. Consequently a fully adequate translation manual should preserve such behavioural relations, and not merely dispositions to assent and dissent. It should translate h into a sentence of J from which J-speakers infer the sentence into which it translates h^*. That is, since we infer h^* from h, an adequate translation, T, should be such that J-speakers infer $T(h^*)$ from $T(h)$. But suppose that $T(h^*) = j^*$ and $T(h) = j$, whereas $T^*(h^*) = j$ and $T^*(h) = j^*$; and suppose that J-speakers infer j^* from j. Then T^* will not correctly predict the inferential relations, even though it may satisfy Quine's adequacy condition (A), preserving all the assertibility facts.

Having argued against the thesis (A), relied on by Quine, that any assertibility-preserving translation is adequate, I would like to end this chapter by sketching what I believe is a more plausible condition of adequacy (judged by Quine's own pragmatic and behavioural standards) and considering where this would leave us with respect to the issues of multiple translation and the existence of meanings.

Suppose translation manual T functions perfectly well in a certain community as a device of expectation replacement. In other words, if we employ T to transform what we would say at home into what to say in that community, and to determine how to react to what others are saying, we find that everything goes smoothly. It follows that the correlations between environmental circumstances, acceptance of sentences, and other states of mind are the same in the two communities, modulo the substitution of their words for ours—i.e. modulo the replacement of each of our words w with $T(w)$. Now these correlational phenomena, within each community, are each the product of certain deeper general facts—explanatorily basic regularities governing the overall use of the words in relation to one another and to other factors. In so far as the correlations produced by these basic facts are the same, modulo T, within the communities, it must be that the basic facts themselves are the same, modulo T. In other words, if the theory that determines the overall use of *our* words is $\$(w_1,$

$w_2, \ldots$), then the theory that determines the overall use of the foreign words is $T\$$—i.e. $\$(T(w_1), T(w_2), \ldots)$. Thus our conception of a functionally adequate translation scheme presupposes that every person's linguistic behaviour is governed by certain universal principles including a set of interconnected basic regularities for the use of words; and that a correct translation schema is one that matches words governed by the same basic regularities. To put it another way, the difference between the theory \$, which accounts for the use of *our* words, and theory $T\$$, which accounts for the use of the foreign words, is merely that the theory structure, $\$(x_1, x_2, \ldots)$, is occupied on the one hand by our words and on the other hand by the associated foreign words. Thus the property which w_1 has, and which any adequate translation of w_1 must also have, is $(\exists x_2)(\exists x_3) \ldots \$(x_1, x_2, x_3, \ldots)$. Therefore an adequate translation manual is one that preserves the explanatory roles of words, i.e. their basic regularities of use.

That this is indeed our conception is borne out in our practice of translation. Consider, for example, the fact that we translate a foreign word as "red" just in case the foreigners are disposed to ascribe it when red things are under observation. What is being supposed in this practice is that the explanatorily fundamental regularity for our word "red" is roughly:

All uses of "red" stem from the tendency to accept "That's red" iff there is something clearly red under observation,

and that the explanatorily fundamental regularity governing the foreign word, say "rouge", is:

All uses of "rouge" stem from the tendency to accept "Ça c'est rouge" iff there is something clearly red under observation,

and that, in a similar way, the laws governing our "That's . . . " match the laws governing "Ça c'est . . . ".

Suppose that this conception of translation is correct, where does it leave us on the issues of indeterminacy and the existence of meanings? Well, as we have seen, Quine's sceptical argument depends on the assumption that any assertibility-preserving manual is adequate. So the question arises as to whether this assumption is consistent with the use-theoretic picture of translation that we have just arrived at.

Clearly, the answer is No. In the first place, the theory we are deploying to explain and predict both within our own community and (relative to a translation manual) within the foreign community is intended to cover, not merely assent/dissent dispositions, but also what is actually held true, and also the causal relations between these states, the inferential processes that engender them. Therefore, for any expression "k", the theoretical roles of "k" and of "k^*" are bound to differ. In the second place, an assertibility-preserving mapping might translate a single word of one language as a complex expression of the other. But it is not possible for a single word to have the same theoretical role (i.e. to be governed by the same basic use regularities) as a complex expression. For complex expressions will participate in regularities which relate the whole expression to its parts; whereas no such regularity can apply to single words. Thus there are at least some assertibility-preserving schemes which are not adequate translations: namely, those that involve mapping words on to complexes. Moreover, it is precisely this type of mapping that is involved in Quine's proxy-function argument. Remember that in this argument the non-standard mapping T^* takes the term "Socrates" to, for example, "the cosmic complement of Socrates" (or, in general, to "the object that bears relation R to Socrates"), and it takes the predicate "red" to "something that is the cosmic complement of a red thing" (or, in general, to "something that bears relation R to a red thing"). Such mappings, let us grant, do preserve assertibility, but they do not preserve meaning in the intuitive sense. More importantly they do not preserve basic regularities of use; hence they do not provide the sort of translation that best serves the needs of prediction; hence, by Quine's own fundamental standards of adequacy, they are inadequate translation manuals.[2]

Finally, let us consider whether there is any scope at all for mul-

---

[2] Granted, we may make do *in practice* with translations of words into complex expressions. But such translations are not regarded as perfect and are tolerated only when no word-to-word mapping is available. (See Chapter 7, response to Objection 3.) One might wonder whether a perfect translation—a perfect match of theoretical roles—is ever possible. But note that the features of a word to be matched in a perfect translation do not concern all facts about it (e.g. its pronunciation), but merely certain facts regarding the acceptance of sentences containing it.

tiple translation from the perspective of the present conception. To repeat: a translation manual, T, is deployed by converting the theory, $\$(w_1, w_2, \ldots)$, which generates behavioural expectations at home, into a structurally identical theory, $T(\$)$ [i.e. $\$(T(w_1), T(w_2), \ldots)$], which applies abroad; and T is adequate just in case $T(\$)$ is as accurate as $\$$. Given the predominantly behavioural character of these theories, what this strongly suggests is that in order for two manuals T and T^* to be equally good, the theories $T(\$)$ and $T^*(\$)$ must be identical. For if they were not identical, then they would to some degree make different behavioural predictions, and so there would be the potential for one to be better than the other. So the question becomes whether this condition—that $T(\$) = T^*(\$)$—leaves any scope for a difference between T and T^*, and hence any scope for a multiplicity of correct translation manuals.

The answer is that it does—but barely. For suppose there were two non-synonymous words whose uses in relation to one another, to other words, and to environmental circumstances, were perfectly symmetrical. In that case, a translation of a foreign term into one of these words would be just as good as a translation into the other; and we would have a real case of indeterminacy of translation. One hypothetical example of such a phenomenon would be provided by a physical theory containing terms "A" and "B" for two types of fundamental particle, where "A" and "B" play qualitatively identical roles in the theory formulation.[3] The postulates might look something like this:

$$A + A \rightarrow X$$
$$B + B \rightarrow X$$
$$A + B \rightarrow Y$$
$$A + C \rightarrow Z$$
$$B + C \rightarrow Z$$

Thus the uses of "A" and "B" would be exactly similar; and if the same physical theory were formulated by foreigners, but using "A^*" and "B^*" instead of our "A" and "B", then both the translation of

---

[3] I owe this example to Tim Williamson. In Chapter 3 (response to Objection 3) I compare such cases—instances of MEANING DISTRIBUTION—with other forms of holism and indeterminacy.

"*A**" as "*A*" and the translation of "*A**" as "*B*" would preserve usage, and hence be perfectly adequate.[4]

More precisely, suppose:

(a) our theory treats words w_1 and w_2 symmetrically: i.e. $\$(w_1, w_2, \ldots) = \$(w_2, w_1, \ldots)$;

(b) $T(w_n) = v_n$ (where w_1, w_2, \ldots, w_n, \ldots are our words and v_1, v_2, \ldots, v_n, \ldots are words of the foreign language);

(c) $T^*(w_1) = v_2$, $T^*(w_2) = v_1$, and, for $n > 2$, $T^*(w_n) = v_n$.

In that case, given (b),

$$T[\$(w_1, w_2, \ldots)] = \$(v_1, v_2, \ldots),$$

and given (c),

$$T^*[\$(w_1, w_2, \ldots) = \$(v_2, v_1, \ldots).$$

Moreover, from (a) it follows that

$$T[\$(w_1, w_2, \ldots)] = T[\$(w_2, w_1, \ldots)],$$

which, given (b), implies that

$$\$(v_1, v_2, \ldots) = \$(v_2, v_1, \ldots).$$

Therefore

$$T[\$(w_1, w_2, \ldots)] = T^*[\$(w_1, w_2, \ldots)].$$

Thus even though the translation manuals T and T^* are divergent

---

[4] Robert Brandom (in his "The Significance of Complex Numbers for Frege's Philosophy of Mathematics", *Proceedings of the Aristotelian Society* 96 (1995–6), 293–315) suggests that "i" and "$-i$" (the square roots of -1) are instances of this phenomena, providing a genuine case of indeterminacy. For the sake of even greater symmetry (hence more plausible indeterminacy), Hartry Field (in "Some Thoughts on Radical Indeterminacy", *The Monist* 81 (1998), 253–73) imagines a community in which the symbols for the square roots of -1 are "/" and "\"—where "\ = −/" and "/ = −\" are both accepted, and neither is regarded as more definitional than the other.

they are equally adequate since they engender exactly the same theory of the foreigners' behaviour.

However, it is not clear that there are any actual examples of this hypothetical situation—any actual English words w_1 and w_2 that we treat so symmetrically that $\$(w_1, w_2, \ldots) = \$(w_2, w_1, \ldots)$. Certainly there are not going to be many such pairs. And, as I argued earlier (in criticizing the third stage of Quine's constructive analysis), even in this sort of case one need not conclude that the words don't have meanings, but merely that the assignment of their meanings to foreign terms is indeterminate. For example, we would not be compelled to admit that "A" and "B" do not possess meanings; it would be enough, rather, to allow that there is no determinate fact as to whether "A"'s meaning is also possessed by "A^*". As we saw in Chapter 3 (response to Objection 3), neither of the meaning properties, 'x means A' or 'x means B', is constituted by an underlying use regularity—although the pair of them may be said to be *jointly constituted* by a regularity that is symmetrical with respect to the use of a pair of words.

Thus my conclusion is that although the basis of Quine's treatment of meaning may be perfectly reasonable—specifically, his insistence that our conception of meaning be extracted from the pragmatic function of translation, and his insistence that the correctness of a translation manual be evaluated solely on behavioural grounds—the surprising, meaning-sceptical conclusion which he draws does not follow. The best translations, from the point of view of prediction, are those that preserve the theoretical roles, the basic use regularities, of words. Such an adequacy condition will not normally be satisfiable by two nonequivalent translation manuals; hence it provides no grounds for the rejection of meanings. On the contrary, what it suggests is a reduction of meaning properties to basic regularities of use.[5]

[5] I would like to thank Paolo Casalegno for his insightful comments on a draft of this chapter.

10

A Straight Solution to Kripke's Sceptical Paradox

Inspired by Wittgenstein's *Philosophical Investigations*, Saul Kripke has given an account of meaning arguing that, in some sense, there is no such thing.[1] But what exactly is Kripke's sceptical conclusion? Just how are we supposed to interpret the thesis that attributions of meaning do not correspond to facts—or, as he puts it, that "There can be no fact as to what I mean by "plus", or any other word at any time"?[2] Let us look at three possibilities for what Kripke has in mind, to be clarified as we proceed:

(A) Words are meaningless.

(B) Meaning a certain thing by a word is not an *intrinsic* property of a person—not a fact about *him alone*.

(C) Meaning attributions are not rendered true, or false, by any collection of natural, non-semantic facts, but have normative and therefore (in some sense) 'non-factual' content.

To start with, it is evident that Kripke's overall conclusion is not intended to be the stunning, self-defeating claim that all language is senseless. This is clear from the two-pronged structure of his discus-

---

[1] Kripke, *Wittgenstein on Rules and Private Language*. It must be emphasized that Kripke does not himself endorse the reasoning that is suggested to him by reading Wittgenstein—though he does admit to finding it somewhat compelling. So when in what follows I refer to something as "Kripke's conclusion", "Kripke's argument", and so on, I mean merely to be labelling the idea in question as one that Kripke presents as an interpretation of Wittgenstein, without suggesting that he fully believes in it.

[2] Kripke, *Wittgenstein on Rules and Private Language*, 21.

sion. He begins by elaborating what he calls a 'sceptical paradox' whose conclusion is that there are no facts about meaning. This argument consists in entertaining a number of plausible candidates for what the facts of meaning might be, together with demonstrations that none of these candidates meet certain adequacy conditions that any account of meaning must allegedly satisfy. The second part of Kripke's line of thought is what he calls a 'sceptical solution' to the paradox. A straight, or normal, solution, he says, would be the discovery of some mistake in the argument—for example, the calling of attention to some further kind of fact, not previously noticed, that would satisfy the adequacy conditions. Kripke's sceptical solution, on the other hand, is not intended to refute the sceptical conclusion or to suggest that it cannot be validly drawn, but rather to show that it is not as paradoxical or radical as it might at first appear to be. Specifically, the idea is to show that the sceptical conclusion does not undermine our ordinary talk about meaning. It need not induce us to reject claims of the form, 'Jones means PLUS by "plus"'. It does not even compel us to deny 'It is a *fact* that Jones means PLUS by "plus"' or 'It is *true* that Jones means PLUS by "plus"'—provided that these are understood (as they *are* in non-philosophical contexts) as saying hardly more than 'Jones means PLUS by "plus"'.

Thus amongst our various construals of the thesis that meaning is nonexistent, there is one—evidently the most dramatic one—that Kripke quite obviously does not have in mind. He is not claiming that meanings, like ghosts and perpetual motion machines, are nothing but illusion. For in that case we would be forced to abandon our ordinary practice of meaning attribution. The moral might perhaps be put as follows. Strictly speaking Kripke is not denying that statements attributing meaning may be true or false, and that when they are true there is a fact corresponding to the statement. His view is rather that there are no facts *of a certain sort*—we could call them 'genuine facts'—regarding meaning; and, moreover, that this is surprising and important. For we are very tempted to think that the facts of meaning are of this special sort and, for this reason, we have been content to employ claims about meaning in linguistics and psychology.

In accordance with this view of the matter, a second possible construal of the sceptical conclusion is that it denies, not the *existence* of meaning, but rather that meaning is a purely personal affair. This idea—that 'meanings are not in the head'—is already implicit is

Kripke's *Naming and Necessity*,[3] and has become familiar through the work of Hilary Putnam and Tyler Burge.[4] It implies that if Jones means addition by "plus" then there is no fact solely about Jones—no intrinsic characteristic of Jones alone—in virtue of which this is the case. This construal of Kripke's thesis employs the old, but hard to explicate, distinction between intrinsic and relational properties. Roughly speaking, the intrinsic properties of an object are those, like 'being spherical' and 'being an electron', that make reference to no other object; whereas relational properties, like 'being one mile from the Earth's surface' or 'being taller than average' do require for their possession the existence of other objects.

Now philosophers have occasionally used "nonexistent" to mean "nonintrinsic". For example, it is sometimes said that there is no such property as redness, where the intention is to claim that a statement of the form "*X* is red" is not simply about *X*, the thing in itself, as one might at first suppose, but is really about relations between the thing and people. For it might be thought that "*X* is red" means something like "*X* would produce such-and-such sensations in such-and-such circumstances". Similarly, the content of Kripke's sceptical conclusion about meaning could be taken as the claim that meaning a certain thing by a word is not an intrinsic property of a person.

It is tempting to think that this is precisely what Kripke has in mind. Many of his formulations in *Wittgenstein on Rules and Private Language* suggest it: for example,

We must give up the attempt to find any fact *about me* in virtue of which I mean PLUS . . . (p. 108)

Wittgenstein's sceptic argues that he knows of no fact *about an individual* that could constitute his state of meaning PLUS . . . (p. 39)

The sceptic holds that no fact *about my past history*—nothing that was ever *in my mind*, or *in my external behavior*—establishes that I meant PLUS . . . (p. 13)

---

[3] Kripke argues in *Naming and Necessity* that the reference of a name is determined, not by anything in the speaker's mind, but by what his teachers were referring to when they introduced him to the name—which, in turn, is determined by what *their* teachers were referring to, and so on. See Chapter 5 for further discussion.

[4] Hilary Putnam, "The Meaning of 'Meaning' "; Tyler Burge, "Individualism and the Mental".

So whatever 'looking into *my mind*' may be, the sceptic asserts that even if God were to do it, he still could not determine that I meant addition by "plus". (p. 14, emphases added in all examples)

However, although Kripke evidently agrees that meaning is not a purely personal property, it emerges that his sceptical conclusion is more radical than this. For the mere fact that meaning is not intrinsic leaves it open that when we say 'Jones means PLUS by "plus"' we are asserting the existence of a certain natural *relation* between Jones and a linguistic community. In other words, the rejection of individualism regarding meaning leaves open the following picture: 'meaning PLUS' is a property of the public word "plus", a genuine, naturalistic property that it has in virtue of a certain communal use; and anyone uses "plus" with that meaning if his usage of the word is in rough accordance with community standards. Here, the fact that Jones means PLUS by "plus" would be partly a fact about Jones and partly a fact about his linguistic community. No wonder God could not determine what Jones means just by looking into Jones's mind.

Although this interpretation is suggested, as I have indicated, by *some* of Kripke's remarks, it is quite clear on balance that it is not what he intends. Most of Kripke's formulations imply the much stronger claim that that there is simply no genuine fact at all—not merely no fact solely about Jones—in virtue of which Jones means PLUS. For example, he says:

[N]o 'truth conditions' or 'corresponding facts' in the world exist that make a statement like 'Jones, like many of us, means addition by "+"' true. (p. 86)

[Wittgenstein] does not give a 'straight' solution, pointing out to the silly sceptic a hidden fact he overlooked, a condition in the world which constitutes my meaning addition by "plus". In fact he agrees with his own hypothetical sceptic that there is no such fact in either the 'internal' or the 'external' world. (p. 69)

It is important to realize that we are *not* looking for necessary and sufficient conditions (truth conditions) for following a rule, or an analysis of what such rule-following 'consists in'. Indeed such conditions would constitute a 'straight' solution to the sceptical problem, and have been rejected. (p. 87)[5]

---

[5] Kripke's discussion is supposed to concern both meaning and rule-following. Indeed he switches between one topic and the other without warning, as if there were no difference between them. He is presupposing, it would seem, that meaning PLUS

Moreover, at the very end of his essay Kripke considers the idea that the meaning of a word might be constituted by facts about its use within a linguistic community, and he rejects it, complaining that "Such a theory would be a theory of the *truth* conditions of such assertions as 'By "plus" we mean such and such a function' "(p. 111). And this he takes to be incompatible with the sceptical conclusion. Thus Kripke does not wish to assert merely that meaning is not a personal matter.

These passages point us towards what I think is the correct interpretation of Kripke's sceptical conclusion. It is intended to deny the reducibility (in *any* sense) of meaning attributions to non-semantic statements. It says that neither conceptual analysis nor empirical theory will permit the constitution of semantic facts by facts about, say, mental processes, overt behaviour, or communal use. The thesis is, in other words, that meaning attributions are not made true by any conglomeration of non-semantic phenomena—so they cannot be incorporated into any grand unified theory of the natural world.

This construal of Kripke's conclusion is suggested in the first place by the shape of his argument. For, as I have said, the strategy of the sceptical paradox is to consider a series of non-semantic candidates for the facts in virtue of which "plus" means what it does, and to argue against each of them, concluding that there are no facts of the right sort to identify with facts about meaning.

In addition, we can perhaps shed light on the character of Kripke's sceptical conclusion by comparing it to the emotivist position on ethics. The general rationale for the emotivist point of view lies in the idea that there are types of utterance—including expressions of value and (perhaps) first-person sensation reports—that, on the basis of their syntactic form, we are tempted to assimilate to

by w is the same thing as following a certain rule for the use of w: namely, to apply w to a triple of numbers, $\langle x,y,z \rangle$, if and only if $x + y = z$. It seems to me, however, that our desire to apply our word "plus" to certain triples and not others is a consequence, partly, of our proclivity for truth, and not merely of our meaning what we do by the word; therefore, meaning does not so obviously reduce to rule-following. This is not to deny that parallel questions may be raised about, on the one hand, what it is to mean a given thing and, on the other hand, what it is to (implicitly) follow a given rule; nor is it to deny that certain parallel difficulties and strategies for overcoming them will arise. Indeed, it seems to me that the straight solution that I will offer to Kripke's problem of meaning will suggest an analogous approach to rule following. In particular, it will be important not to take for granted that the rule that is followed may be 'read off' the dispositions constituting it. But rule-following is too large a topic to address here.

descriptions, expressing 'genuine facts', but that, in light of their role in the language, should properly be regarded as entirely different speech acts. Specifically, it is claimed by emotivists that "X is good" does not ascribe an objective property to X, but rather expresses the speaker's pro-attitude towards X. Similarly, it might be thought that, syntactic appearances to the contrary, attributions of meaning are not used in a way that is characteristic of descriptions, but have, in particular, a normative function, and in that respect are non-factual. As Kripke points out, when we say Jones means PLUS by "plus" we imply not that Jones *will* answer 125 when asked to add 68 and 57 but rather that he *should* answer that way.

Adopting this interpretation of Kripke's position, let us proceed to scrutinize his argument in favour of it. On what basis does he conclude that attributions of meaning are not rendered true or false by natural facts? In particular, what is supposed to be wrong with the view (which, *pace* Kripke, would seem to be Wittgenstein's actual view) that the meaning of a word consists in how we are disposed to use it? Let us review his various arguments to see if they really do undermine the use theory of meaning.

Kripke's first observation about this account of meaning—which he calls "the dispositional theory"—is, as he puts it, that

[a]s a candidate for a 'fact' that determines what I mean, it fails to satisfy the basic condition on such a candidate . . . that it should *tell* me what I ought to do in each new instance. (p. 24)

The point is that we feel *guided* and *justified* in our linguistic behaviour by what we mean, as if directed by a set of instructions; but nothing of this sort could be accommodated by a brute disposition to say certain things and not others.

Now (as we noted in Chapter 8) it might seem odd that Kripke should state this 'guidance requirement' so forcefully. For he himself comes to the view that there are in general no such 'guiding' facts of meaning—the sequence of rules to interpret rules must come to an end somewhere. As he says later in the book, "ultimately we reach a level where we act without any reason in terms of which we can justify our action. We act unhesitatingly but *blindly*" (p. 87), and if this is going to be admitted eventually, then how could it have been insisted at the beginning that facts of meaning must have the character of instructions? The answer is that Kripke never really endorsed the 'guidance' requirement on an account of meaning. Rather, one of the purposes of the initial phase of his discussion—his presentation of the sceptical paradox—was to show that this requirement *cannot* be satisfied; and one of the purposes of the second phase—his sceptical solution—is to show that it *need not* be satisfied. The bottom line is that if the use theory is entirely adequate except for failing to accommodate the intuition that meanings provide guidance, then the proper conclusion is not that meanings are not dispositions, but a strengthened conviction that the naive intuition of guidance should not be taken too literally.

But is the use theory otherwise adequate? Kripke's second concern is that such an account leaves no room for the possibility that someone might use a word *incorrectly*. For if a person's meaning consists in what he is disposed to say, then what he does say (being the actualized part of what he is disposed to say) must be perfectly in accordance with his meaning. For example, if in normal circumstances someone is asked to add 68 to 57 and gets 115 we would be inclined to judge that he has made a mistake—perhaps he has forgotten to carry. But according to the dispositional account we must judge, it seems, that he hasn't made a mistake at all, but rather that he means by the word "plus" some weird function whose value for arguments 68 and 57 truly is 115.

As Kripke acknowledges, this objection works against only a crude form of dispositional analysis, whereby

> S means PLUS by "plus" iff
> S is disposed to apply "plus" to a triple of numbers $\langle x,y,z \rangle$
> iff $x + y = z$,

and, in general,

> S means F by w iff
> S is disposed to apply w to a thing iff it is f.

He proceeds, therefore, to consider more sophisticated dispositional analyses that would make allowances for mistakes. These take the form

> S means F by w iff
> S is disposed, when in 'ideal' circumstances I, to apply w to a thing iff it is f,

where 'ideal' circumstances I are supposed to preclude conditions in which we would be prone to error. However, as Kripke shows, it turns out to be impossible to specify the circumstances I in a satisfactory manner. If we articulate them as "circumstances in which mistakes do not occur", this is tantamount to "circumstances in which S is disposed to apply w to an f iff w means F"—so the analysis becomes circular. But if we insist that the ideal circumstances be spelled out in wholly non-semantic terms—along the lines of "circumstances in which S is not drunk, not tired, has an infinitely large brain, will live forever, . . ."—then we enter the realm of science fiction and have little reason to believe that the resulting biconditional will be true.

Kripke supposes that this argument refutes the dispositional/use approach. In fact, however, there remains the very real possibility that the right dispositional analyses do not have the abstract form he assumes they must have: namely,

S means F by w iff $R(S, f, w)$,

whereby for someone's word to mean F is for it to stand in some relation R to fs. Why could it not be rather that

S means PLUS by w iff $R_1(S, w)$,
S means CHAIR by w iff $R_2(S, w)$,
. . . etc.,

where the use properties, R_1, R_2, . . . etc., make no reference to addition, chairs, . . ., etc.?

The basis for implicitly ruling out this more liberal, non-relational form of use theory is the following assumption:

[The simple dispositional analysis] gives a criterion that will tell me what number theoretic function ϕ I mean by a binary function symbol 'f', namely: The referent ϕ of 'f' is that unique binary function ϕ such that I am disposed, if queried about '$f(m, n)$', where 'm' and 'n' are numerals denoting particular numbers m and n, to reply 'p', where 'p' is a numeral denoting $\phi(m, n)$. The criterion is meant to enable us to 'read off' which function I mean by a given function symbol from my disposition. (p. 26)

Thus Kripke is presupposing that one will be able to 'read off' what S means by w by inspecting S's dispositions for the use of w. And that requires there to be a theory of the form

S means F by w iff $R(S, f, w)$,

where in order to articulate a given meaning-constituting property we have to deploy the very meaning it constitutes. In other words, he rejects the more liberal use-theoretic analyses on the grounds that it would not be possible to tell, merely by scrutinizing a given use property, which meaning property (if any) it constitutes.

However, as we saw in Chapter 2 (section 2) and Chapter 3 (response to Objection 4), the expectation that one will be able to read off (and hence to explain) which particular meaning is engendered by a given meaning-constituting property is misguided. It has its origin in the Constitution Fallacy—the assumption that constituent structure is preserved under reductive analysis. Once we are alert to this mistake and have recognized that the analysis of (for example) 'x means PLUS' need not incorporate any analysis of 'x means y' then we can easily abandon both the reading-off expectation and the associated demand for a theory of the sort that Kripke presupposes.

There is, moreover, no difficulty, within the more liberal use-theoretic approach, in accommodating the phenomenon of mistakes. It is trivial, for example, that

> If S means CHAIR by w, then S's application of w to a thing is correct iff that thing is a chair and mistaken if it is not.

And given our use-theoretic analysis of the property of 'meaning CHAIR' we can infer that

> If $R_2(S, w)$, then S's application of w to a thing is correct iff that thing is a chair and mistaken if it is not.

Thus having acknowledged the Constitution Fallacy and freed ourselves from the requirement that any fact underlying the possession of a meaning must be something from which one can read off what that meaning is, we can see that the need to accommodate mistakes places no constraint at all on what those underlying facts might be.

A third and related argument of Kripke's—one to which I have already alluded—is that the use theorist misconstrues the link between meaning and verbal behaviour, taking the relationship to be descriptive when it really is normative. For the import of meaning

PLUS by "+" is not that one *will* or *would* assent to "68 + 57 = 125", but rather that one *ought to* assent to it.

This point, while correct in itself, can easily lead to two mistakes. The first I have just addressed: it is simply not the case that a use theory implies infallibility. The second mistake is to suppose that the normative implications of meaning cannot be reconciled with a naturalistic reduction: to reason that since, given what Jones means by "plus", "68", and his other words, he ought to affirm "68 + 57 = 125", and since it is impossible for a purely factual antecedent to imply a normative consequent, then it must be that the assumptions about Jones's meaning are not purely factual.

It seems clear (as we saw in detail in Chapter 8) that this argument is no good—specifically, that its final premise is false. For there are numerous cases of obviously pure facts implying obviously normative conclusions. Consider the fairly uncontroversial universal principles: "Human beings should be treated with respect" and "One should believe the truth", which imply respectively "If Jones is a human being, then he ought to be treated with respect" and "If it is true that 68 + 57 = 125, then one ought to believe it". The general point here is that in any normative realm—ethical, pragmatic, aesthetic, or epistemological—there are bound to be principles specifying the normative import of a range of non-normative circumstances. And such principles will entail violations of the crucial premise.

Nor is it hard to see in particular why meaning—construed in terms of use—should have normative implications. For knowledge is valuable (at least for its practical benefits and maybe even for its own sake); so evidently we ought to strive for it: there are certain propositions—namely, true ones—that we ought to believe. Moreover, given our language, we must express each of our beliefs in a particular way. Therefore, within a given linguistic practice, certain sentences ought to be affirmed and others not.

In other words, one ought (other things being equal) to assent to the truth. In particular, one ought to assent to the proposition that 68 + 57 = 125. Therefore one ought to assent to any sentence that one understands to express that proposition. Now, given proficiency and participation in a linguistic practice in which the constituents of the sentence "68 + 57 = 125" are used in certain ways, one will understand that sentence to express the proposition that 68 + 57 = 125. Therefore, given participation in such a linguistic practice, one ought to assent to the sentence "68 + 57 = 125". Thus the use theory has no difficulty in accommodating the normative implications of meaning.

A fourth argument against the use theory, apparently given some weight by Kripke (pp. 77–8), is based on the idea that we should abandon the traditional conception of the meaning of a sentence as consisting in its *truth conditions* in favour of a conception of meaning as consisting in *assertibility conditions*, i.e. circumstances of appropriate use. His implicit line of thought appears to be that since the meaning of the sentence 'Jones means PLUS by "plus"' is given by its assertibility conditions, we should not expect it to have any nontrivial reductive analysis. That is to say, we should not expect there to be any collection of more basic facts—e.g. facts about usage—in virtue of which it is true or false.

The trouble with this reasoning is not merely that it fails to take us to the supposed conclusion (namely that there are no facts to which attributions of meaning correspond), but that it takes us to precisely the opposite conclusion. We may well concede the superiority of 'assertibility conditions' over 'truth conditions' as the central notion in terms of which meaning should be explicated. But all we are entitled to infer from this concession is that *some* sentence might be meaningful yet not have a reductive analysis. It does not follow that, in particular, *meaning-attributions* might not have them. On the contrary, endorsement of the assertibility conception of meaning is a commitment to the view that they *do* have them. According to this conception, the claim that sentence *u* means so-and-so reduces to the claim that *u* has such-and-such assertibility conditions.

To see this more concretely, consider the assertibility conditions that Kripke suggests for meaning attributions:

Smith will judge Jones to mean addition by "plus" only if he judges that Jones' answers to particular addition problems agree with those *he* is inclined to give, or, if they occasionally diverge, he can interpret Jones as at least following the proper procedure . . . If Jones consistently fails to give responses in agreement (in this broad sense) with Smith's, Smith will judge that he does not mean addition by "plus". (p. 90)

Thus what Kripke is maintaining is that we are entitled to say 'Jones means addition by "plus"' whenever we are entitled to believe that his responses more or less coincide with ours—i.e. that his dispositions to use the term match ours. In other words, we may infer that

Jones means addition by "plus" from our belief that his basic use of the term is the same as ours. Thus the 'use-theoretic' truth conditions for attributions of meaning are entailed—and are certainly not precluded—by the assertibility conditions that Kripke endorses.

A final argument, suggested in Kripke's discussion, is that the meaning of a word could not reside in its use, since our dispositions regarding, for example, the predicate "plus" would have been exactly the same even if the meaning and extension of the predicate had been slightly different. For it is possible for there to be a foreign community whose use of the predicate "plus" has been, always will be, and would, in all hypothetical circumstances, be the same as ours, but whose predicate is true of a slightly different set of triples of numbers—the difference concerning only numbers that are ungraspably huge. And if this is so, then usage does not determine extension and so cannot constitute meaning.

The trouble with this reasoning is that it assumes the very thing that it is supposed to establish: namely, that a word whose use is *exactly* the same as the use of our word "plus" might none the less have a different meaning and extension. For to insist, without argument, on there being such a possibility is simply to beg the question against the use theory of meaning. What does seem intuitively right is that there are possible *complex* expressions—definable in terms of "plus"—whose extensions diverge from that of "plus" in the slight way imagined. But no complex expression—since it will inevitably bear certain use relations to its constituents—can have exactly the same use as a primitive expression. Therefore, in order to construct his counter example to the use theory, Kripke must assume in addition that there could be a *primitive* term (on a par with "plus") that is coextensive with one of those possible complex expressions, and that, if there were such a primitive, its use (including dispositions concerning the divergent cases) would be identical to our use of "plus". But it is plausible to suppose that a foreign word could acquire such an extension only if either it were defined in terms of some word meaning the same as "plus", or it were applied in some *definite* way to certain triples that, given our limitations, are beyond our definite range of application of "plus"; and in neither of these cases would it be correct to say that the use of the foreign word is *exactly* like our use of "plus". Thus what Kripke needs to assume in order to construct a counterexample is intuitively implausible and simply begs the question against the use theory of meaning.

Notice, by the way, that in denying the possibility of there being two words with the same use but different meanings, one is not saying that it is an entirely objective, determinate matter which body of facts about use constitutes a given meaning property, and hence which meaning property is constituted by a given body of facts about use. A use theorist could concede that, for all we can know, any of a variety of slightly different meanings might be the one engendered by a given use regularity. But this is not to allow that different instances of that usage, in different communities, might go with different meanings. Similarly, in considering whether to apply a vague predicate to some object, we may feel that there is no determinate fact of the matter as to whether it applies; but this is not a licence to think that it sometimes applies and sometimes does not. Thus in so far as Kripke's point is merely that the match up between meanings and facts of use is somewhat indeterminate, this should be conceded; but it does not conflict with the thesis that meanings are constituted from such facts.[6]

Nor is this 'indeterminacy thesis' especially radical, for such indeterminacy is commonplace even within uncontroversially 'factual' domains. The relations between the length of an object and the (variable) relative location of its atomic constituents, and between the temperature of a gas and the motion of its molecules, are not fully determinate either. But we are not inclined to deny the constitutive relations between these properties, or to suppose that in talking of length and temperature we have left the realm of physical discourse.

Having examined all Kripke's arguments, both explicit and implicit, for the irreducibility of meaning, I conclude that his sceptical thesis is unjustified. He has given no good reason to reject Wittgenstein's view of what the meaning of a word consists in:

For a *large* class of cases—though not for all—in which we employ the word

---

[6] As I argued in Chapter 3, the fact about the use of "plus" that constitutes its meaning is that a certain use regularity is explanatorily basic with respect to overall use of the word: i.e. that a certain generalization regarding its use, together with the analogous generalizations concerning other terms, provide the best account of our deployment of the word. Which such generalizations provide the 'best' explanation may be somewhat indeterminate. This explains how it can sometimes be unclear whether some new deployment of a word amounts to a change in its meaning or not.

"meaning" it can be defined thus: the meaning of a word is its use in the language.[7]

The point of this book has been to clarify and support this idea.[8]

[7] *Philosophical Investigations*, sect. 43. Wittgenstein is sometimes read as allowing here that his account of meaning as use does not apply to all words. But I think that what he has in mind, rather, is that the account does not cover all senses of the word "meaning" (e.g. "I was meaning to send you the cheque").

[8] This chapter is a revised extract from my "Wittgenstein and Kripke on the Nature of Meaning", *Mind and Language* 5 (1990), 105–21. I would like to thank Ned Block, Warren Goldfarb, Itziar Laka, Charles Marks, Gabriel Segal, and Meredith Williams for their help with that paper.

11

Conclusion

Let me summarize what has been done here. The main aim was to demystify the phenomenon of linguistic meaning—to characterize the underlying nature of meaning in such a way that its familiar attributes would become intelligible. And so we had to ask whether a word's meaning derives from what it refers to, from the way it was defined, from some associated mental image, from its evolutionary function, from a prototype structure, an inferential role, or from something else The basic strategy for answering this question was to scrutinize seven general facts about meaning—facts that have often been thought to provide clues to its origin. A striking result, however, was that only one of these facts proved to be capable of guiding us toward a theory of how meaning arises. The other six could be explained quite independently of any such account: in particular—

(1) *Understanding*. When we understand an expression we of course *know* what it means. But this triviality does not yield an epistemological condition on what meaning-constituting properties must be like—because our knowledge that our expressions possess those properties is merely *implicit*. *Whatever* they might happen to be, a speaker of the language — simply in virtue of the fact that his terms do possess those properties, and despite his having no ability at all to articulate such facts—will qualify as implicitly knowing them, and thereby as implicitly knowing the meanings of his terms.

(2) *Relationality*. The fact that a word means what it does is, intuitively, a matter of its standing in the relation of *meaning* or *expressing* to a particular concept: e.g. "chien" is correlated with the concept DOG. It remains to identify what feature of a word is responsible for its being related to its particular meaning, i.e. for its expressing that concept. However, this meaning-constituting property certainly need

not itself be relational. In particular, it need not involve some causal connection between the word and certain things (e.g. dogs) to which the word applies.

(3) *Aboutness*. The reference or extension of a term—what that term is *about*—is determined by the concept it expresses: e.g. x means DOG $\rightarrow$ x is true of dogs. However, the minimalistic/deflationary theory of truth (the theory that designates such conditionals as conceptually fundamental) shows that reference determination will take place regardless of how meaning properties are constituted. Only from an inflationary point of view (in which truth, satisfaction, and reference are *not* defined by such conditionals, but are instead assumed to be susceptible of reductive analysis) can there be a question (the 'problem of error') about how to reconcile the basic nature of meaning (e.g. the analysis of 'x means DOG') with its referential import (e.g. its capacity to ensure that x is true of dogs).

(4) *Aprioricity*. The decision to mean one thing rather than another by a word is not designed to accommodate experience; it is an a priori matter. None the less, one should not require of a theory of meaning that it *explain* the a priori—that it show how certain of our commitments (e.g. in logic, arithmetic, and geometry) are the product of mere meaning, hence knowable a priori. For, in the first place, these commitments might (in light of Quine's web-of-belief model) *not* be a priori. In the second place, even if they are, it would seem perfectly possible for someone (e.g. an intuitionist) to understand them without agreeing that they are correct; thus, substantial (and hence deniable) commitments cannot be essential for the terms in which they are formulated to mean what they do. And in the third place, knowing of some proposition that it is the meaning of a given sentence is orthogonal to, and can have no bearing on, the question of whether that proposition is true; so even though meaning-constituting commitments are a priori, their aprioricity cannot issue from their status as meaning constituting.

(5) *Compositionality*. Each sentence derives its meaning from what its component words mean and from how they are put together. And this is so because (just as 'being red' is constituted by 'emitting light of such-and-such frequency') the meaning property of a sentence (e.g. 'x means DOGS BARK') *is nothing over and above* the property

of being constructed in a certain way from primitives with certain meanings (e.g. '*x* results from substituting words whose meanings are DOG and BARK into a schema whose meaning is *NS V*'). In this explanation of how *sentence* meanings are 'composed', absolutely nothing is presupposed about the source of *word* meaning (e.g. about which properties constitute '*x* means DOG', '*x* means BARK', or '*x* means *NS V*'). Thus the possibility of compositionality imposes no constraint on how the meanings of words are engendered.

(6) *Normativity*. Meaning has normative import: e.g. *x* means DOG → *x should ideally* be applied only to dogs. But even so, it may be in virtue of something entirely *non*-normative that a term means what it does. Given the practical benefits of true belief, and given the correlation between believing a proposition and accepting some sentence that expresses it (or means it), we can easily explain why a word, depending on whether is means DOG, CAT, or ELECTRON, ought to be applied to dogs, cats, or electrons. No assumptions at all need to be made about what type of underlying property of words provides them with their meanings.

Thus, none of these six prominent features of meaning, either separately or jointly, is able to help us in the slightest to narrow down whether a word's meaning stems from its referent, or its inferential role, or its evolutionary function, or whatever; not even a single one of the original candidates can be eliminated. However, in contrast with those pseudo-constraints, there is a further fact about meaning that *does* finally point us towards its basic nature: namely, the fact that all our particular applications of a given word result, in part, from what we mean by it. This characteristic is explained—and I believe can *only* be explained—by the theory proposed here, whereby meaning properties are reduced to regularities of use. More specifically, the theory is that each word means what it does in virtue of the fact that a certain acceptance property of the word is explanatorily fundamental vis-à-vis its overall deployment (where what I call an 'acceptance property' specifies conditions in which designated sentences containing the word are held true). This proposal was forced to confront a formidable barrage of objections; but in every case an adequate reply was shown to be available. Special attention was devoted to the influential sceptical arguments of Quine and Kripke to the effect that *no* account of how word meanings are constituted could ever be forthcoming. But Quine wrongly presupposes that the only types of linguistic behaviour that can objectively pertain to the meaning of an expression are assent/dissent dispositions. And Kripke wrongly presupposes that a word's meaning-constituting property would have to enable us to 'read off' which meaning it engenders.

Having dealt with all imaginable objections to the analysis of meaning in terms of use, and having thereby clarified and supported the theory, it remains to explore its philosophical ramifications. One immediate result, as we saw, is that a radical 'semantic deflationism' becomes viable—a view that combines the use theory of meaning with minimalistic accounts of truth and reference. Therefore, given the heavy role played by our concepts of meaning and truth within just about all areas of the subject, we can expect fresh light to be shed on a considerable number of philosophical problems. But to set out what will then be discerned would require another book.

Bibliography

ADAMS, F., and AIZAWA, K. "Fodorian Semantics", in S. Stich and T. Warfield (eds.), *Mental Representation* (q.v.), 223–42.

AYER, A. J. *Language, Truth and Logic* (1936). New York: Dover, 1952.

BELNAP, N. "Tonk, Plonk and Plink", *Analysis* 22 (1962), 130–3.

BLACKBURN, S. "The Individual Strikes Back", *Synthese* 10 (1984), 281–301.

BLOCK, N. "Advertisment for a Semantics for Psychology", in P. French, T. Uehling, and H. Wettstein (eds.), *Midwest Studies in Philosophy* 10. Minneapolis, Minn.: University of Minnesota Press, 1986.

—— "An Argument for Holism", *Proceedings of the Aristotelian Society* 95 (1994–5), 151–69.

BOGHOSSIAN, P. "Analyticity", in C. Wright and R. Hale (eds.), *A Companion to the Philosophy of Language*. Oxford: Blackwell, 1997.

—— "Analyticity Reconsidered", *Nous* 30 (1996), 360–91.

—— "Does an Inferential Role Semantics Rest upon a Mistake?", *Mind and Language* 8 (1993), 1–27.

—— "The Rule Following Considerations", *Mind* 98 (1989), 507–50.

—— "What the Externalist Can Know A Priori", *Proceedings of the Aristotelian Society* 97 (1996–7), 161–75.

BRANDOM, R. *Making it Explicit*. Cambridge, Mass.: Harvard University Press, 1994.

—— "The Significance of Complex Numbers for Frege's Philosophy of Mathematics", *Proceedings of the Aristotelian Society* 96 (1995–6), 293–315.

BURGE, T. "Individualism and the Mental", in P. French, T. Uehling, and H. Wettstein (eds.), *Midwest Studies in Philosophy* 4: 73–121. Minneapolis, Minn.: University of Minnesota Press, 1979.

—— "Reference and Proper Names", *Journal of Philosophy* 50 (1973), 425–39.

CARNAP, R. "Empiricism, Semantics and Ontology" (1950), repr. in his *Meaning and Necessity*, 2nd edn. Chicago, Ill.: University of Chicago Press, 1956.

—— *Der Logische Aufbau der Welt*. Berlin: Schlachtensee Weltkreis-Verlag, 1928.

CHOMSKY, N. *Knowledge of Language*. New York: Praeger, 1986.

COZZO, C. *Meaning and Argument*. Stockholm Studies in Philosophy, no. 17. Stockholm: Almqvist & Wiksell International, 1994.

CUMMINS, R. "The Lot of the Causal Theory of Mental Content", *Journal of Philosophy*, 94 (1997), 535–42.

DAVIDSON, D. *Inquiries into Truth and Interpretation*. Oxford: Clarendon Press, 1984.

DAVIES, M. *Meaning, Quantification, Necessity*. London: Routledge & Kegan Paul, 1981.

DEVITT, M. *Coming To Our Senses*. Cambridge: Cambridge University Press, 1996.

DONELLAN, K. "Reference and Definite Descriptions", *Philosophical Review*, 75 (1966), 281–304.

DRETSKE, F. I. *Knowledge and the Flow of Information*. Cambridge, Mass.: MIT Press, 1981.

DUMMETT, M. *Elements of Intuitionism*. Oxford: Clarendon Press, 1977.

—— *The Logical Basis of Metaphysics*. Cambridge, Mass.: Harvard University Press, 1991.

—— "Truth", *Proceedings of the Aristotelian Society* 59 (1958–9), 141–62.

EVANS, G. "The Causal Theory of Names", *Proceedings of the Aristotelian Society*, supp. vol. 47 (1973), 187–208.

FIELD, H. "The Deflationary Conception of Truth", in Graham MacDonald and Crispin Wright (eds.), *Fact, Science, and Morality*. Oxford: Blackwell, 1986.

—— "Deflationist Views of Meaning and Content", *Mind* 103 (1994), 249–85.

—— "Logic, Meaning and Conceptual Role", *Journal of Philosophy* 74 (1977), 379–409.

—— "Some Thoughts on Radical Indeterminacy", *The Monist* 81 (1998), 253–73.

—— "Tarski's Theory of Truth", *Journal of Philosophy* 69 (1972), 347–75.

FODOR, J. *Psychosemantics*. Cambridge, Mass.: MIT Press, 1987.

—— "There are no Recognitional Concepts; Not Even RED", in E. Villanueva (ed.), *Philosophical Issues*, vol. 9. Atascadero, Calif.: Ridgeview, 1998.

—— and LEPORE, E. *Holism: A Shopper's Guide*. Oxford: Blackwell, 1991.

—— —— "The Pet Fish and the Red Herring: Why Concepts Aren't Prototypes", *Cognition* 58 (1996), 243–76.

—— —— "Why Meaning (Probably) Isn't Conceptual Role", *Mind and Language* 6 (1991), 328–43.

FOSTER, J. "Meaning and Truth Theory", in G. Evans and J. McDowell (eds.), *Truth and Meaning*. Oxford: Clarendon Press, 1975.

FREGE, G. "On Sense and Reference", *Translations from the Philosophical Writings of Gottlob Frege*, ed. P. Geach and M. Black. Oxford: Blackwell, 1952.

—— "On the Foundations of Geometry", First Series (1903) and Second Series (1906), in his *Collected Papers on Mathematical Logic and Philosophy*, ed. Brian McGuiness. Oxford: Blackwell, 1983.

—— *Philosophical and Mathematical Correspondence.* Chicago, Ill.: University of Chicago Press, 1986.

GIBBARD, A. "Meaning and Normativity", in E. Villanueva (ed.), *Philosophical Issues*, vol. 5: *Truth and Rationality*, 95–115. Atascadero, Calif.: Ridgeview, 1994.

GODFREY-SMITH, P. "A Continuum of Semantic Optimism", in S. Stich and T. Warfield (eds.), *Mental Representation* (q.v.), 259–77.

GOLDFARB, W. "Kripke on Wittgenstein on Rules", *Journal of Philosophy* 82 (1985), 471–88.

GRICE, P. "Meaning", *Philosophical Review* 66 (1957), 377–88.

—— "Utterer's Meaning and Intention", *Philosophical Review* 78 (1969), 147–77.

HARMAN, G. "Conceptual Role Semantics", *Notre Dame Journal of Formal Logic* 23 (1982), 242–56.

—— "Meaning and Semantics", in M. K. Munitz and P. Unger (eds.), *Semantics and Philosophy*. New York: New York University Press, 1974.

—— "(Nonsolipsistic) Conceptual Role Semantics", in E. LePore (ed.), *New Directions in Semantics*. London: Academic Press, 1987.

HIGGINBOTHAM, J. "Knowledge of Reference", in A. George (ed.), *Reflections on Chomsky*. Oxford: Blackwell, 1989.

HORWICH, P. "Chomsky versus Quine on the Analytic–Synthetic Distinction", *Proceedings of the Aristotelian Society* 92 (1991–2), 95–108.

—— "The Composition of Meanings", *Philosophical Review* 106 (1997), 503–31.

—— "Concept Constitution", in E. Villanueva (ed.), *Philosophical Issues*, vol. 9: *Concepts*. Atascadero, Calif.: Ridgeview, 1998.

—— "A Defense of Conventionalism", in G. MacDonald and C. Wright (eds.), *Fact, Science and Morality*. Oxford: Blackwell, 1986.

—— "Deflationary Truth and the Problem of Aboutness", in E. Villanueva (ed.), *Philosophical Issues*, vol. 8: *Truth*. Atascadero, Calif.: Ridgeview, 1997.

—— "Disquotation and Cause in the Theory of Reference", in E. Villanueva (ed.), *Philosophical Issues*, vol. 6: *Content*. Atascadero, Calif.: Ridgeview, 1995.

—— "How to Choose amongst Empirically Indistinguishable Theories", *Journal of Philosophy*, 79 (1982), 61–77.

HORWICH, P. "Implicit Definition, Analytic Truth, and Apriori Knowledge", *Nous* 31 (1997), 423–40.

—— "Meaning and its Place in the Language Faculty", in L. Anthony and N. Hornstein (eds.), *Chomsky and his Critics*. Oxford: Blackwell, 1999.

—— "Meaning, Use and Truth", *Mind* 104 (1995), 355–68.

—— "The Nature of Vagueness", *Philosophy and Phenomenological Research* 57 (1997), 929–36.

—— "Scientific Conceptions of Language and their Philosophical Import", in E. Villanueva (ed.), *Philosophical Issues*, vol. 3: *Science and Knowledge*, 123–33. Atascadero, Calif.: Ridgeview, 1993.

—— *Truth*, 2nd edn. Oxford: Oxford University Press, 1998. (1st edn., Oxford: Blackwell, 1990.)

—— "What is it Like to be a Deflationary Theory of Meaning?" in E. Villanueva (ed.), *Philosophical Issues*, vol 5: *Truth and Rationality*, 133–54. Atascadero, Calif.: Ridgeview, 1994.

—— "Wittgenstein and Kripke on the Nature of Meaning", *Mind and Language* 5 (1990), 105–21.

JACKENDOFF, R. *The Architecture of the Language Faculty*. Cambridge, Mass.: MIT Press, 1997.

JACOB, P. *What Minds can Do*. Cambridge: Cambridge University Press, 1997.

JACKSON, F. *From Metaphysics to Ethics*. Oxford: Clarendon Press, 1998.

JOHNSTON, M. "The End of the Theory of Meaning", *Mind and Language* 3 (1998), 28–42.

KATZ, J. J. "Has the Description Theory of Names been Refuted?", in G. Boolos (ed.), M*eaning and Method: Essays in Honor of Hilary Putnam*, 31–61. Cambridge: Cambridge University Press, 1990.

—— *Language and other Abstract Objects*. Totowa, NJ: Rowman & Littlefield, 1981.

—— *The Metaphysics of Meaning*. Cambridge, Mass.: MIT Press, 1991.

KNEALE, W. "Modality, De Dicto and De Re", in *Logic, Methodology and the Philosophy of Science: Proceedings of the 1960 International Congress*, 622–33. Stanford, Calif.: Stanford University Press.

KRIPKE, S. *Naming and Necessity*. Cambridge, Mass.: Harvard University Press, 1980.

—— "A Puzzle About Belief", in A. Margalit (ed.), *Meaning and Use*, 239–83. Dordrecht: Kluwer, 1979.

—— *Wittgenstein on Rules and Private Language*. Oxford: Blackwell, 1982.

LARSON, R., and Segal, G. *Knowledge of Meaning*. Cambridge, Mass.: MIT Press, 1995.

LEEDS, S. "Theories of Reference and Truth", *Erkenntnis* 13, (1978), 111–29.

LEWIS, D. "How to Define Theoretical Terms", *Journal of Philosophy* 62 (1970), 427–66.

—— "Psychological and Theoretical Identifications", *Australasian Journal of Philosophy* 50 (1972), 249–58.

—— "Reduction of Mind", in S. Guttenplan (ed.), *A Companion to the Philosophy of Mind*. Oxford: Blackwell, 1994.

LOAR, B. "Conceptual Role and Truth Conditions", *Notre Dame Journal of Formal Logic* 23 (1982), 272–83.

—— "Reference from the First Person Perspective", in E. Villanueva (ed.), *Philosophical Issues*, vol. 6: *Content*, 53–72. Atascadero, Calif.: Ridgeview, 1995.

LOEWER, B. "From Information to Intentionality", *Synthese* 70 (1987), 287–317.

MATES, B. "Synonymy", in L. Linsky (ed.), *Semantics and the Philosophy of Language*, 111–36. Champaign, Ill.: University of Illinois Press, 1952.

MCDOWELL, J. "Truth Conditions, Bivalence, and Verificationism", in G. Evans and J. McDowell (eds.), *Truth and Meaning*. Oxford: Clarendon Press, 1975.

—— "Wittgenstein on Following a Rule", *Synthese* 58 (1984), 325–63.

MCGINN, C. "The Structure of Content", in A. Woodfield (ed.), *Thought and Object*. Oxford: Oxford University Press, 1982.

MCKINSEY, M. "Anti-individualism and Privileged Access", *Analysis* 51 (1991), 9–16.

MILLIKAN, R. *Language, Thought and Other Biological Categories*. Cambridge, Mass.: MIT Press, 1984.

PAPINEAU, D. *Reality and Representation*. Oxford: Blackwell, 1987.

PARSONS, T. "Fregean Theories of Truth and Meaning", in M. Schirn (ed.), *Frege: Importance and Legacy*. Berlin: Walter de Gruyter, 1996.

—— "Theories of Meaning and Truth", unpublished.

PEACOCKE, C. "How are A Priori Truths Possible?", *European Journal of Philosophy* 1 (1993), 175–99.

—— "Implicit Conceptions", in E. Villanueva (ed.), *Philosophical Issues*, vol. 9: *Concepts*. Atascadero, Calif.: Ridgeview, 1998.

—— *A Study of Concepts*. Cambridge, Mass.: MIT Press, 1992.

POINCARÉ, H. *Science and Hypothesis*. London: Walter Scott Publishing, 1905.

PRIOR, A. N. "The Runabout Inference-Ticket", *Analysis* 21 (1960), 38–9.

PUTNAM, H. "Does the Disquotational Theory of Truth Solve All Philosophical Problems?", in his *Words and Life*, ed. J. Conant. Cambridge, Mass.: Harvard University Press, 1995.

—— "The Meaning of 'Meaning'", in his *Mind, Language and Reality: Philosophical Papers*, vol. 2. Cambridge: Cambridge University Press, 1975.

—— "On Truth", in his *Words and Life*, ed. J. Conant. Cambridge, Mass.: Harvard University Press, 1995.

QUINE, W. V. "Ontological Relativity", in his *Ontological Relativity and Other Essays*. New York: Columbia University Press, 1969.

—— *Philosophy of Logic*. Englewood Cliffs, NJ: Prentice-Hall, 1970.

—— *Pursuit of Truth*. Cambridge, Mass.: Harvard University Press, 1990.

—— "Reply to Hellman" in L. Hahn and P. Schilpp (eds.), *The Philosophy of W. V. O. Quine*. La Salle, Ill.: Open Court, 1986.

—— "Two Dogmas of Empiricism", in his *From a Logical Point of View*. Cambridge. Mass.: Harvard University Press, 1953.

—— *Word and Object*. Cambridge, Mass.: MIT Press, 1962.

RAMSEY, F. "Theories" (1929), repr. in his *Foundations*, ed. H. D. Mellor. London: Routledge & Kegan Paul, 1978.

REICHENBACH, H. *The Philosophy of Space and Time*. New York: Dover, 1968.

RUSSELL, B. *The Analysis of Matter*. London: Allen & Unwin, 1927.

—— "Knowledge by Acquaintance and Knowledge by Description", repr. in his *Mysticism and Logic*. New York: Norton, 1929.

SAINSBURY, M. "Understanding and Theories of Meaning", *Proceedings of the Aristotelian Society* 80 (1979–80), 127–44.

SCHIFFER, S. "Contextualist Solutions to Scepticism", *Proceedings of the Aristotelian Society* 96 (1995–6), 317–33.

—— *Meaning*. Oxford: Oxford University Press, 1972.

—— "Meanings and Concepts", *Lingue e Style* 33 (1998).

—— "A Paradox of Meaning", *NOW* 28 (1994), 279–324.

—— *Remnants of Meaning*. Cambridge, Mass.: MIT Press, 1987.

SEARLE, J. R. "Proper Names", *Mind* 67, (1958), 166–73.

SELLARS, W. "Empiricism and Abstract Entities", in P. A. Schilpp (ed.), *The Philosophy of Rudolf Carnap*, 431–68. La Salle, Ill.: Open Court, 1963.

—— "Language as Thought and as Communication", *Philosophy and Phenomenological Research* 29 (1969), 506–27.

—— "Some Reflections on Language Games", *Philosophy of Science* 21 (1954), 204–8.

SOAMES, S. "The Truth about Deflationism", in E. Villanueva (ed.), *Philosophical Issues*, vol. 8: *Truth*. Atascadero, Calif.: Ridgeview, 1997.

—— "What is a Theory of Truth?", *Journal of Philosophy* 81 (1984), 411–29.

STAMPE, D. W. "Toward a Causal Theory of Linguistic Representation", in P. French, T. Uehling and H. Wettstein (eds.), *Midwest Studies In Philosophy* 2: 42–63. Minneapolis, Minn.: University of Minnesota Press, 1977.

STICH, S., and WARFIELD, T. (eds.). *Mental Representation*. Cambridge, Mass.: MIT Press, 1994.

THOMSON, J. J. "The Right and the Good", *Journal of Philosophy* 94 (1997), 273–98.

WILLIAMS, B. "Truth in Ethics", *Ratio* 8 (1996), 227–42 (special issue, *Truth in Ethics*, ed. B. Hooker).

WITTGENSTEIN, L. *Philosophical Investigations*. Oxford: Oxford University Press, 1953.

WRIGHT, C. "Kripke's Account of the Argument against Private Language", *Journal of Philosophy* 81 (1984), 759–78.

—— *Truth and Objectivity*. Cambridge, Mass.: Harvard University Press, 1992.

Index

Nozick, R. 116 n

ontology 1

Papineau, D. 5, 23, 24 n, 112 n, 153 n
paradoxes 64
Parsons, T. 183 n
Peacocke, C. 8, 43, 52, 71 n, 99, 131,
   146–8, 153 n
Percival, P. 153 n
Poincaré, H. 131
Pollock, J.-Y. 85 n, 183 n
possible worlds semantics 52
Price, H. 102 n, 114 n
Prior, A. 131, 134
properties 4, 21, 25–6, 44, 178–9
propositions 2, 3, 44 n, 56, 81–5
prototype theory of meaning 36, 52–4,
   159, 161 n, 226
Putnam, H. ii, 2, 56, 85–6, 117 n, 129,
   185 n, 214

Quine, W. V. vii, viii, 2, 6–7, 10, 29 n,
   31, 42 n, 54–6, 60, 62–3, 92, 104 n,
   105, 131, 143, 150–2, 196–211,
   227–8

Ramsey, F. 31, 136
realism 1
recognitional capacities 36, 161 n
reduction 5, 21, 25–6, 65–8; *see also*
   constitution fallacy
reference 3, 29, 68–71, 108, 115–30
representation 27–30, 107–11
rules 58, 194, 215 n
Russell, B. vii, 31 n, 115, 136
Ryan, D. 98 n

Sainsbury, M. 74 n
satisfaction 29, 108; *see also* truth
scepticism 1
Schiffer, S. vii, 64 n, 130 n, 164 n,
   182–3
Searle, J. 116 n
Segal, G. 74 n, 225 n
Sellars, W. 43, 52
semantics 51–4, 168–70
situation semantics 52

Smith, B. C. 102 n
Soames, S. 29 n, 104 n, 114 n
speaker's meaning 3, 85 n
Stalnaker, R. 52
Stampe, D. 23, 24 n, 112
stipulation 149 n; *see also* definition
substitutional quantification 106 n
synonymy 2, 49, 57, 100–1, 163–4
syntax 44, 170
Szabo, Z. 183 n

Tarski, A. 75, 168
teleological theory of meaning 23,
   52–4, 226
Thomson, J. J. 192 n
thought 1, 2, 98–9
tonk 133, 138–9
translation 50–1, 63, 196–211
truth 29, 103–14, 184–92; *see also* satisfaction
truth conditions 9, 23, 55, 71–5,
   168–70, 222–3
twin earth 2
two-factor theory of meaning 58 n,
   87–8
type/token distinction 14–15, 55, 80–1

understanding 8–9, 16–18, 89–90,
   171–3, 226
Usberti, G. 153 n
use theory of meaning
   arguments for 46–51
   defence of 57–102
   Kripke's critique of 217–25
   list of objections to 54–7
   for names 124–30
   summary of 4–10, 44–6, 228–9

vagueness 64
verificationism 151
Voltolini, A. 114 n

Williams, B. 185 n
Williams, M. 225 n
Williamson, T. 109 n
Wittgenstein, L. vii, 2, 3, 43, 52, 58,
   116 n, 194, 215 n, 224–5
Wright, C. 9, 65 n, 184–5 n